Programming

4 Manuscripts in 1 book

-Python For Beginners

-Python 3 Guide

-Learn Java

- Excel 2016

By Timothy C. Needham

Python for Beginners

A Crash Course Guide to Learn Python in 1 Week

Table of Contents

Introduction

Thank you for buying this book. The book has lots of actionable information that will get you started on the journey to becoming a pro at python programming.

Without doubt, code is the language of the future. Think about it, with the ever growing dependency on computers, one of the most critical things that anyone in the world today can learn is how to speak to computers in a language that they understand and have them do anything that you want to do. This skill is one whose demand is increasing at an increasing rate the world over. Whether you want to learn code to pursue a career as a programmer, web developer or graphics designer or want to learn code to be able to develop your own web applications and other computerized systems, the one thing you need to do is to start somewhere. What better place to start than to learn python?

Python is a simple yet powerful programming language that can enable you to start thinking like a programmer right from the beginning. It is very readable and the stress many beginners face about memorizing arcane syntax typically presented by other programming languages will not affect you at all. Conversely, you will be able to concentrate on learning concepts and paradigms of programming.

This book shall introduce you to an easy way to learn Python in just 7 days and in this time, be able to complete your own projects! By reading the book and implementing what you learn herein, you will realize just why major institutions like NASA, Google, Mozilla, Yahoo, Dropbox, IBM, Facebook and many others prefer to use python in their core products, services and business processes. Let's begin. Thanks again for downloading this book. I hope you enjoy it!

Chapter 1

Python: A Comprehensive Background

Before we can get to a point of learning the ins and outs of python programming, let's start by building an understanding of what python programming is and what it is about.

Before we discuss Python programming, especially what python is, let me briefly say something about programming.

Being a good programmer does not simply entail just knowing a vast array of programming languages or how to code fast programs. Instead, it is about:

- Comprehending a problem abstractly and being able to change it into code;
- Looking for new ways to tackle, for instance, a scientific problem and knowing the kind of tools to use;
- Being able to fix a program when it is not working;
- Writing a program that is quick enough, not the quickest possible;
- Writing a program that other people can understand in a short period of time.

Take note of the last point: Reproducible research and open science is becoming the norm in some research fields. This means that other people will probably have to read your code, understand exactly what you are doing and be able to recreate the code so that they can run it themselves.

By the end of this book therefore, we will not only be interested in the correctness of your solutions; we shall also look at whether we can understand how the program you create solves the problem.

This is to mean that you should always write your codes assuming that someone else will read it.

Let's go back to understanding python, the programming language of the future.

What Is Python?

In its simplest terms, python is a general-purpose, multi-paradigm, and interpreted programming language that gives programmers the ability to use various styles of programming to create complex or simple programs, get results faster, and write code in a way that resembles human language (explanation below).

Python is the programming language often used to create algorithms for sorting and analyzing chunks of data that businesses and organizations from all over the world collect. The explanation above brings about some very interesting points about python:

1. *It's a high level language*

Python is a high-level language. This means the code you type to build a program is more like a human language than the typical code created to control machines. This, for one, makes things a lot simpler for you, the programmer, and means that someone else is better placed to understand the code if he/she wants to use it him/herself. The human-like (high-level) code then goes through a software called an interpreter that converts it into machine code, a language that machines can understand.

2. *Its open source*

The software that lets us make programs in Python is open source. This means it is available in the public domain and anyone can freely use it. The greatest advantage of this software is the fact that you can modify it and create your own version to perform particular tasks. This is actually the main reason why many people have openly embraced the open source concept and the use of python is no exception. Let's discuss this briefly:

Associations that Use Python

Many organizations currently use Python to complete major tasks. You will not always hear about their uses since organizations are somewhat reserved about sharing their systems' information, or 'trade secrets.' Nonetheless, Python is still there making a great difference in the way organizations function and many common systems and applications have settled for Python for their development. Some of them include YouTube, Google Search, BitTorrent, NASA, Eve Online, iRobot machines, Yahoo, Facebook, Maya and many others.

Look at the following commercial uses of Python:

Corel: Over the years, people have used products such as PaintShop Pro to grab screenshots, modify pictures, draw fresh images, and perform many other graphic oriented tasks. What is amazing about this popular product is that it heavily relies on Python scripting. This means to automate tasks in PaintShop Pro, you will need a degree of Python knowledge.

D-link: It can be quite problematic to upgrade firmware over a network connection, and this company (D-link) encountered a situation where every upgrade tended to tie up a machine, something they described as a weak utilization of resources. Additionally, a number of upgrades needed extra work since there were problems with the targeted device.

The use of python to build a multi-threaded application that allows for the movement of updates to the devices enables *one machine* to service *several devices,* and a new methodology supported by python decreases all the reboots to one, after the installation of that fresh firmware is done.

Moreover, this company opted for Python over other languages such as Java because Python offers an easy to use serial communication code.

ForecastWatch.com: Have you ever wondered if someone somewhere reviews your weatherman's performance? Well, if you have, look no further; this company does that. This company compares the thousands of weather forecasters produced every day against real climatological data in order to determine their accuracy. The produced report advances weather forecasts.

In this particular case, the software used in the comparisons is a pure Python program since it contains standard libraries that are important in the collection, parsing, and storage of data from online sources. Additionally, the enhanced, multithreaded nature and capability of python gives it the ability to gather the forecasts from about 5,000 sources per day. The code is also a lot smaller than what other languages like PHP or Java would need.

Many other companies, softwares, and programs use Python and to sum this up, I will say that scientists, business people, teachers, governments, and even religious organizations, just to mention the least use python programming in one form or the other.

You too should also get started with learning python if you don't want to be left behind. We'll start from the beginning i.e. downloading the program.

Chapter 2

How to Download and Install Python

We will now discuss how to download Python on your Widows OS and Mac OS X.

Windows OS

If you are a Windows operating system user, you have to note that the program does not arrive prepackaged with windows. As such, you have to install it and ensure you install the latest version.

A number of years ago, Python saw an update that caused a split in the program. This split has become a challenge to many newcomers. However, you should not worry because I will take you through the installation of both versions and talk about some of their important features.

The first thing you have to do is go to the python download page. You'll actually note this division and also see the repository ask whether you want the latest Python 3 (3.6.1) release or Python 2 (2.7.13).

Python ⟫ Downloads ⟫ Windows

Python Releases for Windows

- Latest Python 2 Release - Python 2.7.13
- Latest Python 3 Release - Python 3.6.1

The first question you may ask yourself is which version you should download. While newer means better, naturally, being a Python programmer means you have to make your choice based on your end goal. For instance, python 2.7 is ideal for hobby projects like games (coded in Python) in which you want to introduce new features. If you want to get some project whose extension ends in 'py' running, the best version you can use is Python 2.7.

On the other hand, if your focus is learning Python, you should highly consider installing both versions, something very possible and easy; it also requires minimal risk and very little setup trouble. This will also give you an opportunity to work with the latest Python version and be able to run older scripts of the language while testing for backwards compatibility for fresh projects. Please visit wiki.python.org to get more information about the differences between the two versions.

If you are completely sure you only need a specific version, you can go ahead and download one of them. Just note that you will see an 'x86–64' executable installer under the two versions' main entry.

- Python 3.6.1 - 2017-03-21
  - Download Windows x86 web-based installer
  - Download Windows x86 executable installer
  - Download Windows x86 embeddable zip file
  - Download Windows x86-64 web-based installer
  - Download Windows x86-64 executable installer
  - Download Windows x86-64 embeddable zip file
  - Download Windows help file

The installer will immediately install the suitable 64/32 bit version on your PC. You can also read here for more information about the differences between a 64-bit and 32-bit version.

How to Install Python 2

The installation of this particular version is simple and the installer even sets up the variable that specifies the set of directories where the program is located in your PC known as PATH variable. You only have to run the installer, select 'install for all users' then select 'next'.

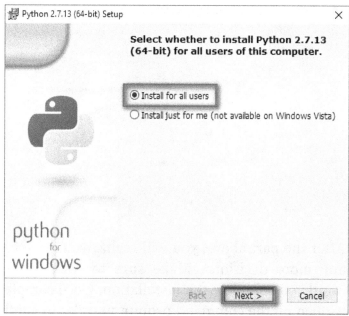

Leave the directory as 'Python27' on the directory selection screen and then click 'next.'

On the window, scroll down and select 'add python.exe to path,' and then click 'will be installed on local hard drive.' When finished, click next.

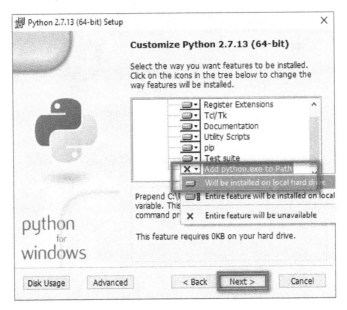

After the part above, you will realize you do not have to make any more decisions. Make sure to click through the wizard until you complete the installation. Once complete, you can now open up the command prompt in order to confirm the installation, and then type the following command: **python -V**

```
C:\Users\Jason>python -V
Python 2.7.13
```

Good job so far! If you wanted 2.7 to complete a pending project, you can stop here. The program is now installed on your device and its path variable set.

How to Install Python 3

Installation of the latest version of Python requires you complete this step, and as I mentioned earlier, you can install this version alongside python 2.7 without experiencing any problems. Go ahead and run the executable now. On the first screen, enable the option labeled 'add python 3.6 to PATH' and then click on 'install now'.

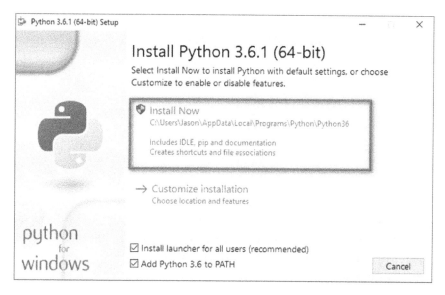

Once you do that, prepare yourself for an important decision. When you select the option 'disable path length limit', you will be taking out the limitation of the MAX_PATH variable. This does not change or distort anything. Actually, it allows the software to use lengthy path names. Currently, we have many programmers working in *nix systems such as Linux where the math name length is largely a negligible issue; therefore, you can turn this one on early enough to help you smooth over whichever issues related to path you may come across as you work in windows.

If you ask me, just go ahead and choose this option. If you are sure you do not want to restrict the path length limit, you can click close and complete the installation there.

In case you are just installing python 3, you can also use the command line trick-'python v' that we used above to confirm its proper installation and that the path variable is set.

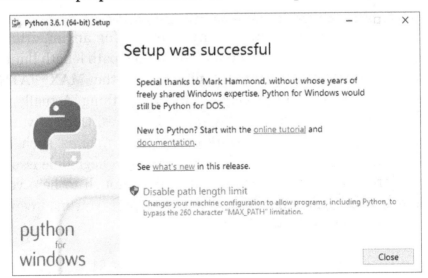

How to Install Python on Mac OS X

Mac OS X typically comes with a pre-installed version of Python. For example, Mac OS X 10.8 comes with version 2.7. You only have to download and install the latest version alongside the one in the system to start enjoying the benefits of the most recent version of this program. Just go to python's <u>official website</u> to get the latest Python 3 version. Remember; you cannot depend on Python 3 to run python 2 scripts.

The Steps

When you use your Mac computer to access the Python download page, it will automatically sense that you are a Mac user and the options given henceforth will reflect that. The steps are simple and in a short while, you will download a file that carries the label '3.x.macosx10.6dmg' that will go directly to your browser's download folder.

When you open the file you downloaded, it will instantaneously mount on your desktop as a volume. Open the file and wait to see some window resembling the one below.

Build.txt   License.txt

Python.mpkg   ReadMe.txt

Before you proceed to install the program, take a few seconds to go through the 'readme.txt' file to learn much including that you may not just double click the installer labeled as 'Python.mpkg' since Apple does not sign it. The settings of your gatekeeper will however determine whether you can double click it or not, and option you will find under systems **preferences>privacy>general**. Ignore the window that appears after you are done, and proceed to the next step.

If your computer is using the gatekeeper default settings, proceed to right click on the installer package and click the option 'open with- installer.app' like this one:

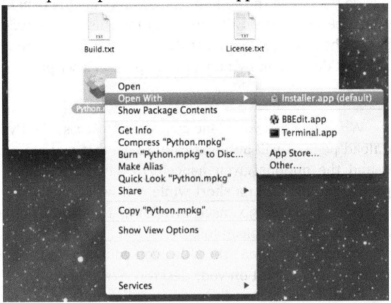

When you complete that, the system will take you through the standard process of installation and the steps are similar to the ones we covered in the Windows section.

Now that you have the program installed and running on your PC, let us go through two very important segments before we continue.

Setting up the PATH

Executable files and programs can be in multiple directories, so operating systems do give a search path listing the directories the operating system looks for executables. The path is kept in an environment variable, a named string that the operating system maintains. This variable has data open to the command shell and the other programs.

In Unix, the path variable is named as PATH (it's case-sensitive) while in Windows, it's referred to as Path (not case-sensitive). The installer in Mac OS manages the path details. If you want to invoke the Python interpreter from any specific directory, just add to your path the Python directory.

How to Set Up Path in Linux/Unix

To add the python directory to the path in Unix for a session, do the following:

1. Type the following in the csh shell: setenv PATH "$PATH:/usr/local/bin/python" and click enter.

2. Type the following in the Linux bash shell export ATH="$PATH:/usr/local/bin/python" then click enter.

3. Type the following in the ksh or sh shell: PATH="$PATH:/usr/local/bin/python" then click enter.

4. Remember that /usr/local/bin/python is the python directory path.

How to Set Up Path in Windows

To add the python directory to the path for a specific session in windows, do the following:

1. Type (at the command prompt) path %path%;C:\Python then click enter.

2. Remember that C:\Python refers to the python directory path.

The Python Environmental Variables to Note

Environmental variables in this regard are system-wide settings living outside python, which you can use to customize the interpreter's behavior every time you ran it on your computer. It is important you know about them before we run our python program. Python recognizes a number of environment variables contained in the following list:

Pythonpath

This one has a role that resembles PATH i.e. informing the Python interpreter the location where it should locate module files, which are usually imported into a given program. It usually contains the python source code as well as the Python source library directory.

Pythonstartup

It has the path of an initialization file that contains the Python source code. It executes each time you start the interpreter.

Pythoncaseok

If you are a Widows user, you will use this variable to ask Python (in an import statement) to search for the first case-insensitive match.

Pythonhome

This one is an alternative module search path typically embedded within the PYTHONPATH directory or the PYTHONSTARTUP directory to ease the process of switching module libraries.By now, you must have come across a number of terms that you are unfamiliar with. To make it easy to understand these and the others that we will discuss as we go on in the book, let's briefly talk about a list of some of these terms.

Chapter 3

Python Glossary

Here is an explanation to some of the common terms that you will find in this book.

Augment: This refers to the supplementary information a computer uses to execute commands.

Class: A class is the template we use to build user defined objects.

Continue: Continue is a function we use to skip an existing block and turn back to the 'while' or 'for' statement

Conditional statement: A conditional statement is a statement containing an 'if/else' or 'if'.

Debugging: Debugging is the process of pursuing and purging errors in programming.

Def: Def is a function that mainly defines a method or function.

Iteration: Iteration refers to the process where instructions or structures are repeated sequentially a set number of times or until some condition is met.

Syntax: A syntax is a set of rules that outline how a python program should be written and interpreted.

Index: Index refers to the position in a well-ordered list assigned to the characters. For instance, each character holds an index beginning from 0 to the length of -1.

Variable: A variable is a reserved memory location a computer uses to store values.

Module: Refers to an object that contains attributes, arbitrarily named, that can reference and bind.

Console: Refers to the terminal where you can execute a command at a time.

Instantiate: The process of generating an instance. An instance is a specific realization of a template, a class of objects or a computer process for example.

Indentation: Refers to the placement of text away to the left or right in order to separate it from the adjacent text.

With that understanding, let's now get to the specifics of using python starting with interacting with python now that you have installed it on your computer.

Chapter 4

Interacting with Python

In this section, you will learn how to use and interact with Python in the number of available ways. Let us begin by talking about the python's interpreter, while using the console of your operating system.

A console is also referred to as a command prompt or a terminal. It is a textual method of interacting with your operating system just as the 'desktop' together with the 'mouse' is the graphical method used to interact with your PC.

How to Open a Console on Mac OS X

The standard console of OS X is a program known as "terminal". To open it, navigate to **applications**, then go to **utilities** and double click the **terminal** program.

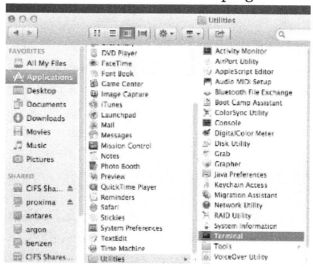

You can also easily search for it in the search tool at the top right of the screen. The command line terminal is a tool you will use to interact with your computer.

A window having a command line prompt message that looks like the code below will open: *mycomputer:~ myusername$*

How to Open a Console in Linux

The different distributions of Linux (such as mint, Fedora, Ubuntu) may have dissimilar console programs, typically known as terminals. The particular terminal you open and how you do so can depend on your distribution.

Let us take one example on Ubuntu; you will probably want to open Gnome Terminal—it presents a prompt similar to this: *myusername@mycomputer:~$*

How to Open a Console on Windows

Window's console is also referred to as the command prompt, or cmd. You can easily get to it by using the key combination 'windows+R' (windows in this case refers to the windows log button), that opens the Run dialog. Just type cmd and press enter or just click okay.

You can also use the start menu to search for it. It should appear like this:

C:\Users\myusername>

The windows command prompt is not as potent as its counterparts on OS X and Linux are; therefore, you should consider directly starting the Python interpreter or use the IDLE program that comes with Python. All these are accessible from the Start menu.

Starting and Interacting With Python

The python program you have installed will act as something we usually refer to as an interpreter. The interpreter picks up text commands and runs them as you write them, which is quite handy for trying stuff out.

At your console, just type 'python' then press 'enter' and you should enter the interpreter.

As soon as Python opens, you will see some contextual information resembling the following:

Python 3.5.0 (default, Sep 20 2015, 11:28:25)
[GCC 5.2.0] on linux
Type "help", "copyright", "credits" or "license" for more information.
>>>

On the last line, we have the prompt >>> which indicates that you are currently in an interactive Python interpreter session known as 'python shell'. You should note that the python shell is different from the normal command prompt. At this point, you can try entering some code for Python to run. Try the following:

Print ("Hello world")

Now press enter and see the result. When you see the results, Python will take you back to the interactive prompt where you can enter another command:

```
>>> print("Hello world")
Hello world
>>> (1 + 4) * 2
10
```

'Help' is a very useful command since it enters a help functionality that lets you explore all the things python enables you to do, right from the interpreter. To close the help window, press 'q' and go back to the Python prompt.

You can also press Ctrl+Z to leave the interactive shell and return to the console or the system shell. On OS X or Linux, press Ctrl+D, or on the Windows button, enter.

Let us now try a simple exercise:

Earlier, I demonstrated entering a command to work out some math. You can now try out some math commands. Do you know any python operations? Tell it to give you the squared result of the sum of 239 and 588.

There are several ways you can get the answer:

```
>>> 239 + 588
827
>>> 827 * 827
683929
>>> (239 + 588) * (239 + 588)
683929
>>> (239 + 588) ** 2
683929
```

Running the Python Files

When you have a large python code to run, you will want to save it into a file. For example, you can modify it into little parts (fix a bug) and re-run the code without having to type the rest repeatedly. You can save your code to a file and pass the name of the file to the python program instead of typing the commands one by one. This executes the file's code instead of launching the interactive interpreter. Let us try that.

Just create a file in the current directory (labelled 'hello.py') with your most preferred code editor and then enter the print command above. Next, save the file. On OS X or Linux, run 'touch hello.py' so that you create an empty file to edit. It is very easy to run this file with Python:

$ python hello.py

Ensure you are positioned at your system command prompt, which will either have $ or > at the end, not at python's (which contains >>> instead). If you are using Windows, you can double click the file to run it.

When you press enter now, the file will execute and you will see the output. This time however, when python has completed the execution of all commands from the file, it exits back to the system command prompt as opposed to returning to the interactive shell.

At this point, we can now get started with the turtle project. Even so, you have to note the following:

NOTE: If you are getting weird errors about 'no such file or directory' or 'can't open file' instead of getting 'hello world', it means your command line is most probably not running from the directory in which you saved your file. You can go ahead and change your current command line's working directory with the 'cd' command—cd stands for 'change directory'. On windows, you might prefer something like:

> cd Desktop\Python_Exercises

If you are using OS X or Linux, you might prefer seeing something like:

$ cd Desktop/Python_Exercises

This changes to 'python_exercises' directory under the desktop folder (or somewhere like that). If unsure of the location directory you saved the file in, simply drag the directory to the command line window. Again, if you are not sure in which directory your shell is currently running, use pwd—it stands for 'print working directory'.

NOTE: When you begin playing around with turtle, avoid naming your file turtle.py. You can try using more apt names like 'rectangle.py' or 'square.py'. Otherwise, each time you refer to 'turtle', python will immediately pick up your file in place of the standard python 'turtle' module.

Before we learn a few more things about python and start handling the intermediate projects, you ought to be able to handle a few basic projects by now, including turtle. Let us cover that one first.

Chapter 5

Using Turtle for a Simple Drawing

Turtle is a python feature resembling a drawing board that lets you command some turtle to draw over it. In this feature, you can use functions such as turtle.left(...) and turtle.forward (...) which can move the turtle around.

Before we can use the turtle, we have to import it first. I recommend playing it in the interactive interpreter first since there is a bit more work needed to make it work from the files. To do so, go to your terminal and type the following:
Import turtle

➤

If you are using Mac OS and are not seeing anything, you can try issuing a command such as turtle.forward(0)' and check whether a new window opens behind your command line.

If you are using Ubuntu and receive the following error message 'no module named _tkinter', it means you have a missing package; just install it with 'sudo apt-get install python3-tk'

While it might be tempting to copy-paste some of the things written in this book into your terminal, I recommend that you type out each command because typing will get the syntax under your fingers (growing the muscle memory) and even assist avoid strange syntax-based errors.
turtle.forward(25)

→

turtle.left(30)

▼

The function 'turtle.forward(...)' will tell the turtle to move forward by a specific distance while 'turtle.left(...)' takes the number of degrees you desire to rotate to the left. We also have the 'turtle.right(...)' and 'turtle.backward(...)' too.

If you want to start afresh, simply type 'turtle.reset()' to clear the drawing your turtle created so far. Do not worry about this though; we will go into more on that shortly.

The standard turtle is a triangle; that is no fun. Instead of using the 'turtle.shape ()' command, let us try making it a turtle: turtle.shape("turtle")

That is so much better. If you placed the commands into a file, you should have noted the turtle window disappear after the turtle completed its movement. This is because python normally exits as soon as your turtle has completed moving. Since the turtle window is innate to python, it will go away as well. To prevent that, you can just put 'turtle.exitonclick()' beneath your file. The window remains open until you click on it.

```
import turtle

turtle.shape("turtle")

turtle.forward(25)

turtle.exitonclick()
```

In Python programming, text's horizontal indenting is important. We will learn all about it as we look at functions later on. For now though, let us consider that stray spaces or tabs can bring an unexpected error. You can even try adding one to see how badly python will react.

Draw A Square

NOTE: I do not expect you to always know the answer immediately. We all learn by trial and error. You need to experiment and see what python does when you feed it different commands, what gives beautiful results (even though sometimes quite unexpected), and what brings errors. It is also okay if you are not prepared to keep playing with something you have learned that generates fascinating results. Overall, do not think twice about trying (and probably failing) and learn something from it.

Let us try the following exercise:

Draw a square that looks like the one below:

For this square, perhaps you will require a right angle that is 90 degrees. This is how you can do this:

```
turtle.forward(50)
turtle.left(90)
turtle.forward(50)
turtle.left(90)
turtle.forward(50)
turtle.left(90)
turtle.forward(50)
turtle.left(90)
```

You can look at how the turtle begins and ends in the same place while facing the same direction before and after drawing the square. This is a very useful convention to follow, and it makes it easier to draw many shapes later on.

If you want to be creative, you can modify the shape using the 'turtle.color(...)' and 'turtle.width(...)' functions. How do you use these functions?

Before you use a function, you need to know its signature. For instance, what to put between the parentheses, and what those things even mean. To find that out, simply key in 'help(turtle.color)' into your Python Shell. If there is a large piece of text, Python will place the text into a pager, which will let you page up and down. To quit (and exit the pager), press the 'q' key.

NOTE: If you are getting an error such as this one: "NameError: name 'turtle' is not defined" when trying to view help, you ought to import names into python before you even refer to them. To do this, in a fresh interactive shell, you will want to import turtle before keying in help(turtle.color).

Alternatively, you can read more about functions on <u>this page</u>. Remember that if you actually misdrew something, you can simply tell turtle to erase the drawing board using the command 'turtle.reset()' or simply undo your most recent step using 'turtle.undo()'

As is detailed in help, you can easily modify the color using turtle.color(colorstring). Among many others, these include 'violet', 'green', and 'red.' For a more extensive list, see <u>this manual</u>.

Do you want to set an RGB value? Just make sure you run 'turtle.colormode (255) first.' After that, you could maybe run turtle.color(215, 100, 170) in order to set a pink color.

Draw a Rectangle

Let us now try drawing a rectangle.

Here is how you do it (the python code):

```
turtle.forward(100)
turtle.left(90)
turtle.forward(50)
turtle.left(90)
turtle.forward(100)
turtle.left(90)
turtle.forward(50)
turtle.left(90)
```

Also, note that when it comes to a triangle, and specifically, an equilateral triangle whose all sides are of equal length every corner has an angle of exactly 60 degrees.

Extra squares

We will now try drawing a tilted square, another one, and another one. It is up to you to decide how to experiment with the angles between the specific squares.

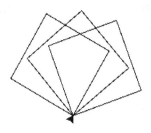

In the picture above, we have three turns of 20 degrees. You could try 30 or even 40-degree turns. For example:

```
turtle.left(20)

turtle.forward(50)
turtle.left(90)
turtle.forward(50)
turtle.left(90)
turtle.forward(50)
turtle.left(90)
turtle.forward(50)
turtle.left(90)

turtle.left(30)

turtle.forward(50)
turtle.left(90)
turtle.forward(50)
turtle.left(90)
turtle.forward(50)
turtle.left(90)
turtle.forward(50)
turtle.left(90)

turtle.left(40)

turtle.forward(50)
turtle.left(90)
turtle.forward(50)
turtle.left(90)
turtle.forward(50)
turtle.left(90)

turtle.forward(50)
turtle.left(90)
```

With that understanding of python, let's now move on to something even more eye opening about python i.e. variables.

Chapter 6

Variables

I'm sure you have noted that experimenting with angles requires changing three different numbers or places in the code each time. Can you imagine trying out all the sizes of squares or with rectangles? Would that not be tedious? Luckily, we have easier ways to do that than changing many numbers each time.

Using variables, we can achieve that sleekly. You will be able to tell python that whenever you refer to a variable, you actually mean something else. When you relate it to symbolic math, where you can write "let x be 5", this concept may be a bit more familiar. In this case, then x*2 is obviously 10. In python syntax, this statement is explained as x = 5. After the statement, if you happen to 'print (x)', it outputs the value -5. We can also use that for turtle as well. turtle.forward(x)

Variables store all sorts of stuff, not just numbers. Another thing you may want to store regularly is a 'string'. A string just refers to a piece of text. These (Strings) usually have a starting as well as an ending double quote (") - we will delve into that, the other data types you can store, and what you can use these for later in the book.

Did you know that you can even refer to the turtle by name using a variable? Here is an explanation of this in play:

john = turtle

Now, each time you type 'john', python thinks you mean 'turtle'. However, you can keep using turtle as well:

```
john.forward(50)
john.left(90)
turtle.forward(50)
```

The Angle Variable

This is an exercise. If you create a variable known as tilt (you could assign it a number of degrees), how could you use that to make your experiment with the tilted squares program much faster? This is the solution:

```
tilt = 20

turtle.left(tilt)

turtle.forward(50)
turtle.left(90)
turtle.forward(50)
turtle.left(90)
turtle.forward(50)
turtle.left(90)
turtle.forward(50)
turtle.left(90)

turtle.left(tilt)
```

- ..and so on!

NOTE: You could also apply this principle to the size of the squares

Santa Claus' House

Now draw a house

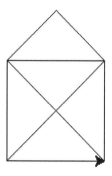

NOTE: You can calculate the diagonal line's length using the Pythagorean Theorem. That is actually a good value to store in as a variable. To determine the square root of a given number in Python, you ought to first import the specific math module then proceed to use this function: 'math.sqrt()'. We exponentiate a number with the ** operator (thus, squaring means **2).

```
import math

c = math.sqrt(a**2 + b**2)
```

Next, we will be discussing loops.

Chapter 7

Loops

You might have noticed something with our programs: there is often some repetition. Python has a strong concept it uses referred to as looping (the jargon is iteration). We will use it to cut all of our repetitive code. Meanwhile, try this simple example:

```
for name in "John", "Sam", "Jill":
    print("Hello " + name)
```

This can prove very helpful if you want to do something many times like when drawing the individual shape borderline but you only want to write the action just once. Look at this other version of loop:

```
for i in range(10):
    print(i)
```

You can see how we use 'i' to write only one line of code, but the values it takes are 10. You can consider the function 'range(n)' a shorthand for 0,1,2...,n-1. You can also use the help in the shell to know more about it; just type 'help(range)'. To exit the help again, use the 'q' key. You can also loop over all the elements you want:

```
total = 0
for i in 5, 7, 11, 13:
    print(i)
    total = total + i

print(total)
```

Write this out, run it, and check how it works. As you can note above, the very lines of code indented are the same ones looped. In python, this is an important concept that allows it to know which lines should be used in the 'for loop' and the ones that come after, as part of the remaining section of the program. To indent your code, use four spaces (by hitting tab).

Sometimes, you may want to repeat some code a particular number of times but do not really care about the specific value of the 'i' variable; it can be good to replace it using _ instead. This shows that you do not care about its value, or do not even desire to use it. Look at this simple example:

```
for _ in range(10):
    print("Hello!")
```

I'm sure you are wondering about the variable 'i' and why we've used it all the time above. This variable stands for 'index' and is one of the most common variable names you will ever find in code. Even so, if you are looping over anything other than just numbers, you can even name it something better- for example:

```
for drink in list_of_beverages:
    print("Would you like a " + drink + "?")
```

You may notice that this is immediately clearer to read than if we had used 'i' instead of 'drink'.

The Dashed Line

Now draw a dashed line. You can use the turtle.penup () function to move the turtle without it drawing its movement. Use turtle.pendown () to instruct it to draw again.

— — — — — — — — →

```
for i in range(10):
    turtle.forward(15)
    turtle.penup()
    turtle.forward(5)
    turtle.pendown()
```

NOTE: you can make the dashes bigger as the line progresses.

If you are feeling lost, inspect 'i' at every loop's run.

```
for i in range(10):
    print(i)
    # write more code here
```

NOTE: You can make use of 'i' (or the index variable/loop variable) to get increasing step sizes.

Comments

In the above example, a comment is the line that begins with #. In this program, the computer ignores everything that goes a line after #. You can use comments to explain what your program does without altering the behavior for the computer. You can also easily use them to 'comment out' or disable some lines of code. The comments can also be at the end of a line; look at this:

```
turtle.left(20)    # tilt our next square slightly
```

More squares

The squares we were drawing at the beginning had many repeated lines of code. You can try writing out a square drawing program in few lines by using loops. Here is the python code for that:

```
for _ in range(4):
    turtle.forward(100)
    turtle.left(90)
```

You can try 'nesting' loops by placing one under (within) the other, with a drawing code that is inside the two. This is how it can appear:

```
for ...:
  for ...:
      # drawing code inside the inner loop goes here
      ...
  # you can put some code here to move
  # around after!
  ...
```

Now replace the...'s with a code of your own to see if you can come up with something different or interesting. Loops aside, the next part will focus on native python datatypes.

Chapter 8

Native Python Datatypes

To have a better understanding of all we have discussed so far (and what is coming), I will introduce a new topic that will go into more detail about specific basic components of python. Besides that, we will also discuss a lot more to make sure you can handle larger projects with the program.

Python Strings

We are now going to discuss how to make, format, change, and delete python strings. You will also learn about the various string operations and functions.

A string is a sequence of characters. A character is a symbol; for instance, we have 26 characters in the English language. Nonetheless, computers do not deal with characters; they deal with binary or numbers. Even though we usually see characters on the screen, internally, they are stored and used as a mixture of zeros (0's) and ones (1's).

The conversion of characters to numbers is also known as encoding and some of the most popular encoding used are Unicode and ASCII (decoding is the reverse process). In Python, the sequence of Unicode character is known as string. At its introduction, encoding was meant to include every character in all languages and bring some uniformity in encoding. To learn more about encoding, read here. That aside, let's discuss how to make strings.

How to Make Strings

You can create strings by enclosing characters within single quotes or double quotes. You can even use triple quotes in Python but generally to represent docstrings and multiline strings.

```python
# all of the following are equivalent
my_string = 'Hello'
print(my_string)


my_string = "Hello"
print(my_string)


my_string = '''Hello'''
print(my_string)


# triple quotes string can extend multiple lines
my_string = """Hello, welcome to
    the world of Python"""
print(my_string)
```

Accessing Characters in a String

You can access particular characters using indexing and an array of characters through slicing. Index starts from 0 and when you try to access a character out of index range, it causes an 'Index Error'. This index must be an integer. We cannot use float or other forms as it will result into Type Error.

In python, negative indexing is used for its sequences. The -1 index refers to the final item, the second last item is represented by -2, and so on. When you use the slicing operator (colon), you can be able to access a range of items.

```
str = 'programiz'
print('str = ', str)


#first character
print('str[0] = ', str[0])


#last character
print('str[-1] = ', str[-1])


#slicing 2nd to 5th character
print('str[1:5] = ', str[1:5])


#slicing 6th to 2nd last character
print('str[5:-2] = ', str[5:-2])
```

If you try accessing index outside the range, or use a decimal number, you get errors.

```
# index must be in range
>>> my_string[15]
...
IndexError: string index out of range

# index must be an integer
>>> my_string[1.5]
...
TypeError: string indices must be integers
```

You can best visualize slicing by considering the index to remain between the elements as illustrated below. If you want to access a range, you will require the index that will help with slicing the portion from the string.

P	R	O	G	R	A	M	I	Z
0	1	2	3	4	5	6	7	8	9
-9	-8	-7	-6	-5	-4	-3	-2	-1

Changing and Deleting a String

Strings are largely immutable; this means you cannot change the string elements once you have assigned it. You can simply reassign various strings to the same name.

```
>>> my_string = 'programiz'
>>> my_string[5] = 'a'
...
TypeError: 'str' object does not support item assignment
>>> my_string = 'Python'
>>> my_string
'Python'
```

You cannot remove or delete characters from a string unless you are deleting the entire string itself; this is possible by using the 'del' keyword.

```
>>> del my_string[1]
...
TypeError: 'str' object doesn't support item deletion
>>> del my_string
>>> my_string
...
NameError: name 'my_string' is not defined
```

Next, we will discuss string operators.

The String Operators

We have numerous operations you can perform with string; this makes it one of the most used python datatypes. For instance, you can do the following:

Concatenation of Multiple Strings

A concatenation is the joining of two or more strings into one string. In Python, we use the + operator to achieve this. When you write two string literals together, it also concatenates them. We use the * operator to repeat the strings a particular number of times.

```
str1 = 'Hello'

str2 ='World!'


# using +

print('str1 + str2 = ', str1 + str2)


# using *

print('str1 * 3 =', str1 * 3)
```

When you write two string literals, this also concatenates them just like the + operator. You can also use parentheses if you want to proceed to concatenate strings in separate lines.

```
>>> # two string literals together
>>> 'Hello ''World!'
'Hello World!'

>>> # using parentheses
>>> s = ('Hello '
...     'World')
>>> s
'Hello World'
```

Iterating Through String

You can also use 'for loop' to iterate through a string. For instance, you can count the sum of '1' in a string.

```
count = 0

for letter in 'Hello World':

  if(letter == '1'):

    count += 1

print(count,'letters found')
```

The String Membership Test

You can test if a substring occurs inside a string or not by using the keyword 'in'. Here is an example:

```
>>> 'a' in 'program'
True
>>> 'at' not in 'battle'
False
```

4. The Built-In Functions to Use with Python

Many built-in functions that work with sequence also work with strings. Some of the most popular functions are len () and enumerate (). The enumerate () function takes back an enumerate object. It has the index and value of every item in the string as pairs, something that can be very useful for iteration. Likewise, len () takes back the number of characters (length) of the string

```
str = 'cold'

# enumerate()
list_enumerate = list(enumerate(str))
print('list(enumerate(str) = ', list_enumerate)

#character count
print('len(str) = ', len(str))
```

Python String Formatting

Here is how python strong formatting works:

Escape Sequence

Say you want to print some text such as 'he said, what's there', you cannot use single or double quotes. Since 'the' text itself has both double and single quotes, it will definitely result into 'SyntaxError'.

```
>>> print("He said, "What's there?"")
...
SyntaxError: invalid syntax
>>> print('He said, "What's there?"')
...
SyntaxError: invalid syntax
```

To dodge this problem, you can simply use triple quotes, or instead, use escape sequences. An escape sequence begins with a backlash and it is interpreted differently. If you use single quotes to signify a string, all the single quotes within the text have to be escaped. This is similar to the case with double quotes. This is how you can do it to represent the text above.

```
# using triple quotes
print("""He said, "What's there?""")


# escaping single quotes
print('He said, "What\'s there?"')


# escaping double quotes
print("He said, \"What's there?\"")
```

The following is a list of the python-supported escape sequence:

Escape Sequence	Description
\newline	Backslash and newline ignored
\\	Backslash
\'	Single quote
\"	Double quote
\a	ASCII Bell
\b	ASCII Backspace
\f	ASCII Formfeed
\n	ASCII Linefeed
\r	ASCII Carriage Return
\t	ASCII Horizontal Tab
\v	ASCII Vertical Tab
\ooo	Character with octal value ooo
\xHH	Character with hexadecimal value HH

Look at the following examples:

```
>>> print("C:\\Python32\\Lib")
C:\Python32\Lib

>>> print("This is printed\nin two lines")
This is printed
in two lines

>>> print("This is \x48\x45\x58 representation")
This is HEX representation
```

Ignoring the Escape Sequence with Raw String

As you will soon realize, there are times when you will just wish to ignore the escape sequences within a string. To do this, you can place R or r before the string. This implies that this is actually a raw string and all escape sequences within are ignored.

```
>>> print("This is \x61 \ngood example")
This is a
good example
>>> print(r"This is \x61 \ngood example")
This is \x61 \ngood example
```

48

Formatting Strings Using the Format () Method

The format () method that is available with the string object is quite versatile and strong in string formatting. Format strings has curly braces {} as replacement fields or placeholders that gets replaced. You can use keyword arguments or positional arguments (explained later) to specify the order.

This 'format ()' method can have discretionary format specifications, and the colon separates them from the field name. For instance, we can right-justify, left-justify or center ^ a string in the set space. We also format integers as hexadecimal, binary and so on, and floats are presentable in the exponent format or rounded.

You can use numerous formatting methods. Visit Pyformat.info for all the available string formatting with the format () method.

```
>>> # formatting integers
>>> "Binary representation of {0} is {0:b}".format(12)
'Binary representation of 12 is 1100'

>>> # formatting floats
>>> "Exponent representation: {0:e}".format(1566.345)
'Exponent representation: 1.566345e+03'

>>> # round off
>>> "One third is: {0:.3f}".format(1/3)
'One third is: 0.333'

>>> # string alignment
>>> "|{:<10}|{:^10}|{:>10}|".format('butter','bread','ham')
'|butter   |  bread   |       ham|'
```

The Old-Style Formatting

You can actually format strings such as the old sprintf () that is popularly used in the C programming language. To achieve this, we use the % operator as shown below:

49

```
>>> x = 12.3456789
>>> print('The value of x is %3.2f' %x)
The value of x is 12.35
>>> print('The value of x is %3.4f' %x)
The value of x is 12.3457
```

The Common Python String Methods

There are various methods available with the string object; the format () method we talked about is one of them. Some of the most popular methods used include upper (), lower (), replace (), join (), split () etc. You can find a complete list of all the Python's built in methods to work with strings here.

```
>>> "PrOgRaMiZ".lower()
'programiz'
>>> "PrOgRaMiZ".upper()
'PROGRAMIZ'
>>> "This will split all words into a list".split()
['This', 'will', 'split', 'all', 'words', 'into', 'a', 'list']
>>> ' '.join(['This', 'will', 'join', 'all', 'words', 'into', 'a', 'string'])
'This will join all words into a string'
>>> 'Happy New Year'.find('ew')
7
>>> 'Happy New Year'.replace('Happy','Brilliant')
'Brilliant New Year'
```

From sequences of characters, let us now try looking at other data structures—all the different collections you have on your computer—the assortment of your files, browser bookmarks, your song playlists, emails, the video collections you can access on a streaming service and many more.

Let us talk about lists.

2. Python Lists

In this section, you will learn all about lists, how they are made, the process of adding or removing elements from them, and so forth.

Python offers many compound datatypes usually known as sequences. Apart from being one of the most frequently used datatype in Python, 'lists' is very versatile.

There are a number of ways to describe lists:
The usual description of a list type is "the container that holds other objects in a particular order." It executes the sequence protocol and lets you add or take out objects from the sequence.

Another description of the list is as a data structure that is a changeable, or mutable, organized sequence of elements. Every element or value within a list is referred to as an item. Just as strings are known as characters in between quotes, lists are characterized by values in between square brackets [ ].

When you want to work with many related values in Python, lists are very handy to use. They will allow you to keep data that belongs together together, condense code, and perform similar methods and operations on different values all at once.

When you are thinking about lists in python, and other data structures that are essentially types of collections, you can try considering all the different collections you have on your computer, the assortment of your files, browser bookmarks, your song playlists, emails, the video collections you can access on a streaming service, and many more.

Creating a List

In Python, you can create a list by placing the elements (or all the items) within a square bracket [], and separating with commas. It can contain any number of items that may be of different types (float, integer, string, etc.).

```
# empty list
my_list = []

# list of integers
my_list = [1, 2, 3]

# list with mixed datatypes
my_list = [1, "Hello", 3.4]
```

Additionally, a list can contain another list as an item in what we call a nested list.

```
# nested list
my_list = ["mouse", [8, 4, 6], ['a']]
```

Accessing Elements from a List

To access list elements, you can use a number of ways:

List index

You can use the index operator [] to get to an item in a list. Index begins from 0, and thus, a list of five items will contain an index from 0 to 4. When you try to access an element other than this, it raises an IndexError. The index should be an integer and we cannot use float or other types because the results will be a TypeError. Nested list are accessed via nested indexing

```
my_list = ['p','r','o','b','e']
# Output: p
print(my_list[0])


# Output: o
print(my_list[2])


# Output: e
print(my_list[4])


# Error! Only integer can be used for indexing
# my_list[4.0]


# Nested List
n_list = ["Happy", [2,0,1,5]]


# Nested indexing


# Output: a
print(n_list[0][1])


# Output: 5
print(n_list[1][3])
```

Negative Indexing

Python programming supports negative indexing within its different sequences. As I mentioned while discussing string, the -1 index is used in reference to the final item, -2 is used in

```
my_list = ['p','r','o','b','e']


# Output: e
print(my_list[-1])


# Output: p
print(my_list[-5])
```

reference to second last one etc.

Slicing Lists in Python

We can access numerous items in a list with the colon/slicing operator.

```
my_list = ['p','r','o','g','r','a','m','i','z']
# elements 3rd to 5th
print(my_list[2:5])


# elements beginning to 4th
print(my_list[:-5])


# elements 6th to end
print(my_list[5:])


# elements beginning to end
print(my_list[:])
```

You can best visualize slicing by considering the index supposed to go between the elements as displayed below. Thus, if you want to access a range, you will need two indexes that will slice that particular portion from the list.

P	R	O	G	R	A	M	I	Z

```
 0  1  2  3  4  5  6  7  8  9
-9 -8 -7 -6 -5 -4 -3 -2 -1
```

Changing or adding elements to a list

I mentioned in the beginning that lists are mutable; this means unlike tuple or strings, their elements can be changed. When changing an item or multiple items, we can use the assignment operator = to do that.

```
# mistake values
odd = [2, 4, 6, 8]


# change the 1st item
odd[0] = 1


# Output: [1, 4, 6, 8]
print(odd)


# change 2nd to 4th items
odd[1:4] = [3, 5, 7]


# Output: [1, 3, 5, 7]
print(odd)
```

You can also use **append ()** method to add one item to a list or use the **extend ()** method to add multiple items.

```
odd = [1, 3, 5]

odd.append(7)

# Output: [1, 3, 5, 7]
print(odd)

odd.extend([9, 11, 13])

# Output: [1, 3, 5, 7, 9, 11, 13]
print(odd)
```

You can also combine two lists using the + operator. This is known as concatenation. The * operator on the other hand repeats a list for the set number of times.

```
odd = [1, 3, 5]
```

```
# Output [1, 3, 5, 9, 7, 5]
print(odd + [9, 7, 5])
```

```
#Output: ["re", "re", "re"]
print(["re"] * 3)
```

Furthermore, you can insert a single item at a desired place by using the **insert ()** method or just insert many items by squeezing it into an empty list slice.

```
odd = [1, 9]
```

```
odd.insert(1,3)
```

```
# Output [1, 3, 9]
print(odd)
```

```
odd[2:2] = [5, 7]
```

```
# Output [1, 3, 5, 7, 9]
print(odd)
```

How to Remove or Delete List Elements

You can delete a single or multiple items from a list by using the 'del' keyword. It can actually delete the list completely.

```
my_list = ['p','r','o','b','l','e','m']


# delete one item
del my_list[2]


# Output: ['p', 'r', 'b', 'l', 'e', 'm']
print(my_list)


# delete multiple items
del my_list[1:5]


# Output: ['p', 'm']
print(my_list)


# delete entire list
del my_list


# Error: List not defined
print(my_list)
```

You can also use **remove ()** to remove the given item or **pop ()** method to get rid of an item at the given index.

The pop () method removes and returns the final item if index is not given. This in particular helps us implement lists just like stacks (first-in, last-out structure). To empty a list, you can also use the **clear ()** method.

```python
my_list = ['p','r','o','b','l','e','m']
my_list.remove('p')

# Output: ['r', 'o', 'b', 'l', 'e', 'm']
print(my_list)

# Output: 'o'
print(my_list.pop(1))

# Output: ['r', 'b', 'l', 'e', 'm']
print(my_list)

# Output: 'm'
print(my_list.pop())

# Output: ['r', 'b', 'l', 'e']
print(my_list)

my_list.clear()

# Output: []
print(my_list)
```

Lastly, you can also delete list items by allocating an empty list to a slice of elements.

```python
>>> my_list = ['p','r','o','b','l','e','m']
>>> my_list[2:3] = []
>>> my_list
['p', 'r', 'b', 'l', 'e', 'm']
>>> my_list[2:5] = []
>>> my_list
['p', 'r', 'm']
```

The Python List Methods

In the following table are the methods available with the Python programming list object. You will access them as list.method (). Note that we have already used some of these methods above.

The list of python Methods
append() – use it to add some element to the end of the list
extend() – use it to add all list elements to the another list
insert() – use it to insert an item at the set index
remove() – use it to remove an item from your list
pop() – use it to remove and return some element at the given index
clear() – use it to removes all your items from the list
index() – use it to return the first matched item's index
count() – use it to returns the count of number of items that have passed as an argument
sort() – use it to sort list items in an ascending order
reverse() – use it to reverse the list's order of items

Look at some examples of python list methods:

```
my_list = [3, 8, 1, 6, 0, 8, 4]


# Output: 1
print(my_list.index(8))


# Output: 2
print(my_list.count(8))


my_list.sort()


# Output: [0, 1, 3, 4, 6, 8, 8]
print(my_list)


my_list.reverse()


# Output: [8, 8, 6, 4, 3, 1, 0]
print(my_list)
```

Creating Lists Elegantly Through List Comprehension

One very elegant and precise way of creating new lists from existing python lists is though list comprehension.

List comprehension comprises an expression that is followed by the 'for statement' within square brackets. The following is an example to make a list with every item assuming an increasing power of 2.

```
pow2 = [2 ** x for x in range(10)]


# Output: [1, 2, 4, 8, 16, 32, 64, 128, 256, 512]
print(pow2)
```

This code is equivalent to

```
pow2 = []
for x in range(10):
  pow2.append(2 ** x)
```


Optionally, the list comprehension can have more 'for' or 'if' statements. An optional 'if' statement will filter out items for the fresh list. Examine these examples:

```
>>> pow2 = [2 ** x for x in range(10) if x > 5]
>>> pow2
[64, 128, 256, 512]
>>> odd = [x for x in range(20) if x % 2 == 1]
>>> odd
[1, 3, 5, 7, 9, 11, 13, 15, 17, 19]
>>> [x+y for x in ['Python ','C '] for y in ['Language','Programming']]
['Python Language', 'Python Programming', 'C Language', 'C Programming']
```

Well, 'lists' just contains values. At this point, I think we should look at something that associates every value with a key: dictionaries. It is also a good time to let the order rest for a while!

Chapter 9

Python Dictionaries

In python, dictionaries refer to the unordered collection of items. We also refer to them as the built-in 'mapping' type of python. Dictionaries are helpful because they map keys to values and these pairs (key-value) offer a convenient way to store python's data. Thus, while other compound types of data contain only a single value as an element, the dictionary contains a key: *value pair.*

We optimize dictionaries to retrieve values when we know the key.

Dictionaries are made with curly braces on both sides since they have to hold related data like the information contained in an ID or a user profile. A dictionary simply looks like this:

```
sammy = {'username': 'sammy-shark', 'online': True, 'followers': 987}
```

Apart from the curly braces, the dictionary also contains colons (:) throughout.

The words to the left of the colons represent keys. Keys can comprise any immutable data type and in the dictionary above, the keys include the following:

- 'username'
- 'followers'
- 'online'

NOTE: Every key in the example above is a string value. The words to the right of the colons represent the values. Values can consist of any data type. In the dictionary above, the values include the following:

- 'sammy-shark'
- True
- 987

Each one of these values is either an integer or Boolean (see next section).

Let us now print the 'sammy' dictionary:

```
print(sammy)
Output
{'username': 'sammy-shark', 'followers': 987, 'online': True}
```

When you look at the output, you may notice that the key-value pairs' order has changed. This is because of the 'unordered' nature of the dictionary data type. Therefore, unlike tuples and lists, dictionaries do not maintain order or the ability to be indexed. Any time you print a dictionary, the order is usually random. However, the key-value pairs usually remain intact all the time thus enabling people to access data according to their relational meaning.

How to Access Elements of the Dictionary

Due to the dictionary data structure's nature of being unordered, you cannot call its values by an index number as you can with tuples and lists. Nonetheless, you can reference the related keys to call its values.

Accessing Data Items Using Keys

In your python program, dictionaries are very important because they provide key-value pairs to store data. If you want to seclude the username 'Sammy', you can do so by calling Sammy['username']. Let us try printing that out:

```
print(sammy['username'])
Output
sammy-shark
```

Like databases, dictionaries are dissimilar to lists in that as opposed to calling an integer in order to get a specific index value, you assign a value to a key and have the option of calling that key to get its related value.

When you invoke the 'username' key, you get the specific value of that particular key i.e. 'sammy-shark'. The values that linger within Sammy dictionary could actually be called using that same format:

```
sammy['followers']
# Returns 987

sammy['online']
# Returns True
```

When you take advantage of the key-value pairs of dictionaries, you can reference keys to retrieve values.

Accessing Elements with Functions

Apart from accessing values using keys, you can also work with a number of built-in functions:

- ✓ dict.keys() isolates keys
- ✓ dict.values() isolates values
- ✓ dict.items() returns items in a list format of (key, value) tuple pairs

To return the keys, you would use the function 'dict.keys()'. In the example, that would take the variable name and thus be 'sammy.keys()'. We'll pass that to a 'print()' function and observe the output:

```
print(sammy.keys())
Output
dict_keys(['followers', 'username', 'online'])
```

We get output that puts the keys in an iterable view object of dict_keys class. The keys are thus printed inside a list format.

You can use this function to query across dictionaries. For instance, you can see the common keys shared between the dictionary data structures:

```
sammy = {'username': 'sammy-shark', 'online': True, 'followers': 987}
jesse = {'username': 'JOctopus', 'online': False, 'points': 723}

for common_key in sammy.keys() & jesse.keys():
    print(sammy[common_key], jesse[common_key])
```

The 'sammy' dictionary and the 'jesse' dictionary are both a user profile dictionary. Their profiles contain different keys. Nonetheless, since Sammy has a social profile carrying associated followers and Jesse carries a gaming profile that has associated points, both keys they have in common are 'online' status and 'username' that you can get when you run this little program:

```
Output
sammy-shark JOctopus
True False
```

You could definitely improve on the program to ensure the output is more readable to the user; however, this illustrates that you can use the 'dict.keys()' to check across different dictionaries to be able to see what they share in common or not. You will find this particularly helpful with large dictionaries.

You can also use the 'dict.values()' function in a similar way to query the values in the 'sammy' dictionary, which you would construct as 'sammy.values'. Let us try printing them out:

```
sammy = {'username': 'sammy-shark', 'online': True, 'followers': 987}

print(sammy.values())
Output
dict_values([True, 'sammy-shark', 987])
```

Both the 'values()' and 'methods()' return unsorted keys lists and values that exist within the 'sammy' dictionary with all the view objects of 'dict_keys' as well as 'dict_values' in that specific order. If you are interested in all the dictionary items, you can simply access them with the 'items()' function.

```
print(sammy.items())
Output
dict_items([('online', True), ('username', 'sammy-shark'), ('followers', 987)])
```

This 'lists' returned format usually has (key, value) tuple pairs containing dict_items view object.

By using a 'for loop', you can actually iterate the returned format list. For instance, you can print every one key and value of a particular dictionary and then make it more readable to any user by adding a string:

```
for key, value in sammy.items():
    print(key, 'is the key for the value', value)
Output
online is the key for the value True
followers is the key for the value 987
username is the key for the value sammy-shark
```

If you check above, the 'for loop' actually iterated over the items in the 'sammy' dictionary and then printed out the keys as well as values line after line, with information to make it simpler to understand by users.

You can utilize the in-built functions to access values, items and keys from the data structures of the dictionary.

Modifying Dictionaries

Dictionaries, as I mentioned earlier, are mutable structures of data that you can modify. In this regard, we will now look at adding and deleting elements in a dictionary.

Adding and Altering Elements

You could add key-value pairs without using a function by using the syntax 'dict[key] = value'. Let us engage in a practical look at how this works by adding a key-value pair to 'usernames' dictionary.

```
usernames = {'Sammy': 'sammy-shark', 'Jamie': 'mantisshrimp54'}

usernames['Drew'] = 'squidly'

print(usernames)
Output
{'Drew': 'squidly', 'Sammy': 'sammy-shark', 'Jamie': 'mantisshrimp54'}
```

As you can see, the dictionary has been updated with the key-value pair 'drew': 'squidly'. This pair can go anywhere in the dictionary since dictionaries are typically unordered. If you can use the dictionary 'usernames' later in your program file, it will contain the additional key-value pair.

Additionally, you can use this syntax to modify the value assigned to a key. In this case, you will reference a key that exists and pass to it a different value.

We will consider a dictionary 'drew' which is one of the users on a given network. Let us say that today, this user had a bump in followers. We have to update this integer passed to the key (followers). We will use the function 'print()' to confirm that the dictionary was indeed modified.

```
drew = {'username': 'squidly', 'online': True, 'followers': 305}

drew['followers'] = 342

print(drew)
Output
{'username': 'squidly', 'followers': 342, 'online': True}
```

In the output, we can see that the number of followers jumped to 342, from the integer value of 305.

We can utilize this method to add key-value pairs to dictionaries with the user-input. Let us now try writing a program (usernames.py), which will run on the command line, as well as allow input from the user to add in more names and linked usernames:

usernames.py

```
# Define original dictionary
usernames = {'Sammy': 'sammy-shark', 'Jamie': 'mantisshrimp54'}

# Set up while loop to iterate
while True:

    # Request user to enter a name
    print('Enter a name:')

    # Assign to name variable
    name = input()

    # Check whether name is in the dictionary and print feedback
    if name in usernames:
        print(usernames[name] + ' is the username of ' + name)

    # If the name is not in the dictionary...
    else:

        # Provide feedback
        print('I don\'t have ' + name + '\'s username, what is it?')

        # Take in a new username for the associated name
        username = input()

        # Assign username value to name key
        usernames[name] = username

        # Print feedback that the data was updated
        print('Data updated.')
```

Let us now use python usernames.py to execute the program: When you run it, you get this output:

```
Output
Enter a name:
Sammy
sammy-shark is the username of Sammy
Enter a name:
Jesse
I don't have Jesse's username, what is it?
JOctopus
Data updated.
Enter a name:
```

After testing the program, press Ctrl+C to escape it, and perhaps set up a trigger that enables you to close/quit the program–like typing the letter 'q'–along with a conditional statement to advance your code. You can interactively modify dictionaries using this approach. With this program in particular, when you press Ctrl+C to exit, you lose all the data unless you find a way to manage <u>reading and writing files</u>.

You can also use the 'dict.update()' function to add and modify dictionaries. This will vary from the 'append()' function available in lists.

We will now add the 'followers' key in the dictionary below and then give it an integer value in 'jesse.update()'. Let's 'print()' the updated dictionary to follow that.

```
jesse = {'username': 'JOctopus', 'online': False, 'points': 723}

jesse.update({'followers': 481})

print(jesse)
Output
{'followers': 481, 'username': 'JOctopus', 'points': 723, 'online': False}
```

You can see from the output that we added the key-value pair 'followers': 481 to the dictionary.

You can as well change the current key-value pair by using the 'dict.update()' method by simply replacing a specific value for a particular key. Let us now change sammy's online status in the 'sammy' dictionary from true to false:

```
sammy = {'username': 'sammy-shark', 'online': True, 'followers': 987}

sammy.update({'online': False})

print(sammy)
Output
{'username': 'sammy-shark', 'followers': 987, 'online': False}
```

The 'Sammy.update({'online':False})'line reference the 'online' key that exists and modifies its Boolean (see next section) value from True to False. When you call to print() the dictionary, you see the update occur in the output.

You can either use the function 'dict.update()' or syntax 'dict[key]=value' to add items to dictionaries, or modify values.

Now, for the easiest part of dictionaries>> Deleting Elements; please go over this information to know how to do that with python.

At this point, you have just covered most of the basic programming topics. It is about time we took all this up a notch. Let us talk about something interesting; what do you think about designing a circuit that gives you an output only when particular combinations are existent? Well, this (and more) is what Boolean logic helps you do.

Chapter 10

Boolean Logic and Conditional Statements

The Boolean type of data can be one or two values, either false or true. In programming, we use Booleans to compare and control the flow of the program.

Booleans symbolize the true values linked with logic in mathematics, which forms the foundation of algorithms in computer science. Booleans are named after George Boole, the mathematician who lived over two centuries ago. Thus, the word Boolean should begin with a capitalized B. The False and True values also have to begin with capital F and T respectively because in Python, they are very special values.

Before we get deeper into the topic, we will start by going over the basics of Boolean logic, including how they work, the Boolean comparisons, truth tables and logical operators.

Comparison Operators

In programming, we use comparison operators to make comparisons of values and evaluate down to one Boolean value of either False or True.

The following is a table showing Boolean comparison operators.

Operator	What it means
==	Equal to
!=	Not equal to
<	Less than
>	Greater than
<=	Less than or equal to
>=	Greater than or equal to

To understand how the operators work in python, you have to assign two integers to two variables:

71

$$x = 5$$
$$y = 8$$

In the example above, x has a value of 5, and is less than y which takes the value of 8. Using the two variables and their connected values, we will go through the operators from the table above. In the program, instruct python to print out 'if' each comparison operator evaluates to true or false. We will have python print a string to show us what it is evaluating so we and other people can understand this output better.

$$x = 5$$
$$y = 8$$

```
print("x == y:", x == y)
print("x != y:", x != y)
print("x < y:", x < y)
print("x > y:", x > y)
print("x <= y:", x <= y)
print("x >= y:", x >= y)
```

Output
```
x == y: False
x != y: True
x < y: True
x > y: False
x <= y: True
x >= y: False
```

Python, following mathematical logic, has evaluated the following in each of the above expressions:

- ✓ Is 5 (x) equal to 8 (y)? **False**
- ✓ Is 5 not equal to 8? **True**
- ✓ Is 5 less than 8? **True**
- ✓ Is 5 greater than 8? **False**
- ✓ Is 5 less than or equal to 8? **True**
- ✓ Is 5 not less than or equal to 8? **False**

Even though we used integers here, we can also utilize float values to substitute them.

Boolean operators are also usable with strings; they are, however, case-sensitive unless you use an extra string method. Let us look at how strings are practically compared:

```
Sammy = "Sammy"
sammy = "sammy"

print("Sammy == sammy: ", Sammy == sammy)
Output
Sammy == sammy: False
```

The string above denoted by 'Sammy' is not equivalent to the 'sammy' string. This is because they are not the same: one begins with the upper case S while the other one begins with a lower-case s. However, if you added another variable assigned to the value of 'Sammy', they will then evaluate to equal.

```
Sammy = "Sammy"
sammy = "sammy"
also_Sammy = "Sammy"

print("Sammy == sammy: ", Sammy == sammy)
print("Sammy == also_Sammy", Sammy == also_Sammy)
Output
Sammy == sammy: False
Sammy == also_Sammy: True
```

You can also use the other comparison operators that include > and < to compare two strings. The program compares the strings using the ASCII values of the characters lexicographically.

You can also evaluate Boolean values with the comparison operators:

```
t = True
f = False

print("t != f: ", t != f)
Output
t != f: True
```

The above code block evaluates that True is not equal to False. Notice the dissimilarity between operators = and ==.

```
x = y   # Sets x equal to y
x == y  # Evaluates whether x is equal to y
```

This one '=' is the assignment operator that sets one value equivalent to another. The other one '==' is the comparison operator that evaluates whether both values are equal.

The Logical Operators

We generally use three logical operators to compare values. These operators evaluate expressions down to the Boolean values and return either False or True. These operators are 'or', 'not' and 'and'. Look at the table below to see their definition:

Operator	What it means	What it looks like
and	True if both are true	x and y
or	True if at least one is true	x or y
not	True only if false	not x

We typically use logical operators to evaluate whether expressions are true or not true. For instance, we can use them to determine if the student has registered for the course and that a grade is passing. If the two cases are true, the student will thus be given a grade in the system. Similarly, we can use it to determine whether someone is a valid active online shop customer based on whether he has a store credit or has purchased goods within the past six months.

To have a better understanding of how logical operators work, we will evaluate some three expressions:

```
print((9 > 7) and (2 < 4)) # Both original expressions are True
print((8 == 8) or (6 != 6)) # One original expression is True
print(not(3 <= 1))       # The original expression is False
Output
True
True
True
```

In the first scenario with 'print((9>7)' and '(2<4))', 9>7 and 2<4 required evaluation to True because the operator being used was 'and'.

In the second scenario with 'print ((8==8))' or (6 != 6)), because 8==8 did evaluate to True, it never made a difference that 6 != 6 evaluates to false since the operator being used was 'or'. Had we used the 'and' operator, it would have definitely be evaluated to False.

In the third scenario with 'print(not(3<=1))', you realize that the operator 'not' negates the False value which 3<=1 returns.

We will now substitute the floats for integers and target False evaluations:

```
print((-0.2 > 1.4) and (0.8 < 3.1)) # One original expression is False
print((7.5 == 8.9) or (9.2 != 9.2)) # Both original expressions are False
print(not(-5.7 <= 0.3))       # The original expression is True
```

In the above example,

• 'and' ought to have at least a single False expression evaluating to False

• 'or' ought to have the two expressions evaluating to False

• 'not' ought to have its inner expression being True for the new expression to evaluate to False

If the above results are not very clear to you, we will shortly go over some truth tables that will bring you up to speed.

You can also use 'and', 'not' and 'or' in writing your compound statements:

not((-0.2 > 1.4) and ((0.8 < 3.1) or (0.1 == 0.1)))

Now, first, focus on the innermost expression: '(0.8 < 3.1)' or (0.1 ==0.1). This particular expression evaluates to True because the two mathematical statements are True.

We can now take the returned 'True' value and merge it with the next inner expression which is '(-0.2>1.4)' and '(true)'. This example in particular returns false because the Mathematical statement '-0.2 > 1.4' is False and obviously, '(False)'and '(True)' returns False.

We finally have the outer expression which is 'not(False)', that evaluates to True, so the last returned value is: (if we print the statement) 'True'.

The logical operators and, not, and, or thus evaluate expressions and return the Boolean values.

Truth Tables

There is definitely a ton of stuff to learn about the branch of mathematics known as logic. However, we can learn some of it selectively to develop our algorithmic thinking for programming.

Look at the truth tables below for the comparison operator ==, and each one of the logic operators 'and', 'not' and 'or'. While it is possible not be able to reason them out immediately, it will prove helpful to work to memorize them so that they quicken your decision-making process.

The truth table for ==

x	==	y	Returns
True	==	True	True
True	==	False	False
False	==	True	False
False	==	False	True

The truth table for 'and'

x	and	y	Returns
True	and	True	True
True	and	False	False
False	and	True	False
False	and	False	False

The truth table for 'or'

x	or	y	Returns
True	or	True	True
True	or	False	True
False	or	True	True
False	or	False	False

The truth table for 'not'

not	x	Returns
not	True	False
not	False	True

Truth tables are logic based mathematical tables-common as they are, they tend to be useful to memorize or always keep in mind when creating instructions or algorithms in any form of computer programming.

Boolean Operators for 'Flow Control'

To control the stream and program outcomes in form of flow control statements, you can use a condition, and then a clause.

A condition essentially evaluates down to a Boolean value of True or False, and presents a point where the program makes a decision i.e. a condition informs you when something evaluates to False or True.

On the other hand, a clause is a block of code following the condition and dictates the program outcome. That is, it forms the 'do this' part of the whole construction- 'if y is True, then do this.'

Look at the block of code below that describes comparison operators working together with conditional statements to control python program flow:

```
if grade >= 65:          # Condition
    print("Passing grade")    # Clause

else:
    print("Failing grade")
```

This program evaluates whether every student's grade is failing or passing. When a student (for instance), gets a grade of 83, the first statement evaluates to True, and the print statement of 'passing grade' is triggered. In case a student registers grade 59, the initial statement evaluates to False and thus, the program goes ahead to implement the print statement attached to the 'else' expression: 'failing grade'.

Since each Python object can be evaluated to False or True, expert python programmers recommend against comparing values to False or True since it is less readable and tends to return an unanticipated Boolean. This means you should try to avoid using something like 'sammy== True' in your programs and alternatively, make a comparison of 'sammy' to some other non-Boolean value that returns a Boolean.

Boolean operators usually present conditions we can use to decide the ultimate program outcome via flow control statements. With all that covered, I know you are ready to make some decisions!

Conditional Statements: If and Else Statements

Every programming language typically has conditional statements. When you have conditional statements, you have code that runs sometimes (not all the time), even though it depends on the conditions of the program at that particular time.

When you execute every program statement fully, moving from the top to bottom with every line implemented in an order, you are not really instructing the program to actually evaluate particular conditions. We can use conditional statements to help programs to actually determine whether specific conditions are really being met.

To gain a better understanding of conditional statements, look at the following examples where they (conditional statements) would be used:

- If the student gets over 70% on his test, report that his grade passed; if not, report that his grade fails.
- If Jane has money in her account, calculate interest; if she does not, charge the penalty fee.
- If he buys 8 mangoes or more, calculate a 5% discount; if he buys less, then don't.

When you evaluate conditions and assign code to run based on whether those conditions are met or not, you are essentially writing conditional code. In this section, I will take you through all you need to know about writing conditional statements in Python.

If Statement

Let us begin with the 'if' statement that will determine whether a statement is false or true, and run code only when the statement is true. Open a file in a plain text editor and write this code:

```
grade = 70

if grade >= 65:
    print("Passing grade")
```

With the above code, you have the variable 'grade' and will give it an integer value of 70; you will then use the 'if' statement to evaluate whether the variable grade is more or equal (>=) to 65 or not. If it fails to meet this condition, you are instructing the program to print the string 'passing grade'.

Now save the program with the name 'grade.py' then use the command 'python grade.py' to run it.

Note that in our case, the grade of 70 does not meet the condition of being more than or equal to 65, and so, when you run the program, you will get the input below:

```
Output
Passing grade
```

We will not try to change the result of this program by altering the value of the variable 'grade' to 60.

```
grade = 60

if grade >= 65:
    print("Passing grade")
```

When you save and run the code, you will not receive any output because the condition was not met and you did not instruct the program to implement another statement. Let us look at another example:

We will calculate whether or not a bank balance is less than 0. We will create a file named account.py and write the program below:

account.py

```
balance = -5

if balance < 0:
    print("Balance is below 0, add funds now or you will be charged a penalty.")
```

When you run the program attached with 'python account.py', you will get the following output:

Output
Balance is below 0, add funds now or you will be charged a penalty.

In the program you initialized, the 'balance' variable with the value '-5' is below 0. The balance did meet the 'if' statement condition (balance<0) and thus, when you save and run the code, you will get the string output. Again, if you alter the balance to 0 or some positive number, you will not get any output.

Else Statement

Even as an 'if' statement evaluates to false, it is possible that you will want the program to do something. In the grade example, you will want an output whether the grade is failing or passing. To do this, let us add an 'else' statement to the above grade condition, which we construct this way:

81

```
grade.py

grade = 60

if grade >= 65:
    print("Passing grade")

else:
    print("Failing grade")
```

The grade variable above contains a value of 60- thus, the 'if' statement will evaluate as false- and the program will not print the 'passing grade'. The subsequent 'else' statement will tell the program to do something anyway.

When you save and run, you will get the following output:

Output
Failing grade

By rewriting the program to give out the grade and a value of 65 or more, you will instead get the output 'passing grade.'

Rewrite the code as shown below to add an 'else' statement to the example on bank account:

```
account.py

balance = 522

if balance < 0:
    print("Balance is below 0, add funds now or you will be charged a penalty.")

else:
    print("Your balance is 0 or above.")
Output
Your balance is 0 or above.
```

Here, we changed the value of the 'balance' variable to a positive number in order for the 'else' statement to print. You can rewrite the value to a negative number to get the first 'if' statement to print.

When you combine the 'if' and 'else' statements, you will be constructing a conditional statement with two parts that will instruct your computer to implement a particular code whether the 'if' condition is met or not.

The else if statement

We have so far learnt a Boolean option for various conditional statements as each statement evaluates to either false or true. In most cases, you will want your program to evaluate more than two possible outcomes. For this, we will proceed to use the else if statement, which in Python, is written as 'elif'. The else if or 'elif' statement resembles the 'if' statement and evaluates another condition.

In our program on bank account, we may want to have some three distinct outputs for three situations that include the following:

- The balance is less than 0
- The balance equals to 0
- The balance is more than 0

The 'elif' statement goes between the 'if' statement and the 'else' statement as is shown below:

account.py

```
...
if balance < 0:
    print("Balance is below 0, add funds now or you will be charged a
penalty.")

elif balance == 0:
    print("Balance is equal to 0, add funds soon.")

else:
    print("Your balance is 0 or above.")
```

Now we have three possible outputs you can receive once you run the program:

- If the 'balance' variable is equal to 0, you will then get the output using the 'elif' statement; this means the balance is 0 and you should add more money to your account.
- If the 'balance' variable is set to a positive number, you will get the output from the else statement; this means that your balance is either 0 or more.
- If the 'balance' variable is fixed to a number that is negative, the output will have to be the string from the 'if' statement; this means that the balance is less than 0 and therefore, you should add funds now or face a penalty.

What about an instance where you want to have over 3 options? This is possible by simply writing more than a single elif statement into your code. In the grade.py program, you can rewrite the code so that you will have a few letter grades agreeing with the ranges of numerical grades.

90 or more is equal to grade A

From 80 to 89 is equal to grade B

From 70 to 79 is equal to grade C

From 65 to 69 is equal to grade D

64 or below is equal to grade F

To run this code, we will require a single 'if' statement, 3 elif statements, as well an else statement to help you handle all the failing cases.

We will now rewrite the code from the above example to have strings printing out every letter grade. We can also keep the 'else' statement the same.

```
grade.py
. . .
if grade >= 90:
  print("A grade")

elif grade >=80:
  print("B grade")

elif grade >=70:
  print("C grade")

elif grade >= 65:
  print("D grade")

else:
  print("Failing grade")
```

The elif statements evaluate in order and thus, you can keep your statements basic. The program is completing the following steps:

- If the grade is more than 90, the program will print grade A; if it is less than 90, the program continues to the following statement...

- If the grade is more than, or equivalent to 80, the program will print grade B; if it is 79 or less, the program continues to the following statement...

- If the grade is more than, or equivalent to 70, the program will print grade C; if it is 69 or less, the program continues to the following statement...

- If the grade is more than or equivalent to 65, the program will print grade D; if it is 64 or less, the program continues to the following statement...

- The program prints 'failing grade' when all the conditions above are not met.

Nested if Statements

When you have started feeling comfortable with the elif, else, and if statements, you can start experimenting with the nested conditional statements. You can use the nested if statements when you want to check for secondary condition if the initial condition implements as true. In this case, you can include an if-else statement right in the middle on another if-else statement. Let us discuss a nested if statement:

```
if statement1:        #outer if statement
   print("true")

   if nested_statement:   #nested if statement
      print("yes")

   else:              #nested else statement
      print("no")

else:              #outer else statement
   print("false")
```

Some possible outputs resulting from this code would be: If the first statement (or statement 1) evaluates to true, the program evaluates whether the nested_statement is also evaluating to true. If both are true, you will get the following output:

```
Output
true
yes
```

However, when the first statement evaluates to true but the nested_statement evaluates to false, the output you get is:

```
Output
true
no
```

If the first statement evaluates to false, it means the if-else statement will not run and thus, the else statement runs alone. In such a case, the output you get is: *false*

You can also have many if statements nested all through your code:

```
if statement1:          #outer if
  print("hello world")

  if nested_statement1:     #first nested if
    print("yes")

  elif nested_statement2:   #first nested elif
    print("maybe")

  else:           #first nested else
    print("no")

elif statement2:          #outer elif
  print("hello galaxy")

  if nested_statement3:     #second nested if
    print("yes")

  elif nested_statement4:   #second nested elif
    print("maybe")

  else:           #second nested else
    print("no")

else:           #outer else
  statement("hello universe")
```

In the above code, there is a nested if statement within every 'if' statement along with the elif statement. This allows for more options inside each condition.

You can look at an example of nested if statement using your grade.py program. You can check for whether or not a grade is passing first (more than or equivalent to 65%), and then look for the letter grade the numerical grade should be equal to. However, if the grade is not passing, you do not need to run through the letter grades. Instead, you can have the program reporting that the grade is failing.

The modified code with the nested if statement will appear like this:

```
...
if grade >= 65:
  print("Passing grade of:")

  if grade >= 90:
    print("A")

  elif grade >=80:
    print("B")

  elif grade >=70:
    print("C")

  elif grade >= 65:
    print("D")
else:
  print("Failing grade")
```

If you run the code with the 'grade' variable set to the integer value of 92, the first condition will be met and your program will print 'passing grade of:'. After that, it checks to find out whether the grade is more than, or equivalent to 90 and since this condition too is met, it prints out A.

If you run the code with the variable 'grade' set to 60, and then the first condition fails to be met, the program skips the nested if statements and moves on to the 'else' statement, and the program prints out 'failing grade'.

You can definitely add more options to this, and use another layer of nested if statements. Maybe you will want to evaluate for A-, A and A+ grades individually. We can also achieve that by first trying to see whether the grade is passing, then trying to check whether the grade is 90 or more, then checking whether (for instance) the grade is beyond 96 for an A+.

```
grade.py
. . .
if grade >= 65:
  print("Passing grade of:")

  if grade >= 90:
    if grade > 96:
      print("A+")

    elif grade > 93 and grade <= 96:
      print("A")

    elif grade >= 90:
      print("A-")
. . .
```

The code above shows that for variable 'grade' set to 96, the program runs the following:

- Check whether the grade is more than, or equivalent to 65; this is true.
- Print out the 'passing grade of:'
- Check whether the grade is more than or equal to 90; this is true
- Check whether the grade is more than 96; this is false
- Check whether the grade is more than 93 and also less than, or equivalent to 96; this is true
- Print A
- Drop these nested conditional statements and move on with the rest of the code

The program output for a grade of 96 will look like this:

```
Output
Passing grade of:
A
```

The nested if statements can give the chance to add a number of particular levels of conditions to your code.

When you use conditional statements such as the 'if' statement, you gain more control over what your program executes. Conditional statements instruct your program to evaluate whether or not a particular condition is being met. If

89

the condition is met, it executes certain code, but if not, the program continues to move down to some other code.

In the next section, we will look at conditional statements that repeat themselves; the repeated implementation of code is mostly founded on Boolean conditions, so nothing new.

Chapter 11

Constructing 'While' Loops In Python

Computer programs come in handy in situations where you want to automate and repeat tasks because in so doing, you won't have to keep doing them manually. A great way to repeat the same tasks is by using loops and in this section of the book, we will be looking at the 'while' loop in Python.

The Boolean condition is the basis on which the 'while' loop executes the repeated implementation of code. The code that contains a 'while' block executes, so long as the 'while' statement is 'true'.

You can think of the 'while' loop as a conditional statement that repeats itself. The program executes the code after the 'if' statement. However, in the 'while' loop, the program goes to the start of the 'while' statement until it finds the condition as 'false'.

The while loops are conditionally based. This is not the same thing when it comes to 'for loops', which usually execute a specific number of times. Therefore, you do not need to know the number of times that you should repeat the code going in.

While loop

Here is how we construct while loops in Python:

```
while [a condition is True]:
    [do something]
```

What is being done in the program will continue to execute until the condition that is under assessment is no longer true.

Let us now try to create a little program for executing the 'while' loop. For this program, we will instruct the user to put in a password. As we go through the loop, there are 2 possible outcomes:

- If the password is right, the while loop exits
- If the password is not right, the while loop continues executing

We will build a file with the name password.py in any editor we choose, and start by initializing the 'password' variable as an empty string:

password.py

```
password = "
```

You will use the empty string to take in input from the user in the while loop. We will now construct the 'while' statement together with its condition.

```
password.py
password = "
```

```
while password != 'password':
```

In this case, the 'while' is followed by the 'password' variable. You are checking to see whether the variable is set to the 'password' string, but you can choose any string you would want. Thus, if the user inputs the 'password' string, then loop will cease and the program continues executing any code outside the loop. Nonetheless, if the string the user inputs is not equivalent to the 'password' string, the loop continues. After that, you will add the block of code that performs something inside 'while' loop:

```
password.py
password = "

while password != 'password':
    print('What is the password?')
    password = input()
```

Within the 'while' loop, the program will run a print statement, which then prompts for the passwords. Afterwards, the 'password' variable is set to the input of the user via the 'input()' function.

The program checks to see whether the 'password' variable is assigned to the 'password' string; if it is, the 'while' loops ends automatically. Now give the program an extra line of code for when that occurs:

```
password.py
password = ''

while password != 'password':
  print('What is the password?')
  password = input()

print('Yes, the password is ' + password + '. You may enter.')
```

The final statement 'print()' is outside the 'while' loop; thus, when the user inputs 'password' as the password, that user will see the last print statement outside the loop. Nonetheless, if the user does not enter the 'password' word at all, he or she will not get to the final 'print()' statement and will thus be stuck in the infinite loop. What is the infinite loop really?

An infinite loop will occur when a program keeps executing within a single loop, at no time leaving it. You can simply press CTRL+C on the command line to exit from the infinite loops. Now save the program and run: python password.py

You will get a prompt for a password, and may then test it with the different possible inputs. Look at the sample output from the program:

93

```
Output
What is the password?
hello
What is the password?
sammy
What is the password?
PASSWORD
What is the password?
password
Yes, the password is password. You may enter.
```

You should remember that strings are case sensitive unless you utilize a string function to change the string to all lower case (for instance) before you check.

A 'while' loop's example program

Now that we are making good progress with the general while loop's premise, we can create a guessing game based on command line, which makes effective use of the while loop. To understand how this program functions, ensure you read and understand the area on conditional statements well.

First, we will start by creating a file with the name 'guess.py' in your preferred text editor. You want your computer to come up with random numbers for the user to guess, and therefore, you will import the random module containing an import statement. If you are not familiar with this package, you can learn a lot about creating random numbers from Python docs.

guess.py

```
import random
```

After that, you will assign to the 'number' variable a random integer, making sure to keep it within the range of 1 through 25, which is inclusive. I hope this will not make the game too hard.

```
import random

number = random.randint(1, 25)
```

Here, you can get into your 'while' loop by first initializing a variable and then generating the loop.

```
guess.py
import random

number = random.randint(1, 25)

number_of_guesses = 0

while number_of_guesses < 5:
  print('Guess a number between 1 and 25:')

  guess = input()
  guess = int(guess)

  number_of_guesses = number_of_guesses + 1

  if guess == number:
    break
```

You have initialized the 'number_of_guesses' variable; this means that you increase it with every iteration of your loop so that you will not have an infinite loop. You then added the 'while' statement so that the variable 'number_of_guesses' is restricted to 5 in total. After making the fifth guess, the user will go back to the command line, and at this moment, if the user inputs something apart from an integer, he or she will get an error.

We added a 'print()' statement within the loop to prompt the user to input a number, which we took in with the function 'input ()' and set to the variable 'guess'. We then converted 'guess' to an integer, from a string.

Just before the loop is over, you also want to raise the 'number_of_guesses' variable by 1 so that you can iterate five times through the loop.

Lastly, you should write a conditional 'if' statement to check whether the 'guess' the user made is equal to the 'number' the computer made, and if so, you will use a <u>break statement</u> to exit the loop.

At this point, the program should be fully functional, and you can run it with this command: python guess.py

Even though it works, the user (at the moment) will not know whether their guess is correct and can even guess the entire five times without knowing whether they got it right. When you sample the current program's output, you get something like this:

Output
Guess a number between 1 and 25:
11
Guess a number between 1 and 25:
19
Guess a number between 1 and 25:
22
Guess a number between 1 and 25:
3
Guess a number between 1 and 25:
8

We will now add various conditional statements that are outside the loop to help the user to get feedback regarding whether or not he/she has guessed the number correctly. These go at the end of the current file:

```
guess.py
import random

number = random.randint(1, 25)

number_of_guesses = 0

while number_of_guesses < 5:
    print('Guess a number between 1 and 25:')
    guess = input()
    guess = int(guess)

    number_of_guesses = number_of_guesses + 1

    if guess == number:
        break

if guess == number:
    print('You guessed the number in ' + str(number_of_guesses) + ' tries!')

else:
    print('You did not guess the number. The number was ' + str(number))
```

Now the program tells the user whether he/she has correctly guessed the number (i.e. whether correct or wrong), which may not necessarily occur until the close of the loop after the user has actually run out of guesses. We will add a couple more conditional statements into the while loop to give the user a bit of help along the way. These will tell the user if the number they chose was too high or too low. This is to ensure they are more likely to guess the right number. Add this right before the 'if guess == number' line

```
guess.py
import random

number = random.randint(1, 25)

number_of_guesses = 0

while number_of_guesses < 5:
    print('Guess a number between 1 and 25:')
    guess = input()
    guess = int(guess)

    number_of_guesses = number_of_guesses + 1

    if guess < number:
        print('Your guess is too low')

    if guess > number:
        print('Your guess is too high')

    if guess == number:
        break

if guess == number:
    print('You guessed the number in ' + str(number_of_guesses) + ' tries!')

else:
    print('You did not guess the number. The number was ' + str(number))
```

When you run the program once more with 'python guess.py', you will note that the user secures a more guided help in their guessing. Thus, if the number generated randomly is 12, and he/she guesses 18, the program will inform the users that the guess is too high, and that they should thus adjust their subsequent guess accordingly.

To improve the code, there is a whole lot more you can do including handling errors for when the user fails to enter an integer. In this example though, you can see a 'while' loop working in a short command line program.

Chapter 12

Constructing 'For Loops' In Python Programming

As I mentioned in the previous section, in programming, the purpose of using loops is to automate and repeat similar tasks many times. In this section, we will be looking at the 'for loop' in python.

A 'for loop' executes the repeated implementation of code according to the loop counter or variable. This means you can utilize 'for loops' especially when the number of iterations is known before you enter the loop, which is nothing like the 'while loops' that are largely conditionally based.

The For Loops

In Python, we construct for loops as follows:

```
for [iterating variable] in [sequence]:
    [do something]
```

What is being done exactly is implemented until the sequence is finished. We will now look at a 'for loop' that iterates through values in a range:

```
for i in range(0,5):
    print(i)
```

By running the program, you get an output that looks something like this:

0
1
2
3
4

'i' is set up by this for loops as its iterating variable, and the sequence occurs in the range of zero to five.

We print a single integer for very loop iteration within the loop. Bear in mind that in programming, it is typical to start at index 0, which is why although five numbers are pointed out, they range from 0-4.

You will generally note and use 'for loops' when your program needs to repeat a block of code a particular number of times.

Using Range () In For Loops

One of Python's in-built types of immutable sequence is 'range ()'. Loops in particular uses 'range ()' to control the number of times the loop is repeated.

When you are working with range (), you can pass between one and three arguments of integers to it:

The value at which the integer starts is denoted by 'start'- if the value is not included, 'start' will start at 0.

The 'stop' integer is always essential and while counted up, it is not included.

'Step' sets how much increasing (or decreasing of negative numbers) the following iteration, - which if omitted, 'step' defaults to 1.

Let us look at a couple of examples of passing various arguments to 'range ()'. First of all, we will only pass the argument 'stop' so that the set up's sequence is 'range(stop)'.

```
for i in range(6):
    print(i)
```

In the above program, 6 is the 'stop' argument, and so the code iterates from 0-6-which is inclusive of 6. The output is:

```
0
1
2
3
4
5
```

Let's now highlight the 'range(start, stop)' with the specific values specified for when the iteration really starts and when they should stop.

```
for i in range(20,25):
    print(i)
```

The range here starts from 20 to 25- both of which are inclusive, so the output looks like this:

20

21

22

23

24

The range () step argument is the same as trying to specify stride while slicing strings; this means you can use it to skip values in the sequence. With the three arguments, 'step' will come in the last position: range(start, stop, step). First, let us use a 'step' that has a value that is positive.

```
for i in range(0,15,3):
    print(i)
```

Here, the for loop is strategically set up so that the numbers ranging from 0 to 15 print out, but a step of 3 so that it is only every third number that gets printed, like this:

0

3
6

9

12

You can also use a negative value for the 'step' argument so as to iterate backwards, but you will have to modify the 'stop' and 'start' arguments accordingly:

```
for i in range(100,0,-10):
    print(i)
```

In this case, 100 is the 'start' value, and 0 is the 'stop' value. -10 is the range; thus, the loop starts at 100 and ends at 0 while reducing by 10 with every iteration. You can see this happening in the output:

```
100
90
80
70
60
50
40
30
20
10
```

When you're using python to program, you will note that for loops usually utilize the range() sequence type as its iteration parameters.

Using Sequential Data Types In For Loops
Lists and other types of data sequence can also be used as iteration parameters in for loops. Instead of iterating through a 'range ()', you can easily define a list and iterate via it. Let us now assign a list to a variable and then try iterating through the list itself.

```
sharks = ['hammerhead', 'great white', 'dogfish', 'frilled', 'bullhead', 'requiem']

for shark in sharks:
  print(shark)
```

Here, we are printing out every item in the list. Even though we used the 'shark' variable, we could have called the variable any other valid name and we would not get any different output as you can see:

Output
hammerhead
great white
dogfish
frilled
bullhead
requiem

The above output clearly shows that the 'for' loop is iterated through the list, and prints every item from the list per line.

List and other sequence based data types such as tuples and strings are ideal to use with loops since they are iterable. You can bring together these datatypes with range () to take in items to a list- for instance:

In this case, I have included a placeholder string of 'shark' with every item of the 'sharks' list length. You can also use a 'for' loop to create a list from scratch.

```python
integers = []

for i in range(10):
    integers.append(i)

print(integers)
```

In the example above, the list 'integers' gets initialized empty; nonetheless, the 'for' loop populates the list this way:
[0, 1, 2, 3, 4, 5, 6, 7, 8, 9]

Likewise, you can iterate through strings like this:
```python
sammy = 'Sammy'

for letter in sammy:
    print(letter)
```

Output
S
a
m
m
y

You can iterate through tuples in the exact same format as iterating through strings or lists.

When you are iterating through a dictionary, it is good to keep the key, the value structure, in mind to make sure you are calling the right dictionary element. Look at this example that calls the key, and also the value:

```
sammy_shark = {'name': 'Sammy', 'animal': 'shark', 'color': 'blue', 'location': 'ocean'}

for key in sammy_shark:
  print(key + ': ' + sammy_shark[key])
```

Output
name: Sammy
animal: shark
location: ocean
color: blue

The iterating variable agrees with the dictionary keys whenever you use dictionaries with 'for' loops. On the other hand, the 'dictionary_variable (iterating variable)' usually agrees with the values. In the above case, the iterating 'key' variable was used to represent key, and 'sammy_shark (key)' was used to represent the values.

We often use loops to iterate and manipulate the sequential data types.

The Nested For Loops

We can nest loops in Python, as we can with other languages. A nested loop is a loop occurring within another loop, and is similar to the nested if statements in terms of structure. We construct them like this:

```
for [first iterating variable] in [outer loop]: # Outer loop
  [do something] # Optional
  for [second iterating variable] in [nested loop]:  # Nested loop
   [do something]
```

The program will first meet the outer loop, implementing its first iteration. This first iteration activates the inner, nested loop that subsequently runs to completion. The program then returns to the top of the outer loop, to complete the second iteration and triggers the nested loop again. Once again, the nested loop runs to the end, and the program goes back to the top of the outer loop up until the sequence finishes or a break or some other statement interrupts the process.

Let us now implement a nested 'for' loop to help us understand more of this. In this case, the outer loop iterates through a list of integers known as 'num_list', and the inner loop iterates through strings list known as 'alpha_list'.

```
num_list = [1, 2, 3]
alpha_list = ['a', 'b', 'c']

for number in num_list:
  print(number)
  for letter in alpha_list:
  print(letter)
```

Upon running the program, you will get this output:

1
a
b
c
2
a
b
c
3
a
b
c

The output will show that the program finishes the outer loop's first iteration by painting 1, which then initiates completion of the inner loop, thus printing a, b, c successively. When the inner loop ends, the program will return to the top of the outer loop and print 2, and then print the inner loop entirely (a, b, c) and so on.

Nested for loops are necessary for iterating through items inside lists that comprise lists. If you use only one for loop, the program gives an output of every list as an item:

```
list_of_lists = [['hammerhead', 'great white', 'dogfish'],[0, 1, 2],[9.9, 8.8, 7.7]]

for list in list_of_lists:
    print(list)
Output
['hammerhead', 'great white', 'dogfish']
[0, 1, 2]
[9.9, 8.8, 7.7]
```

When you want to access every item of the internal lists, you will have to execute a nested 'for' loop.

```
list_of_lists = [['hammerhead', 'great white', 'dogfish'],[0, 1, 2],[9.9, 8.8,
7.7]]

for list in list_of_lists:
    for item in list:
        print(item)
Output
hammerhead
great white
dogfish
0
1
2
9.9
8.8
7.7
```

When you begin utilizing a nested 'for' loop, you become able to iterate over the individual items contained in the lists.

We have gone over how 'for' loops work in this section, and how to create them. For loops, continue looping through a block of code given a particular number of times.

Best for last perhaps... By now you should be looking for a way to make coding easier, and the next topic should help you achieve that—you will be able to group functions that belong together with classes, have a way to inherit other classes, and create a tree search structure for features in the linked classes. Overall, if you want to enjoy the ease of reusing present code as you write large programs, read on.

Chapter 13

Constructing Classes and Defining Objects

As a programming language, Python focuses on building reusable code patterns, which is why it is popularly considered object-oriented. Conversely, procedural programming is focused on explicit sequenced instructions. When you are working on complex programs, object oriented programming allows you to reuse and write code that is generally more readable, thus more maintainable.

Object oriented programming inconspicuously contains the distinction between objects and classes as one of its most important concepts:

• A class is a blueprint a programmer builds for an object. It defines the attributes that will characterize whichever object instantiated from this particular class.

• On the other hand, an object is an instance of a class. It is the realized class version; the class is exhibited in the program.

You will use these to build patterns (with respect to classes) and then utilize the patterns (with respect to objects). In this section, we will discuss about initializing attributes, instantiating objects and creation of classes with the use of the constructor method, and using multiple objects of the same class to work with.

Classes

You can think of classes as blueprints we use to create objects. We use the 'class' keyword to define classes, just as we use the 'def' keyword to define functions.

We will now define a class named 'shark' that contains two functions:
Swimming
Being awesome:

shark.py

```
class Shark:
  def swim(self):
    print("The shark is swimming.")

  def be_awesome(self):
    print("The shark is being awesome.")
```

Since these functions are indented within the class 'shark', we refer to them as methods (special functions defined within a class).

The word 'self' which is a reference to objects made based on this class, are the argument to these functions; 'self' will always be the initial parameter to reference instances, but it does not have to be the only one.

Defining this class then only created a shark object's pattern, which we will define later. It does not create any 'shark' objects. This means if you run your program beyond this stage, there will be nothing returned.

We therefore got a blueprint for an object by creating the 'shark' class above.

Objects

An object is just a class instance. You can take the 'shark' class, which we defined above then use it so as to create an object as well as its instance. We will now make a 'shark' object by the name 'sammy'- Sammy=shark().

In this case, by setting it equal to shark(), we initialized the object 'sammy' as a class instance. Now we will use both methods with the shark object 'sammy':

```
sammy = Shark()
sammy.swim()
sammy.be_awesome()
```

'sammy' is using both methods: be_awesome() and swim(). We called these using the dot operator (.) used to reference the object's attribute. In this case, the attribute is a method called with parentheses just as you would call with a function.

Since the 'self' keyword was a parameter of the methods as is defined in the class -'shark', the 'sammy' object is passed to the methods. The parameter-'self' makes sure the methods have a way of referring to attributes of the objects.

Nonetheless, when we call the methods, there is nothing passed within the parentheses and the 'sammy' object is automatically passed with the dot.

We will now add the object within the program's context:

```
shark.py

class Shark:
    def swim(self):
        print("The shark is swimming.")

    def be_awesome(self):
        print("The shark is being awesome.")

def main():
    sammy = Shark()
    sammy.swim()
    sammy.be_awesome()

if __name__ == "__main__":
    main()
```

When you run the program:

```
The shark is swimming.
The shark is being awesome.
```

The 'sammy' object calls both methods in the program's function 'main()', thus making the methods run.

The Constructor

We use the constructor method to initialize data. The constructor runs when a class object is instantiated. It is also called _init_ method and will be the first class definition; it looks like this:

```
class Shark:
    def __init__(self):
        print("This is the constructor method.")
```

If you add the _init_ method above to the 'shark' class in the above program, you would get an output that looks like the one below without doing any modification inside the 'sammy' instantiation:

```
This is the constructor method.
The shark is swimming.
The shark is being awesome.
```

The reason is that the constructor method is initialized automatically. You should carry out any initialization you want to do with your class objects with this method. Instead of using this constructor method, we can build one that uses a 'name' variable, which we can assign names to objects with. In this case, the 'name' will be passed as a parameter and we will set 'self.name' equivalent to 'name'.

```
shark.py

class Shark:
    def __init__(self, name):
        self.name = name
```

Next, we can modify the strings in our functions to reference the names as below:

```
shark.py

class Shark:
    def __init__(self, name):
        self.name = name

    def swim(self):
        # Reference the name
        print(self.name + " is swimming.")

    def be_awesome(self):
        # Reference the name
        print(self.name + " is being awesome.")
```

Ultimately, you can set the 'shark' object's name 'sammy' as equal to 'Sammy' by passing it as a parameter of 'Shark' class.

```
shark.py

class Shark:
    def __init__(self, name):
        self.name = name

    def swim(self):
        print(self.name + " is swimming.")

    def be_awesome(self):
        print(self.name + " is being awesome.")


def main():
    # Set name of Shark object
    sammy = Shark("Sammy")
    sammy.swim()
    sammy.be_awesome()

if __name__ == "__main__":
    main()
```

Now run the program: python shark.py

```
Sammy is swimming.
Sammy is being awesome.
```

As you can see, the name we passed to the object is printing out. We defined the _init_ method with the name of the parameter (together with the 'self' keyword) and also defined a variable in the method.

Since the constructor method is initialized automatically, we do not need to call it explicitly but pass the arguments within the parentheses that follow the class name when we make a new instance of the class.

We could also add another parameter like age if we wanted to by passing it to the _init_ method too.

```
class Shark:
    def __init__(self, name, age):
        self.name = name
        self.age = age
```

After that, when we build our object 'sammy', we can also pass the age of Sammy in the statement:

```
sammy = Shark("Sammy", 5)
```

We would also need to create a method in the class calling for age in order to make use of it. The constructor method enables us to initialize particular object attributes.

When Working With Multiple Objects

Classes are important because they let you create multiple similar objects on the same blueprint. For a better insight on how this works, we can add another 'shark' object to the program:

shark.py

```
class Shark:
    def __init__(self, name):
        self.name = name

    def swim(self):
        print(self.name + " is swimming.")

    def be_awesome(self):
        print(self.name + " is being awesome.")

def main():
    sammy = Shark("Sammy")
    sammy.be_awesome()
    stevie = Shark("Stevie")
    stevie.swim()

if __name__ == "__main__":
    main()
```

We have created another 'shark' object named 'stevie' and passed to it the name 'stevie'. In this case, we utilized the be_awesome() method with sammy and also the swim() with 'stevie'.

Now run the program: python shark.py

Sammy is being awesome.
Stevie is swimming.

The output shows that we are indeed using two different objects: the stevie and 'sammy' objects both of the 'shark' class. Classes allow you to make more than a single object following a similar pattern without building any of them from scratch.

Conclusion

That has been your guide to understanding programming with python. The book contains a few sections but is very deep. This means that in just a few days, you should be familiar with everything discussed herein, and be able to execute the projects discussed in it comfortably.

You should also note that we have covered a lot but not everything in python programming. Therefore, now that you have finished reading this book, it would be very wise of you to conduct more research on more topics to expand your knowledge of Python and programming as a whole.

Did You Enjoy This Book?

I want to thank you for purchasing and reading this book. I really hope you got a lot out of it.

Can I ask a quick favor though?

If you enjoyed this book, I would really appreciate it if you could leave me a positive review on Amazon.

I love getting feedback from my customers and reviews on Amazon really do make a difference. I read all my reviews and would really appreciate your thoughts.

Thanks so much.

ALL RIGHTS RESERVED.

Python 3 Guide

A Beginner Crash Course Guide to Learn Python 3 in 1 Week

Timothy C. Needham

Table of Contents

Introduction

Have you always wanted to learn how to program in Python? If the answer to that question is yes, you have begun one of the greatest adventures of this century. It is easy to learn to program since there is no specialized equipment that you need to purchase to run the programs. All you need is the right version of the software, a good computer and operating system. You can learn to program from the comfort of your own home.

Python is one of the best languages with which one can learn how to program. There are multiple reasons why, but the simplest explanation is that Python is easy to read and write. It does not take too much time to write a working code since the language has a simple syntax, which makes it easy to write the code. This book acts as a guide for a beginner.

This book provides information on how one should code when using Python and what attributes of Python can be used to make the program simple. You can never trust someone who says they know everything about programming. New versions of Python are built regularly to improve the user experience. This book provides information on different aspects of the language and will help you learn more about different structures and functions in Python.

You have to keep in mind that the more you learn about programming the better you get at it. You will learn different ways to adapt your programming style to overcome some problems. There are a few exercises that have been given in the book to help you improve on writing code. I urge you to try to write the code before you look at the solutions that have been provided in the last chapter.

I hope you enjoy the journey you are about to begin. Power up that computer and prepare yourself for a few solid hours of programming.

122

Chapter One

An Introduction to Python

Running Python

Python is a software that can be installed and run on multiple operating systems including Mac OS X, or OS/2, Linux, Unix and Windows. If you are running Python on GNU/Linus or Mac OS X, you may already have the software installed in the system. It is recommended to use this type of system since it already has Python set up as an integral part. The programs in this book work on every operating system.

Installing on Windows

If you are using Windows, you will need to install Python and configure certain settings correctly before you start working on the examples given in this book. To do that, you must refer to specific instructions provided for your operating system on the following Python web pages:

- http://wiki.Python.org/moin/BeginnersGuide/Download
- http://www.Python.org/doc/faq/windows/
- http://docs.Python.org/dev/3.0/using/windows.html

You will first need to download the official installer. Alternative versions for AMD and Itanium machines are available at http://www.Python.org/download/. This file, which has an .msi extension, must be saved at a location that you can find easily. You can then double-click this file to start the Python installation wizard, which will take you through the installation. It is best to choose the default settings if you are unsure of the answers.

Installing on Other Systems

You may choose to install Python on other systems, if you want to take advantage of the latest versions of Python. The instructions for Unix-like and Linux systems can be found at the following links:

- http://docs.Python.org/dev/3.0/using/unix.html

If you're using OS X, your instructions are here:

- http://www.Python.org/download/mac/
- http://docs.Python.org/dev/3.0/using/mac.html

Choosing the Right Version

Different installers include different numbers after the word Python that refers to the version number. If you look at the archives on multiple websites, the version numbers will range from 2.5.2 to 3.0 where the former is an old but usable version of Python while the latter is the latest version. The Python team released the version 2.6 at the same time that it released the version 3.0, since there are some people who may still want to stick to version 2 of Python since they want to continue to write code the old way but still want to benefit from general fixes and some of the new features introduced in version 3.0.

The Python language is continuously evolving; version 3.0 has become the norm and has evolved into version 3.1.1. The newer versions of 3.0 are refinements of version 3.0. Therefore, the newer versions will continue to be referred to as 3.0 in this book. Version 3.0 includes several changes to the programming language that are incompatible with version 2.0. You do not have to worry about programming using different versions of Python since there is only a subtle difference in the language or syntax.

There may be some differences running Python on other operating systems, which will be pointed out in the book wherever necessary. Otherwise, the codes in the book will work in the same way across different operating systems. This is one of the many good points of Python. For the most part, this book will concentrate on the fun part—learning how to write programs using Python. If you wish to learn more about Python, you should read the documentation prepared by the developers, which is free and well-written. It is available on at http://www.Python.org/doc/.

Learning while having fun

On most occasions, people do not want to have fun when they work on technical disciplines since fun is underestimated. Every human being only learns a subject well when he or she is having fun with it. Developing software using Python is often an engrossing and enjoyable experience, partly because you can test out your changes as soon as you have made them without having to perform any intermediary steps.

Unlike many other languages, Python takes care of most background tasks making it easier for you to focus on the code and the design of your code. This makes it easy for the user to stay in the creative flow and continue to develop and refine the program.

Python is easy to read and is one of many languages that use a syntax that is closer to English. Therefore, you spend less time trying to understand what you have written, which means that you have more time on hand to understand how the code can be improved and how you can expand the code to encompass different aspects.

Another good thing about Python is that it can be used to complete any task, regardless of how big or small the task may be. You can develop simple text-driven or numerical based programs as well as major graphical applications. There are some limitations to the language, but before you identify them you will have already become adept at programming that will help you know how to work around that limitation.

Choosing to Code
Using a Text Editor

People often choose to create or write Python scripts using plain text editors that have basic programming features. Programs like Kate, NEdit, gedit, BBedit and notepad (preferably notepas2/++) are the best ones to use for this task. Multiple editors are available that offer specific enhancements for programmers, such as syntax highlighting, which is useful for showing coding errors immediately as you type. Old-school programmers may choose to use Emacs or Vi. The language does not require specific software that needs to be used to create the code; that choice is up to you. Do not attempt to use word-processing software, such as Word or Open Office for this task; it will mess up badly.

Using an Integrated Development Environment
An integrated development environment (IDE) is a graphical interface with lots of useful features designed to make programming with Python even easier. You still have to type the code in the same way, but you can do all your coding using a single application, and these programming environments can provide some useful shortcuts and reminders. There are now several Python-specific IDEs. Popular applications include IDLE (which is bundled with Python itself), Eric (you may notice a theme here, nudge nudge, wink wink, say no more...), Geany, DrPython and SPE. More general programming environments like Bluefish and a whole host of others also support Python. This book doesn't cover the use of IDEs or any of the alternative distributions of Python, because each of these approaches would require a chapter unto themselves, at the very least. However, the examples contained in this book will still work if you do choose to explore these options. This book will take the simplest

approach, using tools that come as standard with most operating systems; that is, a text editor and the Python Interactive Shell.

Getting Started

When you sit down to write a new program, you must remember that it starts with a problem. Before you write code for anything, you have to develop an idea of what it is that you would like to create and the problem that you are looking to solve. This will help you develop a fair idea on how you would like to solve the problem. Over the course of the next chapter, we will look at the software development cycle, which will help you through the process of designing the software. This is a step that most people will need to learn separately since most programming guides usually switch to the intricacies of the language and focus on how to develop code which can make it difficult for a beginner to understand how to understand the code and what needs to be done to fix that code. Understanding the principles of software design can dramatically speed up the process of creating new software and help ensure that important details are not missed out.

In the subsequent chapters, you will learn to build the designs and ideas in Python and learn to construct the basic units of the codes using words, data and numbers. You will also learn how to manipulate these inputs to refine the code. It is important to learn how to compare different sets of data to make informed decisions. Over the course of the book, you will learn to refine the designs you have created and break them down into portions that can be coded easily. These steps will help to expand your understanding of the language and help you turn your ideas into complete computer programs.

Creating your own files

Python is described as a self-documenting language; it does not mean that the user manual is written for you by Python. However, you can add documentation strings, which are defined as blocks of text, to your script or code. These documentation strings will show up when you open your code that can then be turned into web pages that provide useful references to those looking for similar code. An example of documentation strings has been provided in the subsequent chapters and it is important to learn to include documentation strings in your code at an early stage.

Chapter Two

How to Design a Software

If you were like most programmers, you would have jumped to the third chapter to learn more about how to build a program and may have bumped into an issue. However, this chapter will help you turn your problem into a working program.

Design your software

There are multiple reasons why one may want to write his or her own code to develop an application that does exactly what you want it to do. You may already have an idea of something you wish to achieve, which led you to pick up this book in the first place. You may need to develop a solution for work, you may have an amazing idea in mind that you want to develop or you may want to perform some analyses using Python; you can develop any type of program through Python. You may already have the program you need, if only it would do this one extra thing, or maybe you just enjoy the idea that writing your own software is possible.

The first step that you should take is to ask questions. You must never refrain from asking the right questions. There are times when you may wonder why you should make the effort to ask people questions since there are some people who believe that they should dive into writing code without wasting any time. It is important to break the idea down into smaller fragments to develop a well-structured idea. This will help you develop a strong code. You have to remember that you are trying to make your life easier.

Asking the right questions

It is important to ask yourself why you are developing every module, function, project and line of code. You must ask yourself this right before you begin the process. There are is a possibility that someone out there has already written the code you want to develop or at least has written something very similar to it. You can use this code and convert it to suit your needs.

You have to also ask yourself if there is a simpler way to work on the problem. Every programmer must learn to be lazy since that helps him or her identify a simpler way to work on the code. That way you will not have to work on the program from scratch and you do not need to learn everything from scratch. Most programmers tend to learn as they go along, but the art of programming does not have too much to do with memorizing code. Instead, you must identify the logical procedure and simplify the concept that you have in mind. The first task is extremely simple in the sense that you must only ask the right questions to break your idea down. However, you will encounter more complex problems as you progress and will also learn to develop ideas of your own.

How to use Python to solve problems

Programmers use a language called pseudocode to design software and Python is one of the only fee languages that are synonymous with pseudocode. The difference here is that you can run the code written in Python to obtain a result. This language is easy to read, does not require compiling and is fun to learn. Your scripts can be run immediately once you have saved it since you do not need to call upon the compiler or any other function to run the script. Unlike other languages, Python can be used to solve a wide range of problems easily since there are many preconstructed functions or modules that deal with the menial computer tasks. Experts have said that

Python is similar to playing with building blocks since the elements of the language are easy to grasp and they can be combined in any way possible to create a graceful and complex structure.

A great feature of Python is that it is a self-documenting language. You have to write the documentation yourself but blocks of text called documentation strings or docstrings can be including within the structure of the program. This feature is used by most programmers to keep the design ideas in one file that helps them think about the program and work on the code as they go along. You can also take a look at your old code and understand what it was that you were trying to achieve when you had written that code. These docstrings will help you and other programmers understand how your program functions and what the need for such a program is.

Identifying the problem

Before you start coding anything, you need to have an idea or a problem that you wish to solve. It is quite useful to start with a familiar repetitive task that you suspect could be performed more efficiently using a simple script. Your first problem is to find out how to communicate with your computer using Python and how to get your computer to communicate back. Using this as an example, I will briefly explain the stages of the software development cycle that most programs will go through in course of their development. You don't have to slavishly follow all the suggestions in this chapter, but you may find that they provide a useful structure for developing more complex applications and to get you back on track if you find yourself getting lost. It is also useful to be able to design your program before having to think about the details of coding it in a formal computer language.

The first stage of writing any new program is to grow a design out of the initial problem, a sequence of actions that will calculate the correct result and create the required output. Once the idea has passed the "Why bother?" test, it is necessary to create a simple framework on which to hang the various bits of code that you come up with. Without such a framework, it is virtually impossible and difficult to construct a simple script. We often tend to complicate the code and are left with a messy code in the end. The great news is that no specialized knowledge is required at this stage. The process can be started off by answering a few simple questions:

- What do you want the software to do?
- Who will be using it?
- What system will users be running it on?

What must the software do?

You have to first write the problem you want to tackle down and why you want to solve that problem. This step will help you understand what it is that you want the software or code to do. You can use a simple text editor for this step. Start with some simple tasks that you know a computer can do, like adding a few numbers or updating strings or catalogues. It is difficult to identify the problem in the beginning. It is important to understand the problem better so you can identify the solution. Save the file as plain text (with the .txt extension) and give it the title of your program-to-be. In the next chapter, you will learn to write a code to get your computer to print a statement on your output window.

Who will use the software?

You must then specify your target audience, regardless of whether you are doing it for yourself. Write your target audience down and make a list of every person who will use this program.

- Family
- Relatives

- Friends
- Work mates
- Clients or anonymous users
- Registered users

How do you want the audience to interact with the application you have built?

- Use a text interface
- Click a single button
- Answer a complex form

Do you need this audience to be adept at programming?

- Should the application be self-explanatory?
- Will they need to learn the ropes?

What systems will be used?

You have to know if the program you build will work on different operating systems. If you want it to run only on one operating system, you must let the users know. The program you build may also be accessed by clients through different types of systems through Internet applications and can use different hardware or software in the device. You have to also let the users know if they must download or install software for the computer to decode your script or program.

These questions are important to answer at the initial stages of development since they may have a huge impact on the process in the future. Keep the answers simple ay this stage, but make sure you answer most of them since you will be prepared for any challenges or obstacles. If you can't answer some of the questions yet, that's fine too. This chapter will help you break your answers down into simpler steps, but before you move to that step, you must ask the right questions.

Define the program

It can be useful to create a list of the things you want the software to do and what it is you want to achieve by building this software. You may need to analyze the procedures you would be using and also understand the task you have taken up deeply. It is useful to examine a task that you have already performed before. This can be a task that you have not automated in the past. The following sections will help you generate the list of tasks you must complete to finish your design.

Understanding the Audience

Understand how your target audience performs the task that you have listed down. Sit with them and learn about the sections of the task they want to automate and understand the factors that they would like to control. You have to also make a list of factors that the audience finds confusing and understand how you can help them overcome those difficulties.

There are some people who use a short questionnaire, even if it is them answering the questions, since the answers will help you gain an idea on the problem at hand. You can ask for some detailed answers in the questionnaire to understand what your target audience wants the application to look like and they may want it to behave. You must also understand what file formats they expect to use to read in information from and save it out to, particularly covering any unique or special considerations that you can imagine. File formats could include HTML, XML and plain text for text documents, or your users might have images saved as PNGs or JPEGs audio files (WAV) that they may want to convert to MP3s. A file's extension (the letters after the last dot in the filename) usually provides a clue as to what format a file is in, though there are other ways of finding out this information.

Through this exercise, you will understand how the task if often performed and the information you need to collect before you start the process. You do not need to develop an example or a prototype of the code at this stage since it is invaluable. It is better to have a code written down. You can tweak this code as you go along.

Watching Users

As a developer, you can take the liberty to watch the audience carry out the task and make notes while the tasks are being performed. You do not need a lot of detail at this stage since you only need to gather information that will help you develop your code or software. The alternative approach would be to put yourself in your audience's position and walk through the task. Another technique is to collect up all the pieces of paper that go into or come out of the process and use them to create a storyboard. It is true that this step is more relevant in the future, but it is better to get into the habit of working on this step now.

Compiling User Stories

A user story consists of one or two lines in everyday language that specifies something that the user wants from the software. The idea is that stories should be brief enough to fit on an index card, on a sticky note, or into one cell of a spreadsheet. A user story should indicate the role of the user, what that user wants the software to do, and what benefit might be gained from it. User stories are prioritized by the user to indicate which features are most important and are then used to work out an estimate of the time it will take to develop those features by the developer. The developer may then create use cases out of these stories and tests to determine whether the requirements have been fulfilled. Use cases are longer, more detailed descriptions of features that are required by specific users in specific situations. You just need enough information to work out the basic functionality that will be required from the program you are about to write. Try to keep it concise.

Identifying the Solution

Armed with all this information, let's return to the text file to complete the first stage of the software design. The design stage can often be the most time-consuming part of the programming process. It consists of several stages in which the output from one stage becomes the input to the next. Often, the output from one or more stages is fed back through the same process several times. This process that happens inside the program is termed as recursion. Every software design cycle has a similar recursive nature. So, let us go back to our initial problem now.

Understanding the Problem

This time around, you're going to fill in a little more detail and turn your text file into a very simple user requirements document. In a professional situation, this would become the agreement between the programmer and the client who is paying for the software to be written. For now, you're just going to use it as a means to keep a record of the original purpose of this software. Make sure that the problem is stated clearly and that you have identified the issue you wish to resolve correctly. Often, there can be hidden subtleties in the problem that look straightforward when written down in your natural language but require additional clarification when you come to turn them into programming language, or code. If the problem is not defined well enough to make a decision at that point, you will need to return to this stage and clear up the details before you can make any further progress.

Understanding what the software needs to do

The things you want the software to do are known as functional requirements in the trade. Simple examples include printing a message, adding up some numbers up, or sending an e-mail form. You might have additional details to add; for example, maybe the user must be able to input some text, numbers larger than 200 cannot be entered, or the update must be performed over the Internet. Functional requirements specify how a system should behave. For your first exercise, Hello World! You will be asking the software to print out a simple message, so your first functional requirement is that the computer should print out a message.

Considering Limitations

You may also want to include other needs or limitations of the software, which are called nonfunctional requirements. The remaining constraints are defined by the non-functional qualities and requirements of the software like cost-effectiveness, accessibility and compatibility with other operating systems, performance and usability. You do not have to worry about these aspects if you are developing a code for yourself.

Defining the Results

You need to give some thought as to how the software will be tested. Early on, it will be enough to simply run the program and see if it works, but as your scripts grow in complexity, you will find it useful to formalize the methods used for testing. It may be worth finding or creating some data to use as an example for testing purposes, and you may find it useful to create a table of values that you expect to find at various points in the process. In Chapter 11, I'll be showing you how to create built-in test suites, which can make a large part of the process automatic. It's generally considered good practice to write your tests before you do any coding, but it often happens that the tests and code actually get written at the same time. For now, a note of the expected output will do fine.

Refining the program

Any piece of software that is going to be used more than once will require some degree of maintenance. Issues that are worth thinking about early on are how the software might need to change in future and how to keep track of issues. You might also consider how the application is going to be kept in working condition while you're integrating new possibilities and responding to new challenges. In many cases, the application will be maintained by the person who wrote it, but it is good practice to organize your project and write your code in a way that makes it easy for someone else to understand what you've done and contribute fixes and new features. One day, you might want to pass on the responsibility of keeping it up to date to someone else.

To facilitate maintenance, the software should include some means of contact, such as the author's e-mail address so that users can get in touch if there are any problems. For now, just note your e-mail address. Later on, I'll show you how you can integrate this information into your code, so you don't have to retype this information every time you want to use it. A principle of programming that you must keep in mind is 'Don't Repeat Yourself.' This principle states that every piece of information must have an unambiguous, simple and authoritative representation in the system. No piece of information should ever have to be typed in twice—if you find yourself doing this, it's a sure sign that some part of your script needs redesigning.

Let us take a look at the hello_world txt program.

Problem: Get the computer to output a message.

Target Users: Me

Target System: GNU/Linux
Interface: Command-line
Functional Requirements: Print out a message.
User must be able to input some text.
Testing: Simple run test - expecting a message to appear.
Maintainer: <u>maintainer@website.com</u>

Breaking the Solution Down

Next, you start the process of turning your wish list into a program. In this stage, you will design a logical flow of actions, which will hopefully produce the desired outcome. First, you need to turn the text file into something the Python interpreter can understand by saving it as a Python (.py) file. Use the Save As function in your text editor to save the file with the same name, but this time with a .py extension. This example will become hello_world.py.

Now, the interpreter needs to know what this text is; otherwise, it will attempt to interpret the first thing it finds as a command. There are a variety of ways of marking out blocks of text as comments or text strings so that the interpreter doesn't attempt to execute them.

<u>Comments</u>

The hash symbol, #, is used to mark comments. Comments are completely ignored by the Python interpreter. All text between the # sign and the end of the line is ignored. This formatting is a convenience so you, the programmer, can write little notes to yourself to remind yourself what this part of the code is supposed to do or to flag parts of the code that need attention. These comments will only ever be seen by people who are actually reading the code. If you are writing software as part of a team, comments are a great way of communicating your thoughts and intentions to the other programmers. Good code can often contain more comments than actual lines of code—don't be tempted to remove them once you've coded the design. In a month's time, you are likely to have completely forgotten what this script was intended to do, and you will be thankful for these little reminders.

<u>Text strings</u>

Text strings are delimited by quotation marks. Delimited means the text is enclosed between a matching pair of the specified characters. Python uses a variety of forms of quotation marks, principally 'single' and "double" quotation marks. There is a subtle difference between the two forms, which I'll cover in detail in the section on text strings in Chapter 3. The main reason for the different forms is to allow nesting of quotes. Nesting means putting one inside the other like this: "What on earth does 'nested delimiters' mean?" she asked.

Like comments, quotation marks only work if the text is all on one line. Fortunately, there are a variety of ways to get the interpreter to ignore line breaks. In this example, I shall use the technique of triple quoting, which is explained in later chapters.

Organizing Tasks into Steps

Now, you are prepared to start designing your program. The program design is initially sketched out in pseudocode, which is the design language that can be used as an intermediary step to turn the user requirements document into a piece of Python code. There is nothing special about the form of this language; your own natural way of expressing ideas is exactly what is needed in this situation. Pseudocode is simply a series of logical statements in your own words that describe the actions that the program needs to take in order to produce the desired result.

If you are working as part of a team, your company may have a standard way of writing pseudocode, but you don't need to worry about such considerations while you are learning. Over time, you are likely to find that your pseudocode naturally adopts a Python-like syntax. Initially, the important thing is that you can express your ideas clearly without having to worry about the rules of the language yet.

Using Subgroups and Indentation

Python is very strict about indentation. Python regards any space or tab at the start of a line as an indentation. Every indentation means something. Without going into too much detail at this stage, pay careful attention to how indentation is used in the examples. The most important thing to remember is not to mix tabs with spaces, as the interpreter thinks these are two different things (even if they look the same to you).

In your text editor's Preferences window, set it to insert four spaces instead of using tabs, and you'll avoid so much future grief by doing this. It is always best to keep your designs clear and readable: use blank lines to separate the different sections of your pseudocode and use indentation to show how statements are grouped together. As long as each line is a comment preceded by a #, you are free to format it how you like.

Coding the Design

Now, you are ready to start turning your design into proper Python code. Great!

The data your software will be manipulating will take various forms; these values are assigned to things called variables, which you can think of as a box or a bucket that contains a single piece of information, often a word or a number. Some people find it useful to think of them as slates that can be written on with chalk. The important thing is that the information in the container can be changed by putting a new value into it; this automatically wipes out the old value and replaces it with a new one. The fact that these values can be changed gives rise to the term variable.

There are two stages to creating a variable, the first is to create the container and stick an identifying label on it: this is called initialization. The second is to put a value into it: this is called assignment. In Python, both these things happen in the same statement. Assignment (and therefore initialization) is performed using the = sign like this: variable = value. One of the specific features of Python is that, once a value has been assigned to a variable, the interpreter will then decide what sort of value it is (i.e., a number, some text, or some other relevant piece of information).

Each variable is referred to by a name, known as an identifier, which is rather like a nametag that identifies the variable to the rest of the program. It's a good idea to choose names that give an idea of what sort of values they represent. Python will regard any word that has not been commented out, delimited, or escaped in some other way as either a command or an identifier; for this reason, you need to be careful to avoid choosing words that are already being used as part of the Python language to identify your new variables. Details of which words you cannot use will be covered in the next chapter.

Turning the Design into Executable Code

Now, you have to come up with a strategy for solving the problems you have agreed to tackle.

First, you want to print out a message, and you want the user to be able to input some text. OK, so you're expecting your message and users' text to be strings of text. It would be a very good idea to add this information to the Testing section of your docstrings at the start of the file. Text strings are represented by enclosing the text in quotes.

Now, you just need to know the function that prints things out to the screen, which is called print () in Python. So, your first problem translates fairly easily into executable code as you can see in Listing 2-5. You can print any text you like; "Hello World!" is the default.

Let us take a look at the first version of the Hello_World.py program.

```
"""
```

Problem: Get the computer to output a message.

Target Users: Me

Target System: GNU/Linux

Interface: Command-line

Functional Requirements: Print out a message.

User must be able to input some text.

Testing: Simple run test - expecting a message to appear.

> *- Expecting: message == input text*
Maintainer: maintainer@website.com

```
"""
```

 # 1. Print out a friendly message

Print ("Hello World!")

 # 2. Input some text

 # 3. Print out the text we just entered

This script can be run by typing

$ Python hello_world.py

The only line in this script that is actually executed by the interpreter is print ("Hello World!"). Everything else is either ignored as a comment or assumed to be a docstring, in the case of the block of text at the beginning. If you change the text between the quotes in the call to the print () function, the Python interpreter will print out whatever you tell it to.

Well done! You just wrote your first Python program. It's about as basic as can be, but you can now bask in the satisfaction of having got Python to do something.

Refining the Design

Constantly editing the script to get it to say something different quickly becomes rather tedious. Wouldn't it be great if the program were interactive? In that case, you would need to find a way to get some user input.

The quick-and-dirty method for doing this is to use the built-in input () function. This function takes one argument, a text string that is printed to the screen to prompt the user for input. The function then returns the user's input. All requests for input need a message to tell the user that input is required; this is known as a prompt. I assign this input to a variable called some_text. Then, I can use the print () function to print out the user's input. Notice that this time some_text isn't in quotes, because I want the value contained in the variable called some_text rather than the literal text string "some_text". Variable names aren't allowed to contain spaces, so you'll notice that I've replaced the space with an underscore. It's worth remembering that variable names can't contain dashes either, because Python will assume that the dash is a minus sign. Details of how to name your variables will be covered fully in Chapter 3.

Testing the Design

Now, it's time to save the file again and test it by running the script with the Python interpreter as before. If you get any error messages at this stage, you probably made a mistake typing the script. Common errors include missing quotation marks or spaces in the wrong places. In this case, you will need to go back to the coding stage and correct these errors before you test the code again.

The testing stage involves making sure that the design does what it is supposed to and that it matches the specification that you started with. Compare the actual output from running the program to the output you said you were expecting in your original specification. Are they the same? If not, why not? What could be done better?

Apart from the initial design stage, you will probably spend most of your time cycling around this testing stage. Don't be tempted to view error messages as annoyances or irritations: pay great attention to what they tell you, as they can be one of the most useful aids on the path of learning Python. On some occasions, you will want to deliberately produce error messages to prove that something is working. Try it now. Find out what you have to mess up to get an error message. Take note of what sort of message you get and fix your script so that it runs cleanly again.

Breaking down the Jargon

Some terms that were introduced in the chapter are:

- Argument: This is a value you pass to a function or to a procedure, so it has some data to work with.
- Assignment: This is the operation of setting a variable to a value.
- Delimiter: This punctuation mark is typically used to separate a text string or other piece of data from surrounding characters.
- Escape: This is a method of indicating that the next character in a text string should be processed in a different way.
- Function: A function is a block of code that performs a calculation, accepts zero or more arguments and returns a value to the calling procedure when it is complete.

- Indentation: This refers to the use of spaces and tabs at the start of a line of code or text, except you want to use spaces rather than tabs, remember?

- Identifier: This is a user-defined name; both function names and variable names are identifiers. Identifiers must not conflict with keywords.

- Initialization: This process sets the initial value of a variable. Initialization is done only once for each variable, when that variable is created.

- Module: A module is a Python program that can be imported by another program. Modules are often used to define additional functions and classes.

- Nesting: Put one piece of code inside another similar construct.

- Nonfunctional requirements: These are needs or limitations of the software that are not specifically about what the software will do.

- Program implementation: This is the actual realization of the program, as opposed to the design.

- Prompt: This string of text or punctuation marks indicates that the user needs to input some information or commands.

- Pseudocode: This program design language is intended to be read by humans, not performed by a computer.

- Return: This refers to the process of transferring execution from a function back to the place from which that function was called in the main program. The return statement can also pass a value back to the main program for use in further calculation.

- Statement: This instruction to do something in a programming language manipulates a piece of data, performs a calculation, or produces some output.

- String: This refers to a line of text or other characters intended to be displayed or processed as a single item.

- Top-level design: This is the first stage of a design, and it provides a summary or general description of the actions that the software is intended to perform.

- User story: A user story consists of one or two lines in the everyday language of the user that specifies something desired from the software.

- Validation: This process tests whether a value is what the programmer expects it to be.

- Variables: Use variables as a means of referring to a specific item of data that you wish to keep track of in a program. It points to a memory location, which can contain numbers, text, or more complicated types of data.

Chapter Three
Data Types and Variables

In the last chapter, we learnt that an identifier is a part of a variable, which is a unit of data. These variables and identifiers are held in the computer's memory and its value can be changed by making a modification to a value that is already present in the variable. This chapter will introduce you to the different types of variables that you can use when writing a program in Python. You will also learn how these variables can be used to convert your designs into working codes using Python. This is when you begin real programming. Over the course of this chapter, we will work on two programs – one where we will learn to format and manipulate text strings and another to perform a simple mathematical calculation.

The programs mentioned above can be written easily using different variables. When you use variables, you can specify a function, method of calculation that must be used to obtain a solution without the knowledge of the type of value that the variable must refer to in advance. Every piece of information that must be put into a system needs to be converted into a variable before it can be used in a function. The output of the program is received only when the contents of these variables are put through all the functions written in the program.

Choosing the right identifier
Every section of your code is identified using an identifier. The compiler or editor in Python will consider any word that is delimited by quotation marks, has not been commented out, or has escaped in a way by which it cannot be considered or marked as an identifier. Since an identifier is

only a name label, it could refer to just about anything, therefore, it makes sense to have names that can be understood by the language. You have to ensure that you do not choose a name that has already been used in the current code to identify any new variable.

If you choose a name that is the same as the older name, the original variable becomes inaccessible. This can be a bad idea if the name chosen is an essential part of your program. Luckily, when you write a code in Python, it does not let you name a variable with a name used already. The next section of this chapter lists out the important words, also called keywords, in Python, which will help you avoid the problem.

Python Keywords
The following words, also called keywords, are the base of the Python language. You cannot use these words to name an identifier or a variable in your program since these words are considered the core words of the language. These words cannot be misspelt and must be written in the same way for the interpreter to understand what you want the system to do. Some of the words listed below have a different meaning, which will be covered in later chapters.

- False
- None
- Assert
- True
- As
- Break
- Continue
- Def
- Import
- In
- Is
- And

- Class
- Del
- For
- From
- Global
- Raise
- Return
- Else
- Elif
- Not
- Or
- Pass
- Except
- Try
- While
- With
- Finally
- If
- Lambda
- Nonlocal
- Yield

Understanding the naming convention

Let us talk about the words that you can use and those you cannot use. Every variable name must always begin with an underscore or a letter. Some variables can contain numbers, but they cannot start with one. If the interpreter comes across a set of variables that begin with a number instead of quotation marks or a letter, it will only consider that variable as a number. You should never use anything other than an underscore, number or letter to identify a variable in your code. You must also remember that Python is a case-sensitive language, therefore false and False are two different entities. The same can be said for vvariable, Vvariable and VVariable.

As a beginner, you must make a note of all the variables you use in your code. This will also help you find something easier in your code.

Creating and Assigning Values to Variables

Every variable is created in two stages – the first is to initialize the variable and the second is to assign a value to that variable. In the first step, you must create a variable and name it appropriately to stick a label on it and in the second step; you must put a value in the variable. These steps are performed using a single command in Python using the equal to sign. When you must assign a value, you should write the following code:

Variable = value

Every section of the code that performs some function, like an assignment, is called a statement. The part of the code that can be evaluated to obtain a value is called an expression. Let us take a look at the following example:

Length = 14
Breadth = 10
Height = 10
*Area_Triangle = Length * Breadth * Height*
Any variable can be assigned a value or an expression,

like the assignment made to Area_Triangle in the example above.

Every statement must be written in a separate line. If you write the statements down the way you would write down a shopping list, you are going the right way. Every recipe begins in the same way with a list of ingredients and the proportions along with the equipment that you would need to use to complete your dish. The same happens when you write a

Python code – you first define the variables you want to use and then create functions and methods to use on those variables.

Recognizing different types of Variables

The interpreter in Python recognizes different types of variables – sequences or lists, numbers, words or string literals, Booleans and mappings. These variables are often used in Python programs. A variable None has a type of its own called NoneType. Before we look at how words and numbers can be used in Python, we must first look at the dynamic typing features in Python.

Working with Dynamic Typing

When you assign a value to a variable, the interpreter will choose to decide the type of value the variable is, which is called dynamic typing. This type of typing does not have anything to do with how fast you can type on the keyboard. Unlike the other languages, Python does not require that the user declare the types of the variables being used in the program. This can be considered both a blessing and a curse. The advantage is that you do not have to worry about the variable type when you write the code, and you only need to worry about the way the variable behaves.

Dynamic Typing in Python makes it easier for the interpreter to handle user input that is unpredictable. The interpreter for Python accepts different forms of user input to which it assigns a dynamic type which means that a single statement can be used to deal with numbers, words, or other data types, and the user does not have to always know what data type the variable must be. Not needing to declare variables before you use them makes it tempting to introduce variables at random places in your scripts. You must remember that Python won't complain unless you try to use a variable before you have actually assigned it a value, but it's really easy to lose track of what variables you are using and where you set up their values in the script.

There are two really sensible practices that will help keep you sane when you start to create large numbers of different variables. One is to set up a bunch of default values at the start of each section where you will be needing them, keeping all the variables you are going to use together in one part of the text like an ingredients list. The other is to keep track of the expected types and values of your variables, keeping a data table in your design document for each program that you are writing.

Python needs to keep track of the type of a variable for two main reasons. Chiefly, the machine needs to set aside enough memory to store the data, and different types of data take up different amounts of space, some more predictably than others. The second reason is that keeping track of types helps to avoid and troubleshoot errors. Once Python has decided what type a variable is, it will flag up a TypeError if you try to perform an inappropriate operation on that data. Although this might at first seem to be an unnecessary irritation, you will discover that this can be an incredibly useful feature of the language; as the following command-line example shows:

```
>>> b = 3
>>> c = 'word'
>>> trace = False
>>>
b + c
Traceback (most recent call last):
File "", line 1, in <module>
TypeError: unsupported operand type(s) for +: 'int' and 'str'
>>> c - trace
```

```
Traceback (most recent call last):
File "", line 1, in <module>
TypeError: unsupported operand type(s) for -: 'str' and
'bool'
```

The program above tries to perform operation on data types that are incompatible. You're not allowed to add a number to a word or take a yes/no answer away from it. It is necessary to convert the data to a compatible type before trying to process it. You can add words together or take numbers away from each other, just like you can in real life, but you can't do arithmetic on a line of text. The tracebacks are Python's way of alerting you to a potential error in your logic, in this case a TypeError. This tells me that I need to rewrite the code to make it clear what type of information I want to put in and get out of the equation.

The purpose of data types is to allow us to represent information that exists in the real world, that is, the world that exists outside your computer, as opposed to the virtual world inside. We can have the existential conversation about what is real and what is not some other time. The previous example uses variables of type int (whole numbers) and type str (text). It will quickly become apparent that these basic data types can only represent the simplest units of information; you may need to use quite a complicated set of words, numbers, and relationships to describe even the simplest real-world entity in virtual-world terms.

Python provides a variety of ways of combining these simple data types to create more complex data types, which I'll come to later in this book. First, you need to know about the fundamental building blocks that are used to define your data and the basic set of actions you can use to manipulate the different types of values.

The None Variable

A predefined variable called None is a special value in Python. This variable has a type of its own and is useful when you need to create a variable but not define or specify a value to that variable. When you assign values such as "" and 0, the interpreter will define the variable as the str or int variable.

Information = None

A variable can be assigned the value None using the statement above. The next few examples will use real-world information that will be modeled into a virtual form using some fantasy characters. This example uses some statistics to represent some attributes of the characters to provide data for the combat system. You can use this example to automate your database and your accounts. So, let us take a look at some of the characters in the example.

In the program, hello_world.py, you saw how you could get a basic output using the print () function. This function can be used to print out the value of the variable and a literal string of characters. Often, each print statement must start off on a new line, but several values can be printed on a single line by using a comma to separate them; print () can then be used to concatenate all the variables into a single line only separated by spaces.

> *>>> Race = "Goblin"*
> *>>> Gender = "Female"*
> *>>> print (Gender, Race)*
> *Female Goblin*

Different segments of information can be combined into a single line using multiple methods. Some of these methods are more efficient when compared to others. Adjacent strings that are not separated will be concatenated automatically, but this is not a function that works for most variables.

>>> *print ("Male" "Elf")*

The expression above will give you the following output – "MaleElf"

However, when you enter the following code,

>>> *print ("Male" Race)*

You will receive the following error:

File "<stdin>", line 1

print ("Male" Race)

^

SyntaxError: invalid syntax

This approach cannot be used since you cannot write a string function as a variable and a string together since this is just a way of writing a single line string.

Using Quotes

In Python, a character is used to describe a single number, punctuation mark, or a single letter. A string of characters used to display some text are called strings or string literals. If you need to tell the interpreter that you want a block of text to be displayed as text, you must enclose those characters in quotation marks. This syntax can take multiple forms –

'A text string enclosed in single quotation marks.'

"A text string enclosed in double quotation marks."

"'A text sting enclosed in triple quotation marks.'"

If text is enclosed in quotes, it is considered the type str (string).

Nesting Quotes

There are times when you may want to include literal quotation marks in your code. Python allows you to include a set of quotation marks inside another set of quotation marks, if you use a different type of quotation mark.

>>>*text= "You are learning 'how to' use nested quotes in Python"*

In the example above, the interpreter will assume that it has reached the end of the string when it reaches end of the text at second set of double quotes in the string above. Therefore, the substring 'how to' is considered a part of the main string, including the quotes. In this way, you can have at least one level of nested quotes. The easiest way to learn how to work with nested quotes is by experimenting with different types of strings.

>>> boilerplate = """

... #===(")===#===(*)===#===(")===#

... *Egregious Response Generator*

... *Version '0.1'*

... *"FiliBuster" technologies inc.*

... #===(")===#===(*)===#===(")===#

... """

...

>>> *print(boilerplate)* #=== (") ===#=== (*) ===#=== (") ===#

Egregious Response Generator

Version '0.1'

"FiliBuster" technologies inc.

#===(")===#===(*)===#===(")===#

This is a useful trick to use if you want to format a whole block of text or a whole page.

How to use Whitespace Characters

Whitespace characters are can often be specified if the sequence of characters begin with a backslash. '\n' produces a linefeed character that is different from the '\r' character. In the output window, the former would shift the output to a new line, while the latter would shift the output to a new paragraph. You must understand the difference between how different operating systems use to translate the text.

The usage and meaning of some of the sequences are lost on most occasions. You may often want to use \n to shift to a new line. Another sequence that is useful is \t, which can be used for the indentation of text by producing a tab character. Most of the other whitespace characters are used only in specialized situations.

Sequence	Meaning
\n	New line
\r	Carriage Return
\t	Tab
\v	Vertical Tab
\e	Escape Character
\f	Formfeed
\b	Backspace
\a	Bell

You can use the example below to format the output for your screen:

>>>   *print   ("Characters\n\nDescription\nChoose   your character\n *

.... *\tDobby\n\tElf\n\tMale\nDon\'t forget to escape \'\\\'.")*

- Characters
- Description
- Choose your character
- Dobby
- Elf
- Male
- Don't forget to escape '\'.

You must remember that strings are immutable which means that they cannot be changed. It is possible to use simple functions to create new strings with different values.

How to Create a Text Application

All the information mentioned int his chapter can be used to write the code for our role-playing game. Strings are often simple to use since you must only ensure that you enclose the strings in matching quotes. The script to design the character-description is simple.

 # Prompt the user for some user-defined information

 # Output the character description

You may want to include the following information for the character:

- Name
- Gender
- Race
- Description of the character

For this information, you can create the following variables – Name, Gender, Race and Description. These values can be printed using the following code:

"""

chargen.py

Problem: Generate a description for a fantasy role-playing character.

Target Users: Me and my friends

Target System: GNU/Linux

Interface: Command-line

Functional Requirements: Print out the character sheet

User must be able to input the character's name, description, gender and race

Testing: Simple run test

Maintainer: maintainer@website.com

""" ___

```
version__ = 0.1
Name = ""
Desc = ""
Gender = ""
Race = ""
# Prompt user for user-defined information
Name = input ('What is your Name? ')
Desc = input ('Describe yourself: ')
Gender = input ('What Gender are you? (male / female
/ unsure): ')
Race = input ('What fantasy Race are you? - (Pixie /
Vulcan / Gelfling / Troll/ Elf/ Goblin): ')
# Output the character sheet
character_line                                        =
"<~~==|#|!!++**\@/**++~~==|#|++~~>"
print ("\n", character_line)
print ("\t", Name)
print ("\t", Race, Gender)
print ("\t", Desc)
print (fancy_line, "\n")
```

The program above is a smarter version of the hello_world program written above. However, in this program, there is a new line added _version_ = 0.1 at the start of the program. This is a predefined variable that has a special meaning in Python's documentation. This is the number we will continue to use to record the above example. As we go along, we will continue to increment this number when we make any changes or refine the program. Now, we will need to obtain some numerical information about the characters that will interact in the game.

Working with Numbers

It is straightforward to assign any number to variables.

Muscle = 8

Brains = 13

As mentioned earlier, the interpreter assumes that a set of characters as a number if it starts with a numerical instead of a quotation mark or letter. Therefore, you cannot start any variable with a number. You must learn a few things before you begin to work on mathematics on your computer.

Computers only count to one

All the information in the computer can only be stored in zeros and ones. Every computer stores and processes any volume of data using tiny switches that can either be on (1) or off (0).

Using Boolean

As mentioned earlier, a computer can only register two values – True (value = 1) and False (value = 0). These values are known as Boolean operators and can be manipulated using operators like OR, NOT and AND. These operators are explained in further detail in the following chapter. Boolean values can be assigned as follows:

Mirage = False

Intelligence = True

Using Whole Numbers

Whole numbers, also called integers, do not have decimal points and can be zero, positive and negative. These numbers are used to refer to different things like the recipe example mentioned above.

Performing Basic Mathematical Operations

Now that you know how to store data in a variable, let us take a look at how to manipulate that data. Basic mathematical operations can be performed using operators like +, - and *. These operators create an expression that must be evaluated before you can obtain a value. The following statements can be used to perform these operations.

```
>>>muscle = 2 + 3
>>>brains = 7+4
>>> speed = 5 * 6
>>> weirdness = muscle * brains + speed
>>> weirdness
```

All these operations work using the BODMAS mathematical algorithm.

Working with Floats and Fractions

Most fractions are often expressed using the float type where decimal points can be used. These numbers, like integers, can be both positive and negative. You do not have to assign a variable to the data type float. Python automatically converts a variable into the float type if it is assigned a decimal number.

```
Muscle = 2.8
Brains = 4.6
Speed = 6.8
```

Even if the number before and after the decimal point is 0, it is still considered a fraction. This data type can be manipulated using the same mathematical operations mentioned above.

Converting Data Types

There are different built-in functions that are used in Python to convert a value from one data type to another. The data types often used are:

- int (x) – used to convert any number into an integer

- float (x) – used to convert a number to a float data type
- str (object) – convert any type into a string that can be used to print

>>> *float (23)*
23.0
>>> *int (23.5)*
23
>>> *float (int (23.5))*
23

Breaking down Jargon

This section provides the definition of some new terms that were used in this chapter.

- Binary: In arithmetic, binary relates to the digits 1 and 0. This term responds to the current in a wire.

- Boolean: A Boolean variable can only take two values – True and False which correspond to 1 and 0 respectively. This type of variable is the most appropriate type that can be used to let the user know if a condition holds true or not.

- Characters: A character is anything from a digit, letter, space and a punctuation mark. This data type is anything that can be type using a key on the keyboard, regardless of whether or not an output is printed on the screen.

- Concatenate: When you create a string using different segments of strings or copy two text strings together.

This chapter has helped you understand how to assign different types of variables and how you can manipulate strings and numbers. Let us take a look at the following exercises and see how well you do. The solutions are provided at the end of the book.

1. Write a program to concatenate two strings
2. Write a program to calculate the sum of two numbers

Chapter Four:

Conditional Statements

In the last few chapters, you have learnt how to use Python to manipulate strings and to make simple calculations. More importantly, you have learnt how to design your software. Now, it is time to learn how to refine your code. Therefore, pull out your old scripts and find an effective way to obtain your output.

How to Compare Variables

To generate more accurate answers, you must know how to compare the values and specify what the interpreter must do based on the obtained result. Python allows you to use conditional statements to allow you to make these decisions. A conditional statement can transform the code or script from just being a list of instructions to a code that can be used by the user to make their own decisions. It would be useful to tell the interpreter to perform a different action as per the decisions made by the user. You can write a pseudocode like:

if a certain condition is true:
then the following actions must be performed;
if another condition is true:
then these actions must be performed.

Each pair in the example above is a conditional statement, but before we learn more about these statements, let us take a look at how to specify these conditions. Different values can be compared using the following operators:

- <: Less than
- >: Greater than
- <=: Less than equal to
- >=: Greater than equal to

- ==: Equal to
- !=: Not equal to

These operators affect data types in different ways and give the user answers in the form of the Boolean operators. The data bits on either side of the operator are called operands and these are the variables that are compared. The comparative operator and the operands together form the conditional expression. It is important to check the conditional statements or expressions you are using since you may obtain an error if you compare incomparable data types. The results obtained by comparing these numbers are self-explanatory.

```
>>> -2 < 5
True
>>> 49 > 37
True
>>> 7.65 != 6.0
True
>>> -5 <= -2
True
>>> 7 < -7
False
>>> 23.5 > 37.75
False
>>> -5 >= 5
False
>>> 3.2 != 3.2
False
```

Variables can also be used in conditional expressions.

```
>>> variable = 3.0
>>> variable == 3
True
```

Manipulating Boolean Variables

Before you move onto the different conditional structures used in Python, you must learn how to manipulate the Boolean values True and False. You can use these values to understand the characteristics of any variable. These operators are often used with the terms AND, OR and NOT. The statements below represent some bits of information.

>>> *a = True*
>>> *b = False*
>>> *c = True*
>>> *d = True*
>>> *e = False*

Let us take a look at how AND, OR and NOT can be used.

>>> *a or b*

This operator returns the value True, since for the OR operator either one of the values needs to be true.

>>> *c and e*

This operator returns the value False, since for the AND operator both values must be the same.

>>> *not d*

This operator returns the value False, since the NOT operator provides the opposite of the value.

Combine Conditional Expressions

Conditional expressions can be combined to produce complex conditions that use the logical operators AND and OR. Let us take a look at the following conditions:

(a < 6) AND (b > 7)

This statement will only return True if the value of a is less than 6 and the value of b is greater than 7.

The Assignment Operator

Since you are familiar with the assignment operator (=) which you use to put a value into a variable, let us take a look at how you can use this operator to assign values to variables. This assignment operator can be used to unpack sequences.

>>> *char1, char2, char3 = 'cat'*
>>> *char1*
'c'
>>> *char2*
'a'
>>> *char3*
't'

The assignment operator can also be used to assign different variables with the same value.

a = b = c = 1

The assignment operator can also be used along with mathematical operators.

counter += 1

The statement above is interpreted as counter = counter + 1. Other operators also can be used to either increment or decrement the value of the variable.

How to control the process

You have the liberty to decide what happens next in the program you have written using a control flow statement. The results of the comparison statements can be used to create conditional statements that allow the interpreter to provide the output that is based on whether the predefined conditions hold true. Conditional statements can be constructed using the keywords if, elif and else. Unlike other languages, Python does not use the keyword then. The syntax is very specific therefore you must pay close attention to the layout and punctuation.

if condition:
 # Perform some actions
print "Condition is True"
elif condition != True:
 # Perform some other actions

```
print "Condition is not True"
else:
# Perform default or fall-through actions
print "Anomaly: Condition is neither True nor False"
```

In the syntax above, the first line begins with the word if, which must be followed by a conditional statement that gives a True or False output followed by the colon. This colon means yes. The statements that follow must always start on a new line. The number of spaces doesn't strictly matter so long as all the instructions after the colon are indented by the same amount, though it's good practice to use the same number of spaces to indicate control flow throughout your code. The statements following after the colon are known as a suite.

You can include further conditional sections using the elif keyword (an abbreviation of else-if, which is not a Python keyword); statements following elif will be evaluated only if the previous test fails (i.e., the conditional expression is False).

You can also include a final else: statement, which will catch any value that did not satisfy any of the conditions; it doesn't take any conditional expression at all. This can be used to specify a default set of actions to perform. In our previous example, things would have to go very wrong for us to ever see the final anomaly warning, as the preceding if and elif statements would have caught either of the two possible results. It is possible to nest if statements to allow for more possibilities, and you can leave out the elif or else statements if you don't want anything to happen unless the condition is satisfied. In other words, sometimes you want to do something if a condition is satisfied but do nothing if it is not satisfied.

After the final statement, the indentation must go back to its original level: this will indicate to the interpreter that the conditional block has come to an end. Python marks out blocks of code using indentation alone; it doesn't use punctuation marks like the curly braces you may see in other languages.

This unique feature of Python means you have to be extra careful about indentation. If you do get it wrong, you'll find out soon enough, as the interpreter will complain loudly.

>>> *if c:*
... print(c)
... c += 1
... indent = "bad"
File "<stdin>", line 4
indent = "bad"
^

IndentationError: unindent does not match any outer indentation level

A conditional statement always gives the user the ability to check or validate the data that was used as the input. Validation is often performed when the data is first fed into the computer and also when the information is written out on a database record or file.

How to deal with logical errors

As your applications become more complex, you will need more formal methods of testing your designs. One of the ways of doing this is to construct a trace table. You must trace the values of all the variables and the conditional expressions over the course of the execution of the program.

A trace should be performed with as many different sets of data as is necessary to make sure that all the possible alternatives get tested. Most errors in programming don't occur if the values lie within some expected range, but they often occur for unusual values (also called critical values). Critical values are values that lie outside the tolerances of the program, such a number that the application is not equipped to deal with.

Critical values should be worked out early on in the design process, so that the program can be properly tested against them. In the calculation of the area of the triangle, the value that most needs taking into account is that of the breadth, which has been set at 14 cm. Allowing 8 cm means that the maximum breadth of the triangle can only be 8 cm.

Using the conditional code

Now you can apply your knowledge of conditional statements to allow for different ways of measuring up the material. If the breadth of the triangle were too much, it would become a different type of triangle. Therefore, you need to identify the right code which reflects the right conditions. The first step would be to translate your trace values into a pseudocode. The following example is about measuring the length of a curtain.

if curtain width < roll width:
total_length = curtain width
else:
total_length = curtain length
if (curtain width > roll width) and (curtain length > roll width):
if extra material < (roll width / 2):
width +=1
if extra material > (roll width / 2):
width +=2

LoopsWhile Statement

result = 1
while result < 1000:
result *= 2
print result

To control the number of times the loop is processed, it is necessary to specify a conditional expression; as long as this conditional expression is True at the beginning of an iteration, the loop continues. In the preceding example, our conditional expression is result < 1000. So, as long as the value of result is less than 1,000, the loop will continue processing. Once result reaches 1,024 (210), the program will stop processing the loop body.

The variables used in the conditional expression are often expendable entities, which are only required for as long as the loop is active. Rather than keep thinking up different names, this kind of integer counter is usually named i or j by convention.

Two things are important to remember in this sort of construction: Any variable used in the conditional expression must be initialized before the execution of the loop. Also, there must be some way of updating this variable within the loop; otherwise, the loop will just go around and round forever, which is called an infinite loop.

It is possible to use different sorts of variables in the conditional expression. Let's consider the problem of calculating the average of several numbers input by the user. The main problem here is that I don't know how many numbers will be input. The solution is to use what is called a sentinel value to control the loop. Rather than using the counter in this instance, the script checks the value of the user input number. While it is positive (i.e., $>= 0$) the loop processes as normal, but as soon as a negative number is entered, the loop is broken, and the script goes on to calculate the average. Let us take a look at the following example:

counter = 0
total = 0
number = 0
while number >= 0:
number = int (input ("Enter a positive number\nor a
negative to exit: "))
total += number
counter += 1
average = total / counter
print(average)

There are several methods of getting out of loops cleanly, the chief ones being the use of the break and continue keywords: If you want to get out of a loop without executing any more statements in the loop body, use break. If you just want to get out of this particular iteration of the loop, continue immediately takes you to the next iteration of the loop.

At times, you will want the interpreter to recognize a condition but do nothing. In this case, the pass keyword can be useful; it creates a null statement, which simply tells the interpreter to move on to the next instruction.

Nesting Loops

You are allowed to nest loops and other conditional statements in Python, probably infinitely, but it is best to keep the number of levels of nesting to a minimum. For one thing, it's very easy to get confused about which option the program is taking at any particular point. Also, having lots of indented blocks within other indented blocks makes your code difficult to read, can slow down the program's execution, and is generally considered bad style. If you have come up with a design that involves two or three layers of looping, you should probably start thinking about redesigning it to avoid the excessive depth of nesting.

For

The other control flow statement I want to introduce is the for statement, which is constructed in a similar manner to the if and while statements. Its construction is for element in sequence: followed by an indented suite of instructions. During the first iteration of the loop, the variable element contains the first element in the sequence and is available to the indented suite. During the second iteration, it contains the second element in the sequence, and so on.

To understand how this statement works, you need to know about sequences. The simplest sequence in Python is a string, which is a sequence of individual characters including spaces and punctuation. Other forms of sequence are tuples and lists. Tuples and lists are sequences of data items, the chief difference between them being that lists are editable in place, whereas tuples are not. It's possible to use either in a for statement. They are constructed as follows:

```
# tuple
sequence1 = (1, 2, 3)
# list
sequence2 = [1, 2, 3]
```

Breaking Down Jargon

This section explains some of the terms used in this chapter.

- Assignment operator: The single equals sign (=) is the assignment operator. It can be combined with other operators to perform more complex assignment operations.
- Built-in: A built-in element is an innate part of the programming language, as opposed to something that has to be imported from a module. Built-in elements are part of Python's standard library.
- Comparison operators: These operators compare two values:
- Conditional statement: This section of code is performed if a certain condition evaluates as True. A conditional statement is a form of control flow statement. • Critical values: These values exist at the edges of the permissible ranges set for an application. In particular, these are values that would cause changes or unexpected results from the normal running of the program.
- Loop body: The body is the suite of instructions to be repeated in a loop.

- Null statement: The pass keyword creates a null statement, which tells the interpreter to move on to the next statement.

- Validation: This refers to the process of checking that your data is what you expect.

Now that you have understood how to work with conditional statements and loops, try the following programs. The solutions to these programs have been provided at the end of the book.

1. Write a program to print the Fibonacci series
2. Write a program to print a palindrome
3. Write a program to check if a number is even or odd

Chapter Five:

Data Structures

So far, you have learned to work with individual pieces of data to produce some simple results. Real world data is usually in lumps or groups, and it would be useful to work with such groups without having to make lots of repetitive statements in our code. Fortunately, Python provides a variety of data types that can make handling groups of data much simpler.

The data types that are most used in Python are strings, tuples, lists and dictionaries, which are called data structures. Lists and tuples are a group or ordered data items while strings are pieces of characters or texts that are put together. Strings are just pieces of text. Tuples and lists are ordered groups of individual data items. Dictionaries are groups of pairs that only consist of key variables and values. Strings, tuples, and lists are also called sequences, which are a type of data model. The methods used for accessing the data in a sequence are same, which you will see later in this chapter.

There is another way of looking at these data types— according to whether they can be modified or not, which is called mutability. An existing string and tuple cannot be modified, but new strings and tuples can be created using them which means that both strings and tuples are immutable. Lists are mutable, which means we can add or remove items from a list.

Items in sequences

We can fetch an individual item from a sequence using an index, which is the position of the element. The index is specified as an integer (a whole number) in square brackets immediately following the variable name. So, s[i] will retrieve the item at position i of sequence s. This allows you to access a single character in a string:

>>> *vegetable = 'pumpkin'*

>>> *vegetable [0]*

'p'

Or an item in a list:

>>>*vegetable = ['pumpkins', 'potatoes', 'onions', 'eggplant']*

>>>*vegetable [1]*

'pumpkins'

The first thing you will notice is that indexing is zero-based; that means you start counting at 0. An index of [2] accesses the third item in the list, the first item would be referenced with [0]. So, you can use integers 0 through to the number of elements in the sequence minus one (0 to n − 1) as indices. When you use a negative index, the interpreter counts from the end of the list.:

>>>*vegetable [-1]*

'eggplant'

You can grab sections of a sequence using slices. Slicing is used to fetch multiple items from a sequence. Slices are the same as indices in the sense that the notation used for both is the same. However, slices are written with two or more integers separated by colons. The first value is the inclusive starting point and the second number is the exclusive end point of the slice. So, s [0:2] means that the slice will start from index 0 and stop just before index 2, (i.e., fetch items at positions 0 and 1).

The third value is optional and specifies an additional step value, which may be negative, so instead of picking out a sequential list, you can retrieve every other, or every nth item, and you can also retrieve them backward if you need to. So, s [i: j: step] will retrieve a slice of s starting from i and up to, but not including j, and taking the specified step.If you leave out the starting point, the slice will start at the beginning of the original sequence, and if you leave out the end point, the slice will run to the end of the original sequence.

Indexing and slicing do not modify the original sequence; they make a new sequence from the original. However, the actual individual data items are the same. So, if you modify an individual item in a sequence, you will see the item change in a slice from the sequence as well.

Tuples

A tuple is an immutable ordered group of items or elements. Think of tuples as useful little sealed packets of information. A tuple is specified as a comma-separated list of values, which may be enclosed in parentheses. On certain occasions, the parentheses are required, so when in doubt, use parentheses. The values need not all be of the same type. A value can also be another tuple.

Creating a Tuple

Tuples can be created with no items in it using the round brackets ().

>>>empty_tuple= ()

If you do not want more than one item in the tuple, you should enter the first item followed by a comma.

>>>one_item = ('blue',)

Changing Values in a Tuple

You cannot change the values in a tuple. These tuples are sealed packets of information that are often used in situations where a set of values need to be passed on from one location to another. If you wish to change the sequence of the data, you should use a list.

List

A list is an ordered, comma-separated list of items enclosed in square brackets. Items need not all be of the same type. An item can also be another list.

Lists can be sliced, concatenated, and indexed the same as any other type of sequence. It is possible to change individual items in a list, as opposed to immutable strings and tuples. Where a tuple is rather like a fixed menu, lists are more flexible. It is possible to assign data to slices, which can change the size of the list or clear it completely.

Creating a List

It is easy to create a list.

>>> *shopping_list = ['detergent', 'deodorant', 'shampoo', 'body wash']*

Modifying a List

A new value can be added to a list using the assignment operator.

>>> *shopping_list [1] = 'candles'*
>>> *shopping_list*
['detergent', 'candles', 'deodorant', 'shampoo', 'body wash']

Stacks and Queues

Because lists are an ordered type of data, it is possible to use them to store and retrieve data items in a particular order. The two main models for doing this are described in traditional programming-speak as "stacks" and "queues."

A stack is a last in, first out (LIFO) structure, used rather like the discard pile in a card game. You put cards on the top of the pile and take them back off the top. You can push items onto the stack with list.append () and pop them back off with pop (). Note that there is no additional index argument, so it will be the last item of the list that is popped.

>>> *shopping_list.append ('brush')*
>>> *shopping_list.pop()*
'candles'
>>> *shopping_list*
['detergent', 'deodorant', 'shampoo', 'body wash']

The other approach involves creating a first in, first out (FIFO) structure called a queue. This works more like a pipe, where you push items in at one end and the first thing you put in the pipe pops out of the other end. Again, we can push items into the pipe using append() and retrieve them using pop(0)— this time with an index of 0 to indicate that the data items should be popped from the start of the list

>>> *shopping_list.append ('brush')*
>>> *shopping_list.pop(0)*
'detergent'
>>> *shopping_list*
['deodorant', 'shampoo', 'body wash', 'brush']'

Dictionaries

Dictionaries are like address books: if you know the name of the person, you can get all of that person's details. The name is technically referred to as a key, and any corresponding detail is referred to as the value.

The key must be of an immutable type, that is, a string, number or tuple; the value can be more or less anything you like. The dictionary itself is a mutable data type, which means you can add, remove, and modify key-value pairs. The keys are said to be mapped to objects, hence dictionaries are referred to as "mappings" to remind us that their behavior is somewhat different to sequences.

Dictionaries are used anywhere we want to store attributes and values that describe some concept or entity. For example, we can use a dictionary to count instances of particular objects or states. Because each key has to have a unique identifier, there cannot be duplicate values for the same key. Therefore, we can use the key to store the items of input data, leaving the value part to store the results of our calculations.

Breaking down Jargon

Let us break down some of the new words you have come across in this chapter.

• Arbitrary: In this instance, anything defined by the programmer is arbitrary.

• Complex data types: These are structured or compound types constructed from a sequence of other types of data.

• Constant: A constant value does not change during the execution of the program.

• Constrain: Ensure that the results of a calculation fall between a specified range.

• Hash: A hash is number calculated from a dictionary key to help with storage. This number is designed to be smaller than the key to aid efficiency.

• Immutable: An immutable value that cannot be edited in place.

• Index: An index is a token of an immutable type in square brackets immediately following the variable name, used to point to a specific item in the sequence.

• Iterable: This refers to a code object that can be iterated.

• Iterate: When you loop through items in a sequence one item at a time, you iterate it.

• Iterator: This construct is designed to allow looping.

• Mapping: This refers to a sequence that maps hashable values to arbitrary objects.

• Matrix: A matrix is a multidimensional sequence.

• Method: A method is a function specifically attached to an object or class of objects.

• Mutable: A mutable value can be changed.

• Operation: This action is performed on two variables (operands), usually of a mathematical or logical nature.

• Queue: A queue is a first in, first out (FIFO) structure. You push things in at one end and pop values out of the other.

• Resultant: This value is returned as the result of a process.

• Separator: This text string is used to distinguish between items of data.

• Sequence: A sequence is the simplest sort of complex data type in Python. Lists, strings, and tuples are the types of sequences.

• Sequence packing: Sequence packing is the action of assigning a sequence of comma-separated values to a variable.

• Slice: This refers to a smaller segment of a sequence.

Here are a few exercises that will help you master data structures.

1. Write a program to access the elements in a list
2. Write a program to slice a list in Python.
3. Write a program to delete elements in a List.
4. Write a program to access elements in a tuple.
5. Write a program to change a tuple.

TIMOTHY C. NEEDHAM

Chapter Six:

Working with Strings

Most commands in Python 3 will work in exactly the same way as in Python 2. There are, however, some important changes. Probably the most fundamental change is the rationalization of the string data type. In previous versions of Python, strings were coded as a sequence of single bytes, using the limited American Standard Code for Information Interchange (ASCII) character set to represent text, this 7-bit encoding allows for up to 128 characters including uppercase and lowercase letters, numbers, punctuation, and 33 invisible control characters. While ASCII is OK for representing languages that use Latin script, such as English and most European languages, it is completely useless when it comes to representing the 2,000 basic ideograms of the Chinese language. To deal with these sorts of problems, the Unicode standard was created to cover all written languages, so Python 3 has brought itself up-to-date by switching to Unicode as its default text encoding. The str type is what used to be the unicode type, and a new type, byte, has been introduced to represent raw text strings and binary data. Previous versions of Python went through all sorts of contortions in order to deal with text encoding; fortunately, all you really need to know is that the str type in Python 3 supports international characters by default, so you don't have to do anything special if you want to write a string.

To go along with the string type changes, the print statement in Python 2.x has been replaced with the print() function which is a built-in function in version 3.0. this function replaces most of the earlier syntax with keyword arguments. To balance this, the old raw_input() is replaced by input(), and you have to use eval(input()) to get the old functionality of input().

Splitting Strings

As strings are immutable, you will often want to split them up into lists in order to manipulate their contents. Quick reminder—a delimiter is a character or string of characters that are used to separate words or units of data. The list will be split up to maxsplit times, so you'll end up with a list that's maxsplit + 1 items long. If no separator is specified, the string will be split up by whitespace characters as if they are words.

>>>*sentence = 'This is a long sentence'*

>>> *sentence.rstrip('sentence').split()*

['This', 'is', 'a', 'long']

Python has an alternative string splitting method, string.partition(sep), which returns a tuple: (head, sep, tail). The method identifies the separator within the string and then returns the section before the separator the separator and the part of the string that is separated from the string. If the separator is not found, the method will return the original string and two empty strings.

Concatenation and Joining Strings

Using the + operator to join strings together is very inefficient; combined with lots of calls to the print() function (or statement in Python 2), using the + operator can potentially slow your program's execution to a crawl. Python isn't that slow. Often, it works out better to manipulate a list of words and then use string.join(sequence) to return a string that is a concatenation of the strings in the sequence. This method is the opposite of string.split(): the data you want to manipulate is in the sequence of the argument, and the string that you call the method on is just the string of characters you want to use to separate the items. This could be a space or an empty string.

```
>>> s1="example"
>>> s2 = "text"
>>> s3 = " "
>>> s3.join([s1,s2])
```
'example text'

You must remember that the function string.join() always expects a sequence of strings as the argument.

```
>>> s3 = "-"
>>> s3.join ('castle')
```
'c-a-s-t-l-e'

You also may have the need to convert different data types into strings by using a sublist.

Editing Strings

Strings, as you have probably gathered by now, can't be edited in place, but they do have some useful methods that will return a new edited version of the string.

You often need to clean up the beginning and end of the string to remove extraneous whitespace or punctuation, especially if you're trying to compare some user input with a stored value. This is done with the string.strip([chars]) method. This returns a copy of the string with chars removed from the beginning and the end if the sequence is found. If no arguments are given, string.strip() will remove whitespace characters by default.

```
>>> sentence = 'This is a long sentence'
>>> sentence.strip('A')
```
' This is long sentence'

How to Match Patterns

Sometimes, the basic string methods just aren't enough. For example, you may need to retrieve values that appear within a regular pattern in a piece of text, but you don't know what those values are going to be or just have a rough idea of what they should not be. This is where regular expressions come in. A regular expression (regex, for short) is a pattern that can match a piece of text. In its simplest form, a regular expression could just be a plain string of ordinary characters that matches itself. Regular expression syntax uses additional special characters to recognize a range of possibilities that can be matched. These expressions can be used in search and replace operations and to split up text in different way than string.split().

Regular expressions are complex, powerful, and difficult to read. Most of the time, you can manage without them, but they are particularly useful when dealing with complex, structured pieces of text. It's best to take regular expressions slowly, learning a bit at a time. Trying to learn the whole regular expression syntax all in one go could be quite overwhelming.

Regular expression matching operations are provided by the re module. As re is not built in by default, it is necessary to import the module first before it is possible to use it.

>>> *import rein*

The module supports both 8-bit and Unicode strings, so it should be possible to recognize any characters that you can type in from the keyboard or read from a file.

Next, you need to construct a regular expression string to represent the pattern you want to catch. Let's use the rather colorful string from earlier in the chapter again.

Creating a Regular Expression Object

You can compile a regular expression pattern into a regular expression object using re.compile(pattern[, flags]). This returns a pattern object on which you can call all the previous methods, but you no longer need to provide the pattern as an argument. You might want to do this if you need to use this pattern to perform lots of matches all at once;

compiling the pattern into an object speeds up the pattern comparison process, because the pattern does not have to then be compiled each time it is used. You might also need to use this approach where a function specifically requires a regular expression object to be passed to it rather than just a pattern string.

Exercises:

1.　　Write a Program to create a string.

Chapter Seven:

How to Use Files

So far, data has either been written into the program itself or received via the input() function and printed out using the print() function. Once the program has finished its execution, the data is lost. In order for an application to have any practical value, it is necessary to be able to store that information and retrieve it the next time the program is run. The vast majority of computer information is stored in files on a hard drive or similar storage medium or can be transmitted via some file-like object. File-like objects share some similar properties with files and can often be treated with the same methods; streams are an important kind of file-like object.

How to Open Files

File objects can be created with the built-in open(filename[, mode[, buffering]]) function. Built-in functions and methods also return file objects. Let us open a plain text file in the same directory where we started the interpreter.

>>> *open('Python.txt')*

<io.TextIOWrapper object at 0xb7ba990c>

The example above uses another Python object which says it is an io.TextIOWrapper; in plain language, that's a file object. If the file doesn't exist, you'll get an IOError. IO stands for input/output, in other words, reading and writing to files. The file object now holds the contents of story.txt, but in order to do anything with it, you need to learn some file methods.

I hope you're getting used to the concept that everything in Python is some type of object and that any type of object will usually have several methods that you can use to access its values or edit it. Before you can make use of the different file methods, it is important to understand the different ways that Python can open a file to create a file object.

Modes and Buffers

Opening the file by just passing the filename to open() creates a read-only file object. If you want to be able to write to that file as well, it is necessary to set the optional mode argument. This argument can be a single character: r (read), w (write), or a (append), any of which may be followed by b (binary) or + (read/write). If you don't provide a mode argument, Python will assume your file is a text file, and mode r will be assumed.

>>> *open('Python.txt', 'rb')*
<io.BufferedReader object at 0xb7ba990c>

The b mode returns a different kind of object to the default file object—one that contains the same information in byte format. You might want to use this if you wanted to handle image or audio data. Write mode (w) lets you change the contents of the file completely. Append mode (a) only lets you add information to the end. This last option is useful for creating log files.

The buffering argument, used with w or a, can either be 0 or 1. If it's 0, your data is written straight to your hard-drive. If it's 1, Python creates a temporary file to store the text in before it gets written out. The data is not written to disk unless you explicitly call file.flush() or file.close(). You probably won't need this option immediately.

Reading and Writing

The most basic method you can use to access the file's contents is file.read([size]). This reads up to size bytes from the file (less if the read hits the end of the file before it gets to size bytes). The complete file is read as one string if there is no size argument provided or if it is negative. Unless the file is opened as a binary object, the bytes are returned as string objects. In such cases, you will only have raw bytes as output. If you are reading a plain text file containing ordinary characters, you might not notice a great deal of difference.

>>> *text = open('Python.txt')*

>>> *text.read()*

'Are you keen to learn the Python language

[... pages more text here ...]

Thank you for purchasing the book.\n'

If you are dealing with a large body of text like the following example, you may wish to deal with it in smaller pieces. file.readline([size]) reads a single line from the file (up to the next newline character, \n). An incomplete line may be returned in an iteration. The size argument is defined as the number of bytes that the interpreter must read. The bytes also include the trailing newline. If the interpreter reaches the end of the file, an empty string is returned.

>>> *text = open('Python.txt')*

>>> *text.readline()*

"Are you keen to learn more about the Python language. Thank you for purchasing the book. I hope you gather all the information you were looking for."

Files are their own iterators, so you can also iterate through lines in a file using a for loop. The same result as the file.readline() method is returned at each iteration and the loop only ends when the method returns a null or empty string.

Try the following code out:

>>> *for line in text:*

... print (line)

Closing Files

It is a good idea to use file.close() to close a file after you are finished with it. Python will probably notice that you're not using the file anymore and free up the memory space eventually, but explicitly closing it is cleaner. Often, the data in a file.write() operation is stored in a buffer until the file is closed. You can make sure the data gets written out to the file without closing it by using file.flush(). A file once closed cannot be further read or written. You are allowed to call close() more than once.

Chapter Eight:

Working with Functions

The first design considerations in making a new function are what kind of input it needs and what information the function will return. Of close importance are the type and structure of the data that will be fed in and retrieved. Data supplied to a function are called parameters, and the final information that is returned is known as results, or output. Our initial specification for the function design should also include a general description of the function's specific purpose.

Defining a Function

A function is always defined using the def statement. The word def is followed by the function name, an optional list of parameters and the line ends with a colon which indicates that the subsequent lines should be indented as a suite or block of instructions. Let's start with a function that takes no parameters:

```
>>> def generate_rpc():
... """Role-Playing Character generator
"""

... profile = {}
... print "New Character"
... return profile
```

This block of instructions proceeds in exactly the same way as a complete script. So, in essence, we give a name to each piece of functionality, and they are called functions.

If you want to provide some notes on what the function does, you can do so in the docstring, which must be the first thing in the function. The docstring is then followed by a series of statements that are the core functionality. The function can also return some data using a return statement.

The function's last line specifies which variables get returned to the main program. If there is nothing to return, you do not have to use a return statement, and Python will assume None as the default return value.

Up to this point, the block of code in our function has not yet been run; it has simply been assigned to the function definition. To get the code to run, you need to call the function from the main body of the program. (This is called a function call.) Since we have given names to functions, we can call those functions any number of times:

>>> generate_rpc()
New Character
{}

We haven't specified any parameters in this example, hence the empty parentheses after the function name.

Defining Parameters

Most functions work on some data that they have been given by the main program. In order for the function to receive data, it needs to set up some empty containers to hold the data. These become variables unique to the function and are known as formal parameters, and it's best if they don't use the same names as in the main program. These formal parameters have to be specified in the parentheses after the function name on the first line of the function definition.

import random
def roll(sides, dice):
result = 0 for rolls in range(0,dice):
result += random.randint(1,sides)
return result

This function might be called from the main program in the following way:

muscle = roll(33,3)

The values in parentheses in the function call are known as arguments; they correspond to the formal parameters in the function definition. In this case, the first argument, 33, is bound to the parameter sides, and the second argument, 3, is bound to the parameter dice. This effectively creates two variables, sides and dice, to be used inside the function. If you just send the function values like this, there must be the same number of arguments as parameters, and they have to be in the right order, so these are known as positional arguments. You could substitute the actual values in the function call with variables if you prefer. Just remember that the function is going to refer to that value by the name of the parameter that receives it, and the original variable will remain unaffected; only the value gets passed on.

Documenting your Function

Once a function is fully coded and passes the tests you have set for it, it is a good time to edit its docstring to fit with the expectations of Python's documentation tools.

Docstrings are expected to follow convention: The first line of a docstring should be a short description of the function that makes sense by itself and fits on only one line (usually a maximum of 79 characters, including any indentation). The next line should be left blank. After that, the body of the docstring should contain a description of the function's parameters, a longer description of the function, notes about the algorithm used, and an example of how to use the function that includes details of optional arguments, keyword arguments, and its return values. You might also want to include information about possible side-effects, exceptions, and restrictions on when the function can be called (these matters will be covered later in this book). In short, all the information that another programmer would need to be able to use the function. It is very important to update your docstrings and comments every time the code changes.

Working with Scope

One way of conceptualizing functions is to think of them as black boxes that take in source data, process it and pass it back. The code in the main program that sends the source data and receives the result is known as the calling procedure. It doesn't need to know what is inside the black box, so long as the source data and results are clearly identified.

Understanding Scope

When you write a function, you should not have to worry about using names that will clash with names used in the other parts of the program. This is why we have the concept of scopes.

When any program is run, the interpreter keeps track of all the names that are created and used in the program. These names are tracked in a table referred to as a symbol table and can be viewed as a dictionary using the built-in vars() function. The variables created in the main program's symbol table are known as global variables, because any part of the program can access these variables. These can be viewed with the built-in globals() function. You will notice that the result of running vars() with no arguments inside the main program is the same as running globals(). So far, the script examples in this book have only used global data.

Any variable that is created in a function is stored in a symbol table unique to that function; this data is known as local data and can be accessed within that function using the locals() function. The main body of the program (global scope) cannot access the variables set inside the function (local scope). The function, however, is still able to access names in the main body, that is, globals. Hence, you have two ways to get at a function to process some data: The correct way is to take that data as a parameter for the function; the function will process it and then return the result, which will be collected by the main program. The other way is to let the function directly access and process the global data, but this second way is discouraged because the function works with only particular variable names and cannot be reused anywhere else.

Manipulating Dictionaries and Lists

Parameters to a function are passed by value. However, in the case of objects (unlike simple types such as integers and strings), if you modify the parts of an object, including items in a list or a dictionary, the changes are reflected outside the function as well. This means that a function can be used to modify a mutable data type such as a dictionary or list. Technically, such a modification procedure is not a pure function, as it neither needs a return value or indeed, any input parameters.

In order to avoid strange side-effects, a good general policy is to send and return immutable values from functions and keep any modification procedures for your mutable types separate. If you send a list or dictionary to a function, all you are doing is sending it a pointer to the same global instance of that object, just as if you had written local_list = global_list.

Abstraction

This round of testing may bring new issues to light. In order to help you keep track of what's going on with your code, do the minimum necessary to get the new code to pass its tests. If the new code fails, you should roll back the changes to the point where the code passes again. Also, if using the function doesn't work, don't sweat it: reverse the changes and move on. There is no rule that says you have to abstract everything into a function.

The processes of placing code into functions (abstraction) and turning code that deals with specifics into general-purpose code (generalization) can also be applied to your testing procedures, and this is a good thing to do. All these test procedures will eventually get moved outside the program into a separate module, so abstraction and generalization are also good preparation. The rule to remember is to write your tests first and then make sure your existing code still passes before attempting to refactor it. Although this might seem like a laborious approach, in fact, it speeds up the development of new code and provides a mechanism for flagging up which part of the code needs fixing next, rather than having to keep all the details in your head. This has to be a good thing.

Chapter Nine:

Solutions

Concatenate two strings

```
# Python Program - Concatenate String
print("Enter 'x' for exit.");
string1 = input("Please enter the first string: ");
if string1 == 'My name is Dobby':
    exit();
else:
    string2 = input("Please enter the second string: ");
    string3 = string1 + string2;
    print("\nString after concatenation =",string3);
    print("String 1 =",string1);
    print("String 2 =",string2);
    print("String 3 =",string3);
```

Sum of Two Numbers

```
# Program to add two numbers

number1 = input(" Please Enter the First Number: ")
number2 = input(" Please Enter the second number: ")

# Using the arithmetic operator to add two numbers
sum = float(number1) + float(number2)
print('The sum of {0} and {1} is {2}'.format(number1,
number2, sum))
```

Even and Odd Numbers

```
# Program to check whether a number is even or odd
# When a number is divided by 2 and the remainder is
0, the number is even.
# If remainder is 1, the number is odd.
```

```python
num = int(input("Enter a number: "))
if (num % 2) == 0:
   print("{0} is Even".format(num))
else:
   print("{0} is Odd".format(num))
```

Fibonacci Series

```python
# Program to display the Fibonacci sequence up to n-th
term where n is provided by the user
# change this value for a different result
nterms = 10
# uncomment to take input from the user
#nterms = int(input("How many terms? "))
# first two terms
n1 = 0
n2 = 1
count = 0
# check if the number of terms is valid
if nterms <= 0:
   print("Please enter a positive integer")
elif nterms == 1:
   print("Fibonacci sequence upto",nterms,":")
   print(n1)
else:
   print("Fibonacci sequence upto",nterms,":")
   while count < nterms:
     print(n1,end=' , ')
     nth = n1 + n2
     # update values
     n1 = n2
     n2 = nth
     count += 1
```

Palindrome

```
# Program to check if a string is a palindrome or not
# change this value for a different output
my_str = 'I need to save Harry Potter'
# make it suitable for caseless comparison
my_str = my_str.casefold()
# reverse the string
rev_str = reversed(my_str)
# check if the string is equal to its reverse
if list(my_str) == list(rev_str):
  print("It is palindrome")
else:
  print("It is not palindrome")
```

Access Elements in a List

```
my_list = ['p','r','o','b','e']

# Output: p
print(my_list[0])
# Output: o
print(my_list[2])
# Output: e
print(my_list[4])
# Error! Only integer can be used for indexing
# my_list[4.0]
# Nested List
n_list = ["Happy", [2,0,1,5]]
# Nested indexing
# Output: a
print(n_list[0][1])
# Output: 5
print(n_list[1][3])
```

Slice a List

```
my_list = ['p','r','o','g','r','a','m','i','z']
# elements 3rd to 5th
print(my_list[2:5])
# elements beginning to 4th
print(my_list[:-5])
# elements 6th to end
print(my_list[5:])
# elements beginning to end
print(my_list[:])
```

Delete Elements in a List

```
>>> my_list = ['p','r','o','b','l','e','m']
>>> my_list[2:3] = []
>>> my_list
['p', 'r', 'b', 'l', 'e', 'm']
>>> my_list[2:5] = []
>>> my_list
['p', 'r', 'm']
```

Access Elements in a Tuple

```
my_tuple = ('p','e','r','m','i','t')
# Output: 'p'
print(my_tuple[0])
# Output: 't'
print(my_tuple[5])
# index must be in range
# If you uncomment line 14,
# you will get an error.
# IndexError: list index out of range
#print(my_tuple[6])
# index must be an integer
# If you uncomment line 21,
# you will get an error.
```

```python
# TypeError: list indices must be integers, not float
#my_tuple[2.0]
# nested tuple
n_tuple = ("mouse", [8, 4, 6], (1, 2, 3))
# nested index
# Output: 's'
print(n_tuple[0][3])
# nested index
# Output: 4
print(n_tuple[1][1])
```

Change a Tuple

```python
my_tuple = (4, 2, 3, [6, 5])
# we cannot change an element
# If you uncomment line 8
# you will get an error:
# TypeError: 'tuple' object does not support item assignment
#my_tuple[1] = 9
# but item of mutable element can be changed
# Output: (4, 2, 3, [9, 5])
my_tuple[3][0] = 9
print(my_tuple)
# tuples can be reassigned
# Output: ('p', 'r', 'o', 'g', 'r', 'a', 'm', 'i', 'z')
my_tuple = ('p','r','o','g','r','a','m','i','z')
print(my_tuple)
```

Create a String

```python
# all of the following are equivalent
my_string = 'Hello'
print(my_string)
my_string = "Hello"
print(my_string)
```

```python
my_string = '''Hello'''
print(my_string)
# triple quotes string can extend multiple lines
my_string = """Hello, welcome to
        the world of Python"""
print(my_string)
```

Conclusion

Thank you for purchasing the book. This book acts as a guide for those who are working with Python for the first time. Over the course of the book, you will gain information on what Python is and how to code in Python. Before you begin to program, there are some questions you must ask yourself to understand the right code you must write. This is called the software development stage and is one of the most important steps to complete when writing a code. Python is a simple language and is written as a pseudocode. As a programmer, you will find that it is easy for you to code in Python.

You will gather information on different aspects of Python including – data types, structures, functions, how to work with files, how to work with strings including others. There are some exercises given at the end of the chapters which can be used to practice. The solutions to these exercises are provided in the last chapter of the book. The exercises provided in the book are simple but they will help you learn how to write simple code in Python. Once you understand the language better, you can go onto developing larger and more complex programs. Try to work on the exercises before you look at the solutions in the last chapter.

You must remember that it is practice that will help you become the best programmer in any language. It is okay to make mistakes when you write code, but it is important that you learn from those mistakes. Keep a notepad close to you and make note of all the variables and functions you have declared in your code to ensure that you do not overwrite them with new code.

I hope you gather all the information you are looking for. Good luck on your new adventure.

Other Books By Timothy C. Needham

Python For Beginners: A Crash Course Guide To Learn Python in 1 Week

Click here to download:

https://www.amazon.com/Python-Beginners-Crash-Course-Guide/dp/1549776673

Excel 2016: A Comprehensive Beginner's Guide to Microsoft Excel 2016

Did you enjoy this book?

I want to thank you for purchasing and reading this book. I really hope you got a lot out of it.

Can I ask a quick favor though?

If you enjoyed this book I would really appreciate it if you could leave me a positive review on Amazon.

I love getting feedback from my customers and reviews on Amazon really do make a difference. I read all my reviews and would really appreciate your thoughts.

Thanks so much.

Timothy C. Needham

p.s. You can click here to go directly to the book on Amazon and leave your review.

ALL RIGHTS RESERVED.

Sources

https://www.programiz.com/Python-programming/first-program

https://www.programiz.com/Python-programming/keywords-identifier

https://www.programiz.com/Python-programming/variables-datatypes

https://www.programiz.com/Python-programming/if-elif-else

https://www.programiz.com/Python-programming/while-loop

https://www.programiz.com/Python-programming/while-loop

https://www.programiz.com/Python-programming/string

http://interactivePython.org/runestone/static/Pythonds/Introduction/GettingStarted.html

http://interactivePython.org/runestone/static/Pythonds/Introduction/WhyStudyDataStructuresandAbstractDataTypes.html

http://interactivePython.org/runestone/static/Pythonds/Introduction/ReviewofBasicPython.html

http://interactivePython.org/runestone/static/Pythonds/AlgorithmAnalysis/Lists.html

https://docs.Python.org/3/tutorial/datastructures.html

http://thomas-cokelaer.info/tutorials/Python/data_structures.html

https://www.datacamp.com/community/tutorials/data-structures-Python

https://www.learnPython.org/en/Loops

https://www.w3schools.com/Python/Python_for_loops.asp

Learn Java

A Crash Course Guide to Learn Java in 1 Week

Timothy C.Needham

Timothy C.Needham

This document is geared towards providing exact and reliable information in regards to the topic and issue covered. The publication is sold with the idea that the publisher is not required to render accounting, officially permitted, or otherwise, qualified services. If advice is necessary, legal or professional, a practiced individual in the profession should be ordered.

- From a Declaration of Principles which was accepted and approved equally by a Committee of the American Bar Association and a Committee of Publishers and Associations.

Table of Contents

___Introduction___

I want to thank you and congratulate you for buying the book, *"Java for Beginners: A Crash Course Guide to Learn Java in 1 Week."*

This book is the ultimate beginners' crash course to Java programming, as it will help you learn enough about the language in as little as 1 week!

We all have dreams. My dream could be to become a great teacher, and chances are that your dream is to have a great career in IT or develop your skills and knowledge in IT for self-fulfillment (or something close to that). Without a doubt, the hands-on experience and expertise Java Programming Language offers is an essential requirement for anyone who's ardent about becoming a professional programmer.

But while you might be motivated enough to learn the language, I'm sure you must have asked yourself some questions severally: *why programming? Or why choose Java?* There are many reasons as to why you should learn programming- and Java in particular- most of which I'm sure you already know. If you ask me though, I'd be mean enough to say that some of us learn to earn. There are definitely many self-actualization and fulfillment related benefits that come with learning the art and trade of programming but the fiscal benefits are simply too conspicuous to ignore.

For one, Java is arguably the most acclaimed skill and is in demand nearly everywhere. IBM, Infosys, Twitter, Netflix, Google, Spotify, Uber, Amazon, Target, Yelp, Square, and other big players are always in need of a great Java programmer. Going by PayScale.com (the website that offers information about salary), an average Java developer earns about $70,000 annually. As a pro in the field, you have the entire globe to work over, as the demand is never restricted to a particular geographical area.

This book is the ultimate guide specially designed to help you move from a person largely unacquainted with programming to a person who can actually teach the subject and complete good programming projects. Here's the cool part: you get to learn the whole thing in ONE WEEK! It is updated to the latest versions (8 and 10) and the main topics of what the book will be about include:

- Variables
- Conditions
- Loops
- Arrays
- Operators
- User input
- Classes
- Objects
- Methods
- Object Oriented Programming which includes:
- ✓ Inheritance
- ✓ Encapsulation
- ✓ Polymorphism
- ✓ Compositions

And much, much more! Let's begin our learning.

Thanks again for downloading this book. I hope you enjoy it!

Before we get to the specifics, let's start by learning some of the common terms that you will encounter as you learn about Java, whether in this book or in any other learning material.

Understanding the Lingo: A Glossary

While the following list is in no way comprehensive of all terms that you will come across when using and learning Java, it will give you a good starting point to ensure you understand what is being talked about.

- **IDE (Integrated Development Environment) -** this refers to a software application that offers you comprehensive facilities for software development or basic programming. It usually comprises built automation tools, source code editor and a debugger.

- **PATH-** in its general form (of a directory or file), path refers to the specific location in a file system.

- **Source code repository-** this refers to a file archive and web hosting facility in which a huge amount of source code for web pages or software is stored, either privately or publicly. They are usually used by open-source software projects as well as certain multi-developer projects to deal with various versions.

- **Refactoring-** this refers to a process of altering a software system in a way that it doesn't change the external behavior of the code, but improves its internal structure.

- **Unicode-** this refers to a 16-bit character encoding standard that is able to represent nearly all characters of well-known languages of the world.

- **Compiler-** a compiler is a special program that is tasked with processing statements written in a programming language, and turns them into code (or machine language) that is used by the computer's processor.

- **Heap-** refers to a part of pre-reserved computer main storage or memory that a process of a program can access to store data in a given variable amount that cannot be known until the program runs.

- **Syntax-** refers to the general set rules in a programming language that describe the combinations of symbols considered to be rightly structured programs in that particular language.

- **Constructors-** they are special methods that are called when objects are instantiated, or, when you make use of the new keywords.

- **Modifiers-** these are keywords in Java that you add to classes, variables and methods to change their meaning

- **Naming convention-** refers to the rule that you follow to determine what to name your identifiers like package, class, constant, method or variable and so on.

- **Object oriented programming (OOP) -** is a kind of computer programming in software design that allows programmers to define the data type of a data structure as well as the functions or types of operations that are applicable to the data structure.

- **Access modifiers-** also referred to as access specifiers, access modifiers are keywords that set the accessibility of methods, classes among other members. They are a specific part of programming language syntax that facilitates component encapsulation.

As I stated earlier, the above list is in no way comprehensive. It will however, prove useful at this point, as a larger list would have been overwhelming. You can always refer to this list if something is not clear.

With that in mind, let's start our learning. In case you are completely new to this, we'll start with the basics:

Java Programming: A Background

Before we get into Java programming, let's first make sure you understand what computer programming (or coding) really is.

What Is Programming?

By definition, programming is the process of building software, which is made up of instructions. These instructions are basically referred to as the *source code*. The *source code* is a set of written instructions that a computer understands. Throughout this book, we'll be using this concept so you need to understand it before we begin.

What does the source code really look like?

Code doesn't typically follow the rules of natural languages, such as English. Take a look at this small program to understand what I mean:

```
require 'open-uri'
require 'json'
FRONT_PAGE_URL = 'https://reddit.com/r/all.json'
front_page = JSON.load(open(FRONT_PAGE_URL).read)
top_post = front_page['data']['children'][0]['data']
puts 'The top post on reddit is:'
puts top_post['title']
puts top_post['url']
```

A computer actually takes everything literally- for instance, when you ask a computer if a number is even or odd, it will always respond with a 'yes'. Don't believe me? Take a look at the code below:

```
puts (5.odd? or 5.even?)
```

The code will display 'true', which is, technically speaking, right. The number 5 is either even or odd- even though that's not what I really meant.

Programming also entails Testing and debugging

When code is written, it has to be tested because just writing it does not guarantee that it is correct. The code could crash from time to time, or display incorrect results, freeze or any other problem like that. Professional programmers usually employ different methods to test their code to try to avert such problems.

Lastly, we have a term referred to as ***debugging***- this is the process of investigating a problem, diagnosing it and fixing it in source code- as you will soon find out in the course of this book, this is actually a skill in itself.

So, what is Java programming language?

Java programming language is a computer programming language that uniquely lets you write the computer instructions using English-based commands as opposed to writing them in the usual numeric codes. It is referred to as high-level language due to the fact that human beings can read and write it easily. Just like English though, Java has some rules, which determine how these instructions are written; these rules are referred to as its **syntax**. Basically, when the program is written, the high-level instructions are translated into numeric codes that are understandable and executable to computers.

So, Who Created Java?

Java was created in the early 90s by a man known as James Gosling for a company called Sun Microsystems (which is currently owned by Oracle). The program was originally called Oak, and then Green.

Java was originally designed to be used to program home appliances controlled by different computer processors and then later, mobile devices like cell phones. Soon enough, there came the realization that the language needed to be accessible by various computer processors. In 1994, the language was seen as ideal for use with web browsers and in no time, its connection to the internet started. In 1995, the latest version of the Netscape browser capable of running Java programs was released by Netscape Incorporated and in 1996, when Java 1.0 was released to the public, its main focus had already shifted to use on the internet, thus offering interactivity with users by providing developers a good way to create animated web pages.

Since the 1.0 version, we have seen many updates and developments such as:

✓ J2SE 1.3 released in 2000
✓ J2SE in 2004
✓ Java SE 8 in 2014
✓ Java SE 10 in 2018

Java has undeniably evolved over the years as a great and successful language you can use on and off the internet. Let's touch on the benefits of using Java programming language:

The Benefits

Each programming language has been introduced with a purpose and has some benefits. Even though each language creates the opportunity to begin a flourishing career, Java is usually given preference. The benefits of Java in particular are indeed countless but I will mention a few briefly.

✓ *You get rich information*

While there is no obvious competition between existing programming languages, Java is considered the best-sometimes owing to its wealth of information. Java has been existing for many years so you can expect a quick answer to nearly all queries that come to mind with regards to programming. Thus, you can solve each one of your problems easily as you hone your skills in the process.

✓ *Ease of learning*

Sometimes beginners tend to think that the better a language is, the harder it's probably going to be to learn it.

However, that is not true- at least not with Java. There are definitely some unavoidable initial hurdles but the fact that the language uses ordinary and simple English in place of generics or multiple brackets makes the language easy to learn. When you learn how to install JDK and the installation of PATH the right way, the rest will be fun to learn and implement.

✓   *You get a great toolset*

You will often hear that in programming, the toolset of a language has a major role to play in determining its overall success. Java undeniably has an upper hand in this respect because it comes with a complete support for *open source systems*. This means that as a user, you can get tools for nearly everything you require. We have a number of open source libraries that provide information on all topics to do with Java programming. Also, there are a number of communities-especially online to guide new programmers.

✓   *You get to learn from your mistakes*

We have a few languages that are designed to teach or allow you to learn from your own mistakes and let you build up your base. Java contains some great *IDEs (IDE refers to Integrated Development Environment* – see glossary) that are tasked with updating you of your errors as soon as you make them. Besides that, the language also suggests for you to reformat the codes and gives you the reason for doing that. That way, you get a clear understanding of coding right from the basic stage and barely get yourself making any mistakes as you begin your journey as a professional.

✓   *The language is free*

To get Java, you don't have to incur any cost from the very beginning. Therefore, whether you are in the learning stage or professional stage, you can create or develop an application using Java without paying anybody any cash at all. All you need to learn is how to get the program, set it up and begin.

✓   *Better scope for the professionals*

As you intend to learn a programming language to start a professional career, Java remains your best bet. It is applied in most existing apps and its scope is still being increased further. Therefore, by learning this language, you can expect a better career in the industry compared to another programmer specialized in another language.

With all that in mind, let's move on to actually getting started with Java.

The Fundamentals/Prerequisites

This section describes the things you need to get before you begin coding anything. To get started, you should download Java (Java runtime environment -JRE/ Java Development Kit- JDK), and the Integrated Development Environment -IDE.

How To Download And Install Java

Downloading and installing Java is simple for any kind of operating system. I will show you how you can download and install this program using Linux and Windows operating systems as examples.

1: Linux

By the end of this section, you will have Java well installed and configured for your Linux machine- whether it's Debian, Mint or Ubuntu. I will, however, be using Ubuntu 14.04 for the duration of the guide and also mention the terminal and non-terminal ways of going about the process to help you follow in case you are a complete newbie.

You are going to be installing either Oracle JRE or Oracle JDK so you need to really understand the difference between the two.

Oracle JRE (Java Runtime Environment)

JRE is the minimum requirement to be able to execute a Java program. It entails the JVM (Java Virtual Machine), supporting files and core classes. In other words, when all you care about is running Java programs on your computer or browser, you'll install JRE.

Oracle JDK (Java Development Kit)

This is a software development kit that comprises the JVM, JRM (Java Runtime Environment), as well as the entire list of class libraries present in the production environment to build and compile programs. Thus, if you want to do some Java development, you'll require JDK.

Having said that, let's start.

Create the Java Folder

As an example, we'll begin by creating an empty folder called 'Java' for your JRE/JDK files in the directory /usr/local which makes the path of the folder: /usr/local/java. Get to the terminal and type the command below then press okay:

sudo mkdir -p /usr/local/java

```
😵😑🙂  kross@com-ubun: ~
kross@com-ubun:~$ sudo mkdir -p /usr/local/java
[sudo] password for kross:
kross@com-ubun:~$ █
```

Check the Linux version

Before you download the java files, you have to understand the Linux version you are running (32 bit or 64 bit).

The terminal method

Open the terminal and type the command below, then press okay:

file /sbin/init

```
😵😑🙂  kross@com-ubun: ~
kross@com-ubun:~$ file /sbin/init
/sbin/init: ELF 64-bit LSB  shared object, x86-64, version 1 (SYSV), dynamically
 linked (uses shared libs), for GNU/Linux 2.6.24, BuildID[sha1]=7d9cc5d4d6cb68ae
de9400492a7c5942c55c7598, stripped
kross@com-ubun:~$ █
```

For instance, you can see in the above image that the result received before the command execution informs me that the Linux version I am running is 64 bit.

Try doing the same without the terminal:

Non-terminal method

As a user of Ubuntu, you can check your version by checking the *details* under *systems* panel in the *system settings*.

As you can see, the dialog box called 'details' will pop up. You'll see the Linux version beside the OS type in the 'overview' tab.

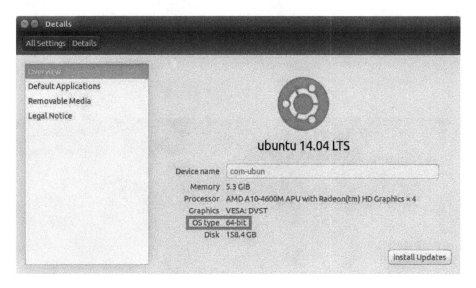

Download Oracle JRE/JDK

Head on to the Java <u>Download Page</u> and choose either JRE. Since you are only running Java programs on your computer (as I mentioned earlier) and don't require the full-featured Software Development Kit for Java in JDK (even though it also includes JRE) which is only useful for application development like android development, JRE (and not JDK) is good enough.

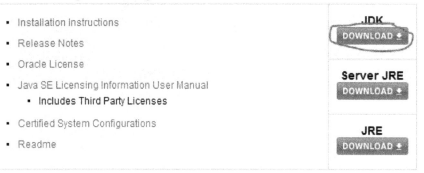

| Overview | Downloads | Documentation | Community | Technologies | Training |

Java SE Development Kit 10 Downloads

Thank you for downloading this release of the Java™ Platform, Standard Edition Development Kit (JDK™). The JDK is a development environment for building applications, and components using the Java programming language.

The JDK includes tools useful for developing and testing programs written in the Java programming language and running on the Java platform.

See also:

- Java Developer Newsletter: From your Oracle account, select **Subscriptions**, expand **Technology**, and subscribe to **Java**.
- Java Developer Day hands-on workshops (free) and other events
- Java Magazine

JDK 10.0.2 checksum

Java SE Development Kit 10.0.2

You must accept the Oracle Binary Code License Agreement for Java SE to download this software.

○ Accept License Agreement   ⦿ Decline License Agreement

Product / File Description	File Size	Download
Linux	306 MB	jdk-10.0.2_linux-x64_bin.rpm
Linux	338.43 MB	jdk-10.0.2_linux-x64_bin.tar.gz
macOS	395.46 MB	jdk-10.0.2_osx-x64_bin.dmg
Solaris SPARC	207.07 MB	jdk-10.0.2_solaris-sparcv9_bin.tar.gz
Windows	390.25 MB	jdk-10.0.2_windows-x64_bin.exe

If you choose Java JRE, a screen like the one below will pop up. Just below Java SE Runtime Environment, you'll see 'Accept License Agreement'; check the box.

| Overview | Downloads | Documentation | Community | Technologies | Training |

Java SE Runtime Environment 10 Downloads

Do you want to run Java™ programs, or do you want to develop Java programs? If you want to run Java programs, but not develop them, download the Java Runtime Environment, or JRE™.

If you want to develop applications for Java, download the Java Development Kit, or JDK™. The JDK includes the JRE, so you do not have to download both separately.

JRE 10.0.2 Checksum

Java SE Runtime Environment 10.0.2

You must accept the Oracle Binary Code License Agreement for Java SE **to download this software.**

○ Accept License Agreement   ◉ Decline License Agreement

Product / File Description	File Size	Download
Linux	60.36 MB	jre-10.0.2_linux-x64_bin.rpm
Linux	83.91 MB	jre-10.0.2_linux-x64_bin.tar.gz
macOS	78.49 MB	jre-10.0.2_osx-x64_bin.dmg
macOS	73.87 MB	jre-10.0.2_osx-x64_bin.tar.gz
Solaris SPARC	53.35 MB	jre-10.0.2_solaris-sparcv9_bin.tar.gz
Windows	100.57 MB	jre-10.0.2_windows-x64_bin.exe
Windows	75.38 MB	jre-10.0.2_windows-x64_bin.tar.gz

If you are running a 32-bit Linux, choose the Linux x86 link. If you are running a 64-bit Linux, choose the Linux x64 link.

The file will be downloaded to the directory: home/*unsername*/downloads. For instance, if your username is panda, it will be home/panda/downloads.

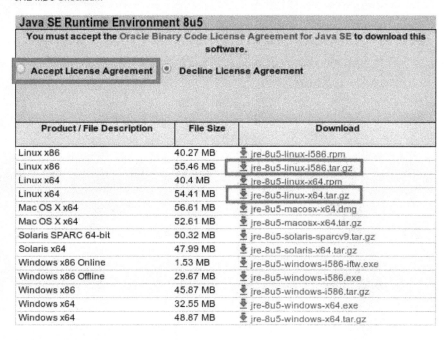

Copy the tar,gz JRE/ JDK files to the directory /usr/local/java

Type the code below and tap enter:

cd ~/Downloads

If you downloaded the 32 bit Oracle JDK, you will type the code below and tap Enter:

sudo cp -r jdk-8u5-linux-i586.tar.gz /usr/local/java

```
kross@com-ubun: ~/Downloads
kross@com-ubun:~$ cd ~/Downloads
kross@com-ubun:~/Downloads$ sudo cp -r jdk-8u5-linux-i586.tar.gz /usr/local/java

[sudo] password for kross:
kross@com-ubun:~/Downloads$
```

Enter the code below and tap Enter.

cd ~/Downloads

If you downloaded the JRE (32 bit), just type the code below and tap Enter:

sudo cp -r jre-8u5-linux-i586.tar.gz /usr/local/java

```
kross@com-ubun: ~/Downloads
kross@com-ubun:~$ cd ~/Downloads
kross@com-ubun:~/Downloads$ sudo cp -r jre-8u5-linux-i586.tar.gz /usr/local/java
[sudo] password for kross:
kross@com-ubun:~/Downloads$
```

How To Copy The Oracle JDK (64-Bit) In A 64-Bit Linux

Like usual, type the code below and tap Enter:

cd ~/Downloads

In case you downloaded the Oracle JDK (64-bit), simply type the code below and press Enter.

sudo cp -r jdk-8u5-linux-x64.tar.gz /usr/local/java

```
kross@com-ubun: ~/Downloads
kross@com-ubun:~$ cd ~/Downloads
kross@com-ubun:~/Downloads$ sudo cp -r jdk-8u5-linux-x64.tar.gz /usr/local/java
[sudo] password for kross:
kross@com-ubun:~/Downloads$
```

How To Copy Oracle Java JRE In A 64-Bit Linux

Type the code below and tap Enter:

cd ~/Downloads

If you downloaded the oracle JRE (64-bit), you can type the code below and press Enter:

sudo cp -r jre-8u5-linux-x64.tar.gz /usr/local/java

```
kross@com-ubun: ~/Downloads
kross@com-ubun:~$ cd ~/Downloads
kross@com-ubun:~/Downloads$ sudo cp -r jre-8u5-linux-x64.tar.gz /usr/local/java
[sudo] password for kross:
kross@com-ubun:~/Downloads$
```

Extract the tar.gz JDK/JRE files to the directory: usr/local/java

Copying oracle Java in a 32-bit Linux

Type the code below and tap Enter:

cd /usr/local/java

In case you downloaded the oracle JDK (32-bit), simply type the code below and press Enter.

sudo tar xvzf jdk-8u5-linux-i586.tar.gz

```
kross@com-ubun: /usr/local/java
kross@com-ubun:~$ cd /usr/local/java
kross@com-ubun:/usr/local/java$ sudo tar xvzf jdk-8u5-linux-i586.tar.gz
[sudo] password for kross: 
```

Extract the Java JRE (32-bit) in a 32-bit Linux by typing the code below, and then press Enter:

cd /usr/local/java

If you downloaded oracle JRE (32-bit), type the code below and tap Enter:

sudo tar xvzf jre-8u5-linux-i586.tar.gz

```
kross@com-ubun: /usr/local/java
kross@com-ubun:~$ cd /usr/local/java
kross@com-ubun:/usr/local/java$ sudo tar xvzf jre-8u5-linux-i586.tar.gz
[sudo] password for kross: 
```

How about the Java JDK (64-bit) in a 64-bit Linux? Just type the code below and tap Enter:

cd /usr/local/java

For the Oracle JDK (64-bit), type the code below and tap Enter.

sudo tar xvzf jdk-8u5-linux-x64.tar.gz

```
kross@com-ubun: /usr/local/java
kross@com-ubun:~$ cd /usr/local/java
kross@com-ubun:/usr/local/java$ sudo tar xvzf jdk-8u5-linux-x64.tar.gz
[sudo] password for kross: 
```

Extract the oracle Java JRE (64-bit) in a 64-bit Linux by typing the code below:

cd /usr/local/java

If you have the oracle JRE (64-bit), just type the code below and tap Enter:

sudo tar xvzf jre-8u5-linux-x64.tar.gz

Edit the system path
Start by opening the terminal and typing the following:
sudo gedit /etc/profile

By doing so, you'll have opened a text editor that has all the Linux system wide and startup programs.

Scroll down all the way to the end of the file and append the lines below to the end of the /etc/profile file:

If you're dealing with JDK, just add the code below:

JAVA_HOME=/usr/local/java/jdk1.8.0_05

PATH=$PATH:$HOME/bin:$JAVA_HOME/bin

JRE_HOME=/usr/local/java/jdk1.7.0_05/jre

PATH=$PATH:$HOME/bin:$JRE_HOME/bin

export JAVA_HOME

export JRE_HOME

export PATH

```
# The default umask is now handled by pam_umask.
# See pam_umask(8) and /etc/login.defs.

if [ -d /etc/profile.d ]; then
  for i in /etc/profile.d/*.sh; do
    if [ -r $i ]; then
      . $i
    fi
  done
  unset i
fi
JAVA_HOME=/usr/local/java/jdk1.8.0_05
PATH=$PATH:$HOME/bin:$JAVA_HOME/bin
JRE_HOME=/usr/local/java/jdk1.8.0_05/jre
PATH=$PATH:$HOME/bin:$JRE_HOME/bin
export JAVA_HOME
export JRE_HOME
export PATH
```

In the instance you are installing JRE, you should write the code below:

JRE_HOME=/usr/local/java/jre1.8.0_05

PATH=$PATH:$HOME/bin:$JRE_HOME/bin

export JRE_HOME

export PATH

```
⊗ ⊖ ⊙   *profile (/etc) - gedit
File  Edit  View  Search  Tools  Documents  Help

  📄  📁  Open  ▾   💾  Save   🖨   ↩ Undo  ↪    ✂  📋  📋    🔍  🔧

 📄 *profile  ✕
       ' J⊥  J
      fi
    fi
 fi

 # The default umask is now handled by pam_umask.
 # See pam_umask(8) and /etc/login.defs.

 if [ -d /etc/profile.d ]; then
   for i in /etc/profile.d/*.sh; do
     if [ -r $i ]; then
       . $i
     fi
   done
   unset i
 fi

 JRE_HOME=/usr/local/java/jre1.8.0_05
 PATH=$PATH:$HOME/bin:$JRE_HOME/bin
 export JRE_HOME
 export PATH
```

```
        Plain Text ▾    Tab Width: 8 ▾        Ln 32, Col 1        INS
```

Save the file and exit.

Inform Linux about your Java's location

The commands below will let your system know that your java JRE/JDK is accessible or available for use.

For 32 or 64 bit JDK

In this case, just type the code below and tap enter.

sudo update-alternatives --install "/usr/bin/java" "java" "/usr/local/java/jdk1.8.0_05/jre/bin/java" 1

Type the code below and tap enter:

sudo update-alternatives --install "/usr/bin/javac" "javac" "/usr/local/java/jdk1.8.0_05/bin/javac" 1

Type the code below and tap enter:

sudo update-alternatives --install "/usr/bin/javaws" "javaws" "/usr/local/java/jdk1.8.0_05/bin/javaws" 1

```
kross@com-ubun: ~
kross@com-ubun:~$ sudo update-alternatives --install "/usr/bin/java" "java" "/us
r/local/java/jdk1.8.0_05/jre/bin/java" 1
[sudo] password for kross:
kross@com-ubun:~$ sudo update-alternatives --install "/usr/bin/javac" "javac" "/
usr/local/java/jdk1.8.0_05/bin/javac" 1
update-alternatives: warning: alternative /usr/local/java/jdk1.8.0/bin/javac (pa
rt of link group javac) doesn't exist; removing from list of alternatives
update-alternatives: warning: /etc/alternatives/javac is dangling; it will be up
dated with best choice
update-alternatives: using /usr/local/java/jdk1.8.0_05/bin/javac to provide /usr
/bin/javac (javac) in auto mode
kross@com-ubun:~$ sudo update-alternatives --install "/usr/bin/javaws" "javaws"
"/usr/local/java/jdk1.8.0_05/bin/javaws" 1
update-alternatives: using /usr/local/java/jdk1.8.0_05/bin/javaws to provide /us
r/bin/javaws (javaws) in auto mode
kross@com-ubun:~$
```

For 32 or 64 bit JRE

If you are dealing with JDK, just type the code below and press enter:

sudo update-alternatives --install "/usr/bin/java" "java" "/usr/local/java/jre1.8.0_05/bin/java" 1

Type the code below and tap enter.

sudo update-alternatives --install "/usr/bin/javaws" "javaws" "/usr/local/java/jre1.8.0_05/bin/javaws" 1

```
kross@com-ubun: ~
kross@com-ubun:~$ sudo update-alternatives --install "/usr/bin/java" "java" "/us
r/local/java/jre1.8.0_05/bin/java" 1
[sudo] password for kross:
kross@com-ubun:~$ sudo update-alternatives --install "/usr/bin/javaws" "javaws"
"/usr/local/java/jre1.8.0_05/bin/javaws" 1
kross@com-ubun:~$
```

Make oracle Java JRE/JDK the default Java

If you are dealing with JDK, just type the code below and press enter:

sudo update-alternatives --set java
/usr/local/java/jdk1.8.0_05/jre/bin/java

Do the same (type the code below) for JDK and tap Enter:

\sudo update-alternatives --set javac
/usr/local/java/jdk1.8.0_05/bin/javac

Type the code below as well and tap Enter:

sudo update-alternatives --set javaws
/usr/local/java/jdk1.8.0_05/bin/javaws

```
kross@com-ubun: ~
kross@com-ubun:~$ sudo update-alternatives --set java /usr/local/java/jdk1.8.0_0
5/jre/bin/java
[sudo] password for kross:
update-alternatives: using /usr/local/java/jdk1.8.0_05/jre/bin/java to provide /
usr/bin/java (java) in manual mode
kross@com-ubun:~$ sudo update-alternatives --set javac /usr/local/java/jdk1.8.0_
05/bin/javac
kross@com-ubun:~$ sudo update-alternatives --set javaws /usr/local/java/jdk1.8.0
_05/bin/javaws
kross@com-ubun:~$
```

For oracle JRE (32 or 64 bit)

For the installation of JRE, type the code below and tap Enter:

sudo update-alternatives --set java
/usr/local/java/jre1.8.0_05/bin/java

For the installation of JDK, type the code below and tap Enter:

sudo update-alternatives --set javaws
/usr/local/java/jre1.8.0_05/bin/javaws

Reload the system path file/etc/profile

Type the following and tap enter:

. /etc/profile

You need to note that the system-wide path file will reload once you reboot your Linux system.

Test a successful installation

Open your terminal, type and tap enter: java –version

You get the something like this if your installation of 32 bit Java is successful.

```
● ● ●   kross@com-ubun: ~
kross@com-ubun:~$ java -version
java version "1.8.0"
Java(TM) SE Runtime Environment (build 1.8.0-b132)
Java HotSpot(TM) 32-Bit Server VM (build 25.0-b70, mixed mode)
kross@com-ubun:~$
```

If you are using a 64-bit java, you'll get something like this:

```
kross@com-ubun: ~
kross@com-ubun:~$ java -version
java version "1.8.0"
Java(TM) SE Runtime Environment (build 1.8.0-b132)
Java HotSpot(TM) 64-Bit Server VM (build 25.0-b70, mixed mode)
kross@com-ubun:~$ 
```

If the tests mentioned above work as depicted above, you can be sure that your Java is successfully installed on your system.

2: *Windows*

The process of downloading and installing Java in Windows is even easier than in Linux. Let's go through the steps:

Click <u>this link</u> to download the latest version of Java JDK.

Java SE Downloads

Java Platform (JDK) 9

NetBeans with JDK 8

Java Platform, Standard Edition

Java SE 9.0.1
Java SE 9.0.1 includes important bug fixes. Oracle strongly recommends that all Java SE 9 users upgrade to this release.
Learn more ▸

- Installation Instructions
- Release Notes
- Oracle License
- Java SE Licensing Information User Manual
- Third Party Licenses
- Certified System Configurations
- Readme

JDK
DOWNLOAD ⬇

Server JRE
DOWNLOAD ⬇

JRE
DOWNLOAD ⬇

Now accept the license agreement and download the latest JDK according to your version (that is 64 or 32 bit) of Java for windows.

When your download is complete, run the exe file to install JDK, and click next.

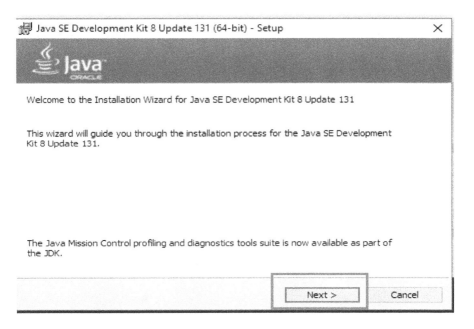

Click close when the installation completes.

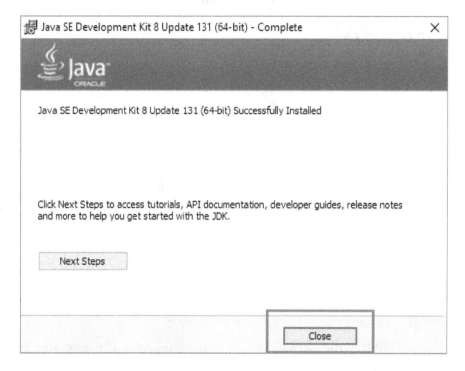

Set Java environment variables: classpath and path

The path variable offers the location of executables such as java, javac and so forth. You can be able to run a program without specifying the PATH but you'll require a full path of executable such as

C:\Program Files\Java\jdk1.8.0_131\bin\javac as opposed to the simple *javac A.Java*

The variable 'CLASSPATH' provides the library files' location. We'll now look at the steps to set the CLASSPATH and PATH.

Right click on 'My Computer' and then select 'properties'

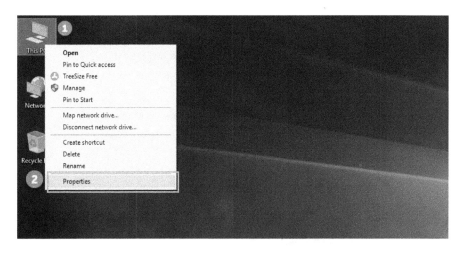

Select 'advanced system settings' and then 'environment variables'.

Control Panel Home

Device Manager

Remote settings

System protection

Advanced system settings

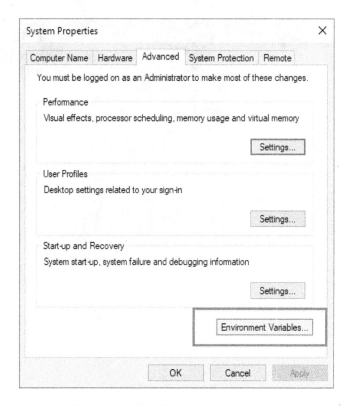

In the 'user variables', select the 'new' button.

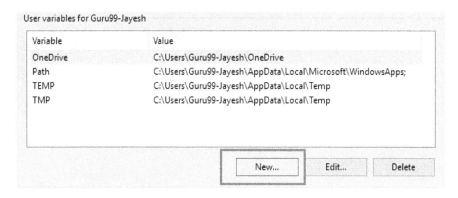

In the 'variable name', type PATH.

Copy the bin folder's path that is installed in the JKD folder:

Paste the bin folder's path in variable value and then click on the 'ok' button.

If you have a PATH variable set in your PC already, just edit the PATH variable to the following:

PATH = <JDK installation directory>\bin;%PATH%;

In this case, the %PATH% joins the existing path variable to your new value

To set CLASSPATH, just follow the same process.

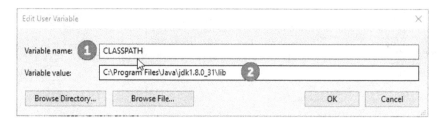

If you realize your installation is not working after you complete, just change the classpath to the following:

CLASSPATH = <JDK installation directory>\lib\tools.jar;

Now tap the 'ok' button.

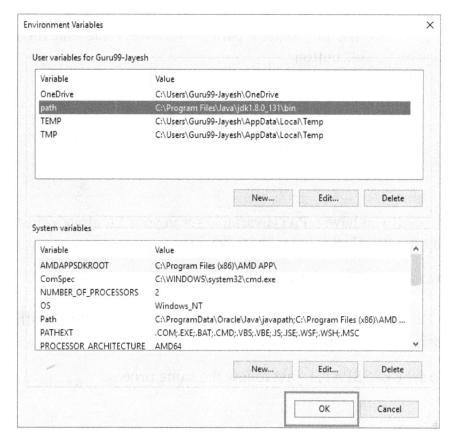

Now go to your command prompt and enter javac commands. If the screen is similar to the one below, Java has been installed successfully.

```
C:\Users\Guru99-Jayesh>javac
Usage: javac <options> <source files>
where possible options include:
  -g                         Generate all debugging info
  -g:none                    Generate no debugging info
  -g:{lines,vars,source}     Generate only some debugging info
  -nowarn                    Generate no warnings
  -verbose                   Output messages about what the compiler is doing
  -deprecation               Output source locations where deprecated APIs are used
  -classpath <path>          Specify where to find user class files and annotation processors
  -cp <path>                 Specify where to find user class files and annotation processors
  -sourcepath <path>         Specify where to find input source files
  -bootclasspath <path>      Override location of bootstrap class files
  -extdirs <dirs>            Override location of installed extensions
  -endorseddirs <dirs>       Override location of endorsed standards path
  -proc:{none,only}          Control whether annotation processing and/or compilation is done.
  -processor <class1>[,<class2>,<class3>...] Names of the annotation processors to run; bypasses default discovery process
  -processorpath <path>      Specify where to find annotation processors
  -parameters                Generate metadata for reflection on method parameters
  -d <directory>             Specify where to place generated class files
  -s <directory>             Specify where to place generated source files
  -h <directory>             Specify where to place generated native header files
  -implicit:{none,class}     Specify whether or not to generate class files for implicitly referenced files
  -encoding <encoding>       Specify character encoding used by source files
  -source <release>          Provide source compatibility with specified release
  -target <release>          Generate class files for specific VM version
  -profile <profile>         Check that API used is available in the specified profile
  -version                   Version information
  -help                      Print a synopsis of standard options
  -Akey[=value]              Options to pass to annotation processors
  -X                         Print a synopsis of nonstandard options
  -J<flag>                   Pass <flag> directly to the runtime system
  -Werror                    Terminate compilation if warnings occur
  @<filename>                Read options and filenames from file

C:\Users\Guru99-Jayesh>
```

Getting Eclipse IDE

An IDE (for Integrated Development Environment) makes you productive in development, as it helps you in handling important tasks such as coding, refactoring, debugging, running web apps and testing.

Nonetheless, the most important factor it offers- according to me, is speed (days of sitting around and waiting for stuff to compile or load are long gone). An good IDE such as Eclipse is extremely fast, doesn't suck up memory and takes short time to load, and doesn't take lots of time to synchronize changes. A good programming expert would also mention other features you get to enjoy such as 'integration with *code repositories' (see glossary)* and checking of errors- such as static code analysis and highlighting unused references.

Steps Of Installing Eclipse For Java On Windows
Download Eclipse
Go to <u>this link</u> and download the latest version:

Get Eclipse **PHOTON**

Install your favorite Eclipse packages.

Download 64 bit

Download Packages | Need Help?

Click 'download packages' under 'get eclipse photon'. As a beginner, you should select the fourth entry *'eclipse IDE for Java Developers'* (32-bit or 64-bit).

Click download.

The next step entails unzipping the downloaded file to install it. Unzip the file into a designated directory (for instance, c:\javaproject).

You don't need to run any installer. What's more, you can just delete the whole eclipse directory when you don't need it anymore (without having to run the 'un-installer'). Feel free to rename or move the directory. Also, note that you can unzip (install) more than one copy in the same machine.

Installing Eclipse on Mac OS X

Repeat the same process of downloading and installing Eclipse for windows explained above using this link. Just ensure to select Mac OS X (cocoa). When you select 'eclipse IDE for Java Developers', you'll get a DMG file. Double click this downloaded file (DMG) and follow the instructions given thereafter to install the program. The program will be installed in the location: /applications/eclipse.

Note that you may alternatively download a TAR ball (.tar.gz); double click to be able to expand into a folder known as 'eclipse' and then drag this expanded folder into the 'applications' folder.

Installing Eclipse on Ubuntu Linux

Install Eclipse for java by downloading from this page. As usual, download the 'packages' and for platform, select 'Linux', then 'eclipse IDE for Java developers' for Java SE program development. You will get a .tar ball in the downloads folder and the installation will be under /usr/local

```
1.  // Unzip the tarball into /usr/local
2.  $ cd /usr/local
3.  $ sudo tar xzvf ~/Downloads/eclipse-java-oxygen-2-
    linux-gtk-x86_64.tar.gz
4.  // Extract the downloaded package
5.  // x: extract, z: for unzipping gz, v: verbose, f: filename
6.  // Extract into /usr/local/eclipse
7.  // You can also unzip in "File Explorer" by double-clicking
    the tarball.
8.
9.  // (Optional) Change ownership
10. $ cd /usr/local
11. $ sudo chown -R your-username:your-groupname
    eclipse
12. // Change ownership to your chosen username and
    groupname
13. // -R recursive
14.
15. // Set up a symlink to /usr/bin (which is in the PATH)
16. $ cd /usr/bin
17. $ sudo ln -s /usr/local/eclipse/eclipse
18. // Make a symlink in /usr/bin, which is in the PATH.
19. $ ls -ld /usr/bin/eclipse
20. lrwxrwxrwx 1 root root 26 Aug 30 11:53 /usr/bin/eclipse ->
    /usr/local/eclipse/eclipse
21. $ which eclipse

    /usr/bin/eclipse
```

To run Eclipse, just open the folder '/usr/local/eclipse' and then click on the icon 'Eclipse'; or just start a terminal and enter 'Eclipse'.

Lock Eclipse on the launcher

Just start the program and right click the Eclipse icon and then click lock to launcher. If you are using an older version (and thus the above is not working), just create a file '/usr/share/applications/eclipse.desktop' with the contents below:

```
[Desktop Entry]
Name=Eclipse
Type=Application
Exec=eclipse
Terminal=false
Icon=/usr/local/eclipse/icon.xpm
Comment=Integrated Development Environment
NoDisplay=false
Categories=Development;IDE;
Name[en]=Eclipse
```

You can now write your first Java program or project in Eclipse

Launch Eclipse (run 'eclipse.exe') from the Eclipse installed directory and then select an appropriate directory for your workspace- i.e. where you would want to save your files (such as c:\javaproject\eclipse for windows).

If the screen named 'welcome' pops up, click the button labelled 'cross' next to the 'welcome' title.

For all Java applications, you have to create a project to have all the classes (discussed in a bit), source files and important resources.

Do the following to create the project:

• Select 'file' menu then 'new', then 'java project' (or 'file' then 'new' then 'project' then 'java project.')

• The dialog named 'new java project' will pop up.

• Enter 'firstproject' in the 'project name'

• Check the 'user default location'

- Select 'use default JRE' in JRE.
- Check the 'use project folder as the root for sources and class files' in the 'project layout' and then push the button labeled 'finish'.

Before we continue (write our first project), let's go over some of the basic concepts of Java.

Basic Concepts In Java.Java Tokens

Tokens are basically the tiniest logical components of Java and any other program. The first step of the compiler is to separate the whole program into smaller bits known as tokens. You can think of them as the building blocks of a program.

Tokens are basically anything in a program that a compiler can identify during the compilation process or tokenization. Let's take a look at the types of tokens:

- Keywords
- Operators
- Literals
- Separators
- Comments
- Literals

Let's have a brief description of each one of them so that you get a better understanding.

Keywords

Keywords are special words or what are known as 'reserved' words in Java as they have a special meaning. We have a list of 50 keywords, which are highlighted below:

byte	short	int	long	double	float	char	boolean	void	public
private	static	import	package	class	interface	extends	implements	if	else
for	do	while	switch	case	instanceof	return	native	new	synchronized
strictfp	super	this	volatile	try	catch	finally	final	protected	transient
default	assert	break	continue	throw	throws	goto	abstract	const	enum

Identifiers

Identifiers are those names programmers use in program to any method, class, variable, packages, objects, labels or interfaces in Java programs (you'll learn more on the meaning of these terms in due course).

We have *rules of naming identifiers,* which include the following

• You cannot have any special symbols in Java identifiers apart from the dollar sign $ and the underscore (_)

• Identifiers need to begin from digits

• The keywords are reserved already and contain special meaning – so they can't be used as identifiers.

• The reserved literals are also allowed as identifiers; for instance- null, false and true

• You cannot use one name for multiple identifiers. Identifiers also have to be case-sensitive thus the Mf and mf variables are very different.

Some good examples of valid identifiers in this case include the following:

pasa 1, Name, roll_no, $raju, string

Invalid identifiers would include something like:

True (reserved literal), Roll-no (a special character has been used), 16sita (begins with a number) and try (this is a java keyword).

NOTE: reserved literals and keywords in Java are those words you cannot use as variables or function names.

Operators

Operators are the symbols you'll use to produce some result as you apply with some operands. We have different types of operators in Java. As you will note, some strings can also be used as operators. Essentially operators are important in Java when it comes to building expressions and statements – some of them include: -, +, *, =, >= and so forth.

Separators

Separators are also referred to as punctuators. These special characters and symbols separate different parts of code from others. Sometimes, they connect and separate either one or multiple tokens or organize a code block – that's why we call them separators.

In Java, punctuators that are used include semi-colon (;), period (.), comma (,), pair of square brackets (**[,]**), group of parenthesis (**(,)**), pair of braces (**{,}**).

Literals

Literals refer to any values in Java programming that don't change in the process of program execution. You can think of them as constants for literals. These are constant values of some string type or primitive type. Any literal that is used in Java needs to be one of the types mentioned below:

- *Character*

This is what stores the Character constants in the memory. It basically takes up a size of 2 bytes but can hold only one character since char stores Unicode sets of characters. It contains a maximum value of 65,535 and a minimum of 0.

- *Integer*

Integer types can basically hold whole numbers like -96 and 123. The values sizes that can be stored mainly depends on the type of integer we select.

Type	Size	Range of values that can be stored
byte	1 byte	- 128 to 127
short	2 bytes	- 32768 to 32767
int	4 bytes	- 2,147,483,648 to 2,147,483,647
long	8 bytes	9,223,372,036,854,775,808 to 9,223,372,036,854,755,807

This calculation – (2^{n-1}) to (2^{n-1}) −1 is used for the range of values. Here, n represents the number of bits required- for instance, the byte data type requires 1 byte= 8 bits. Thus, the range of values, which can be kept in the byte data type is as follows:

$$-(2^{8-1}) \text{ to } (2^{8-1})-1 = -2^7 \text{ to } (2^7) -1$$

Floating point numbers/data types

These are data types we use to denote the numbers with a fractional part. The single precision floating point numbers usually use up 4 bytes while the double precision floating point numbers use up 8 bytes. We have two sub-types here:

Type	Size	Range of values that can be stored
float	4 bytes	3.4e- 038 to 3.4e+038
double	8 bytes	1.7e- 308 to 1.7e+038

- *Boolean*

The Boolean data types basically store values with two states: false or true

Take the examples below to understand better:

- 34.43
- 5322
- 'd'
- Null
- True

Comments

In Java, comments are used in the process of documentation. Some people don't place comments in the category of tokens because the compilers usually ignore them during tokenization. In Java, multi-line comments begin with the following:

/* ...

The single line comments begin with:

//....

What we've discussed is just a basic overview of Java tokens. I hope you understood what tokens mean. Let's now write a little java program and separate it into distinct tokens that specify their token type:

```
class Test{
    public static void main(String args[]){
        int w,x=10,y=20;
        w=x+y; // This line add x and y, then assign to w
    }
}
```

In the program written above,

•   The keywords include public, class, void, static and int.

•   The identifiers include: Test, main, args, x, w

•   The operators include: + and =

•   The literals include: 20 and 10

The separators include:

{, (...

The comment is described by: //this line add x and y...

As you can see here, the compiler breaks down the program into tinier logical individual parts known as tokens.

Variables

Variables are *containers* that store data in programming. When a variable is declared, it is initialized with some value and then changed to another value later on. A variable can be further used to do any calculations, printing and so forth. Each variable needs to have a datatype such as Boolean, int and so on, and that type needs to be specified at the time the variable was declared. Each variable needs to have a non-duplicate or unique name to identify it.

Let's take an example of a student program. In such, we can have a single variable to store 'the student section', another one for 'student roll number' and so forth.

```
char section;
int roll_number;
```

In this case, 'char' is used to specify the variable's data type while the 'section' is used to specify the variable name. That's not all; 'int' is the datatype and 'roll_number' is the variable name. You can assign some value to a variable at the same moment it is declared, in a process known as initialization.

```
char section = 'C';
int roll_number = 76; //assign 76 to roll number
```

In this case, 'int' is used to define the variable data type while the 'roll_number' is defined by the variable name, where 76 is the variable's current number. As seen above, one variable- or roll_number in your program can store numerical data whereas another variable- or section can store the char data. The special keywords in Java signify the type of data that every variable stores. This means that we can actually declare variables with the types/keywords and initialize the variable's value.

The Types of Variables In Java

In Java, variables can be divided into four categories namely:

- Static variable
- Instance variable
- Method parameter
- Local variable

Instance Variable

Also known as non-static fields, instance variables are used to store states of objects. The variables that are defined without the static keyword, and are outside any declaration method automatically are object-specific, and are referred to as instance variables due to the fact that their values are instance specific and their values don't get shared among instances. Some people look at non-static fields as instance variables because their values tend to be unique to each class instance. For instance, the currentSpeed of a certain bicycle is independent from another's currentSpeed.

Further, you need to note the following:

- When a space is assigned for an object in the heap (see glossary), a slot for every instance variable value is made.

- These variables are made when objects are created using the keyword 'new' and destroyed when the object gets destroyed.

- Instance variables hold values that have to be referenced by multiple methods, block or constructor, or the essential parts of the state of an object that need to be present throughout the class.

- Instance variables could as well be declared within the class level right before use or after use.

- Keywords used to specify accessibility of a class or type and its members, which are also known as access modifiers could be given for different instance variables.

- Instance variables contain default values. For the numbers, zero is the default value; it's false for the Booleans and null for the object references. During declaration (or within the constructor), the values can be assigned.

- The instance variables are also visible for all constructors, block and methods in the class. Typically, it's recommended to make these variables private or access level. Nonetheless, subclasses' visibility can be provided for these variables using access modifiers.

- The instance variables can be directly accessed by calling the name of the variable within the class. Nonetheless, within the static variables – that is when the instance variables are offered accessibility- they need to be called with the fully qualified name. Let's take an example:

```java
import java.io.*;
public class Employee {

    // this instance variable is visible for any child class.
    public String name;

    // salary  variable is visible in Employee class only.
    private double salary;

    // The name variable is assigned in the constructor.
    public Employee (String empName) {
        name = empName;
    }

    // The salary variable is assigned a value.
    public void setSalary(double empSal) {
        salary = empSal;
    }

    // This method prints the employee details.
    public void printEmp() {
        System.out.println("name : " + name );
        System.out.println("salary :" + salary);
    }
```

From this, you'll get the following result:

name : Ransika

salary :1000.0

Class Or Static Variables

Also known as static variables, class variables are declared using the static keyword in a class, but outside a method, block or constructor. Regardless of the number of objects created from it, there would only be a single copy of each class variable per class.

Static variables are seldom used – that is besides being declared as constants. Constants are variables essentially declared as private/public, static and final. Constant variables will never change from their first value.

The static variables are kept within the static memory, and it is not common to use static variables as private or public constants. Static variables are actually created when the program starts up and killed when the program stops.

Visibility is similar to instance variables. Nonetheless, most static variables get declared public because they need to be available for the class users. The default values are similar to instance variables and for the numbers, zero represents the default value. It is false for the Booleans and null for the object references. The values can get assigned either within the constructor or during the declaration. What's more, the values can get assigned in distinctive static initializer blocks.

Calling with the class name is what is required to access the static variables –className.VariableName.

Lastly, if we declare the class variables as public static final, this essentially means that the constants or variable names are all in the upper case. Moreover, if the static variables aren't public as well as final, this means that the naming syntax is similar to the instance and the local variables.

Let's take an example:

```
import java.io.*;

public class Employee {

    // salary variable is a private static variable
    private static double salary;

    // DEPARTMENT is a constant
    public static final String DEPARTMENT = "Development";

    public static void main(String args[]) {
        salary = 1000;
        System.out.println(DEPARTMENT + "average salary:" + salary);
    }
}
```

The following result will be given:

-Development average salary: 1000

You need to note that if the variables are accessed from an outside class, the constant needs to be accessed as the Employee Department.

Local Variables

Local variables are used to store a method in its temporary state. The syntax used to declare a local variable is the same as declaring a field- for instance, int count=0;. You won't find a particular keyword that designates a variable as local as such a determination comes entirely from the location in which the variable is declared- that is between the method's closing and opening braces. Thus, local variables can only be seen by the methods, which they are declared in- so they cannot be accessed from the rest of class.

In short, local variables are referred to as 'local' because they can only be referenced and locally used in the method that they are declared in. Below is a method where 'miles' is a local variable.

```
private static double convertKmToMi(double kilometers) {

    double miles = kilometers * MILES_PER_KILOMETER;

    return miles;

}
```

Parameters

Parameters are also methods passed in Methods. For instance, in the main method, the string args [] variables is a parameter.

```
 1. package com.jbt;
 2.
 3. /*
 4.  * Here we will discuss about different type of Varia
        available in Java
 5.  */
 6. public class VariablesInJava {
 7.
 8. public static void main(String args[]) {
 9. System.out.println("Hello");
10. }
11. }
```

Conditional Statements In Java

Every day in life, we come in contact with different kinds of objects as you try to get things done; at the same time, we use these objects to carry out different tasks. The one type of objects we tend to come in contact with are digital or analog devices such as phones, computers, cars, self-opening doors in malls and offices, and televisions.

In relation to the example above, you'll realize that the concept of conditional statements in Java depicts the way we go about our daily lives. Conditional statements, with regards to Java programming, are all about making decisions that are directed towards a desired result. Each day, we make decisions, and for these decisions, we get particular result.

In Java programming, we have two types of decision making statements to use when programming a software or device that you can run on any device like the ones I've stated above. These statements basically assist the device and the device's user as well to do something according to a particular state or condition.

The IF-STATEMENT is the first conditional statement. You need to note that the if-statement contains three versions, which include the following:

- IF—STATEMENTS
- ELSE—IF STATEMENTS
- IF / ELSE STATEMENTS

Let's see how an IF-statement works using the first device we mentioned.

```
if(batteryIsLow) {
    // Alert the user to charge
}

if(phoneStorageIsFull) {
    // Alert the user to delete contents
}

if(softwareUpdateIsAvailable) {
    // Alert the user to download
}

if(incomingCall) {
    // Ring Ring Ring
}

if(userPressPowerOffButton) {
    // Alert the user that phone is going off
}
```

In Java, we use the IF-statements to check for a condition or state of the phone and when that condition happens to be true, the action thus becomes executed. If the condition is not true, nothing will happen. Now let's consider the phone; if the condition or state of the phone is battery low, then the phone will inform you to charge it. If the phone storage is full, you can get a notification is to fix it just the same way it informs you to download a software update when it's available.

The if/else statements

Let's now use the second device to see how the if/else statement on the other hand works.

```
if(loginPaswwordIsCorrect) {
    // Grant the user access
} else {
    // Deny the user access
}


if(batteryIsLow) {
    // Alert the user to charge
} else {
    // Shutdown
}


if(laptopIsInactive) {
    // Enter sleep mode
} else {
    // stay on screen active
}
```

When you look at the image above, you'll see that the 'if conditional' statements are extended to complete another action in the instance the first one is false. You can also define another action that can be completed (in the if/else statements) if the first condition isn't true – in this case, the first condition is false. The conditions above are quite self-explanatory since they are evident in our day-to-day use of computers.

The other version of these statements is known as:

The If-Statements

Let's use the device we mentioned third to look at how an else-if statement works.

```
if(temperatureIsHot) {
    // Turn on the Air conditioner
} else if(temperatureIsWarm) {
    // Turn on the fan
} else {
    // Turn on the heater
}


if(speedIsGreaterThan80km/hr) {
    // Switch to gear 3
} else if(speedIsGreaterThan120km/hr) {
    // Switch to gear 5
} else {
    // Switch to gear 1
}


if(carIsNotInMotion) {
    // Open all doors
} else if(carIsInMotion) {
    // Lock all doors
} else if(carIsMovingSlow) {
    // Leave all doors open
}
```

Besides the if/else, Java also lets you test other conditions by using the **else if** keyword. Let's take the first case as an example; you can see that once you test the first condition, it was decided to test for two more conditions which are likely consequences in our day-to-day use of air conditions. Basically therefore, we are able to give actions to be carried out according to any possible condition- with the java else if statements that is.

Switch case

Lastly, we also have the 'switch case', another type of conditional statements used in Java. Just as the name implies, it is some kind of a 'switch case' that controls a light bulb. Therefore, it essentially means that you can have multiple switches to act as conditions that light up different 'bulbs' (or perform actions). See the image below.

Using the last device mentioned, we'll take a look at how a switch case statement functions.

```
int televison = 0;

switch(television) {
    case 0:
        // Off mode activated;
        break;
    case 1:
        // On mode activated;
        break;
    case 3;
        // Scan for channels activated;
        break;
    defualt:
        // Sleep mode activated;
        break;
}
```

When you look at the image above, it is pretty obvious that the distance needed to open the door automatically is stowed in the distance variable. Following the declaration and initialization of variables, the switch case comes next to test all possible distances that are having their corresponding actions. What exactly happens is that you store the major variable required to perform a certain action and then go on to include other cases that can carry out other actions.

You need to note that you don't always need to use a switch case for purposes of calling just a single specific method as you can use it to create a scenario where a number of actions can be carried out based on what the user desires.

The switch case can also have as many cases as required and additionally, the default statement can be used to perform an action in the instance the rest of the cases don't equal the action required. See the image below.

With the device I mentioned last, we'll be able to see how a switch case statement functions alongside a default statement.

```
int televison = 0;

switch(television) {
    case 0:
        // Off mode activated;
        break;
    case 1:
        // On mode activated;
        break;
    case 3;
        // Scan for channels activated;
        break;
    defualt:
        // Sleep mode activated;
        break;
}
```

At this point, I'm sure you know how you can create conditional statements in Java. It's now up to you to go ahead and include it in your programs when you finally begin coding.

Loops In Java

In Java or any other programming language, looping is a feature that facilitates the execution of a set of instructions or functions recurrently as some condition evaluates to true. Java offers three ways to execute the loops.

Even as all the ways offer the same basic functionality, they usually differ in terms of syntax and the condition checking time.

While Loop

The while loop, to begin with, is a flow control statement that lets code to be repeatedly executed according to a particular Boolean condition. You can think of the while loop as repeating the IF statement.

```
while (boolean condition)
{
    loop statements...
}
```

Take a look at the flowchart below:

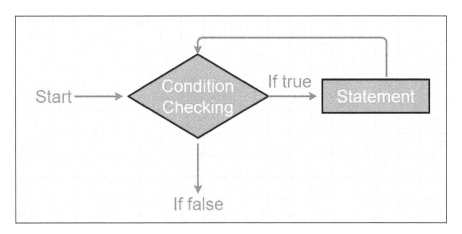

The while loop begins by checking the condition. If it evaluates to true, the loop body statements automatically become executed, if not, the first statement following the loop becomes executed. Therefore, it is for this reason that it is known as entry control loop. When the condition evaluates to true, the loop statements get executed. Usually, the statements have what's known as an update value for the specific variable that is under processing for the subsequent iteration. If the condition turns false, the loop then terminates thus killing its life cycle.

```java
// Java program to illustrate while loop
class whileLoopDemo
{
    public static void main(String args[])
    {
        int x = 1;

        // Exit when x becomes greater than 4
        while (x <= 4)
        {
            System.out.println("Value of x:" +
x);

            // Increment the value of x for
            // next iteration
            x++;
        }
    }
```

When you run it on IDE, you get the following output:

Value of x:1

Value of x:2

Value of x:3

Value of x:4

For Loop

This type of loop offers a concise way to write the loop structure. Unlike the while loop, the for statement uses up the initialization, increment and decrement, and condition in one line, thus giving a shorter, easy to debug looping structure.

for (initialization condition; testing condition;

                increment/decrement)

{

   statement(s)

}

The flowchart is as follows:

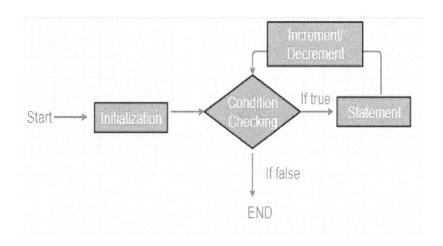

Initialization condition

In this case, you initialize the variable being used. It marks the beginning of a for loop. A variable that is already declared can be put to use or a variable can get declared, that is local to loop alone.

Testing condition

This one is used to test a loop's exit condition. It must take back a Boolean value. It also acts as an entry control loop

269

as the condition gets checked before the loop statements are executed.

Statement execution

When the condition evaluates to true, the loop body statements become executed.

Increment/decrement

This one is used to update the variable for the subsequent iteration.

Loop termination

If the condition is false, what happens is that the loop terminates to mark the end of its lifecycle:

```java
// Java program to illustrate for loop.

class forLoopDemo
{
    public static void main(String args[])
    {
        // for loop begins when x=2
        // and runs till x <=4
        for (int x = 2; x <= 4; x++)
            System.out.println("Value of x:" + x);
    }
}
```

When you run it on IDE, you get the following output:

```
Value of x:2
Value of x:3
Value of x:4
```

The enhanced For Loop

Java also entails another for loop version that was introduced in Java 5. Enhanced for loop offers an easier way of iterating through the elements of a collection or array. It is rigid and you should use it only when you really need to iterate through the elements in a sequence without being aware of the index of the currently processed element.

```
for (T element:Collection obj/array)
{
    statement(s)
}
```

As an example (a demonstration of how you can use the enhanced for loop to simplify the work), assume you have an array of names and want to print all the names contained in the array. Let's take a look at the difference between these two examples. The enhanced for loop makes things easier in the following manner:

Running it on IDE will give you the following output:

Ron

Harry

Hermoine

Do while

The do while loop is largely the same as the while loop. The only difference however is that it checks for condition once it executes the statements and thus, it is a good example of the exit control loop.

```
do
{
    statements..
}
while (condition);
```

The flowchart is as follows:

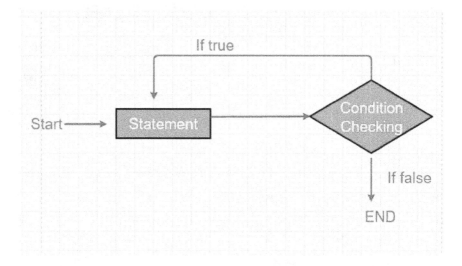

The do while loop begins with the statement(s') execution. For the first time, there usually isn't any checking of any condition.

Once the statements are executed, and there is the update of the variable value, the condition gets checked for a true or false value. In case it gets evaluated to true, the next loop iteration commences.

When the condition turns out to be false, the loop is terminated and just like that, its life cycle comes to an end. You need to remember that the do-while loop executes its statements not less than once before checking of any condition; therefore, it is a good example of the exit control loop.

```java
// Java program to illustrate do-while loop
class dowhileloopDemo
{
    public static void main(String args[])
    {
        int x = 21;
        do
        {
            // The line will be printed even
            // if the condition is false
            System.out.println("Value of x:" + x);
            x++;
        }
        while (x < 20);
    }
}
```

When you run it on IDE, you get the following output:

Value of x: 21

With that, I think you are ready to learn something about Arrays in Java.

Java Arrays

When you hear the name 'arrays', think about a *container* that holds values or data of one type. For instance, you can have an array that holds 100 int type values. Array is an important Java construct that basically lets you store and conveniently access many values.

Declaring Arrays

Let me now explain how you can declare arrays in Java:

dataType[] arrayName;

In the example above, the dataType refers to a primitive data type such as char, int, byte, double and so forth or an object.

The 'arrayName' on the other hand is an identifier. Let's look at the example above once more:
Double[] data;

In this case, data refers to an array that is able to hold values of the type 'double'.

many elements therefore can this array hold? Since this hasn't been defined yet, our next step will be allocating memory for the array elements.
data = new Double[10];

The data array length is 10- this means that it can hold ten elements (in this case, it is 10 double values). You need to note that when the array length is defined, it can't be changed in the program. We'll take another example:

int[] age;

age = new int[5];

In this example, the age array is able to hold five values of the *int* type. You can be able to allocate and declare memory of an array in a single statement. You can also replace two statements above with one statement.

int[] age = new int[5];

The Java Array Index

You can use indices to access the array elements-consider the (previous) example below:

int[] age = new int[5];

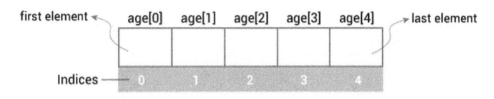

Array age **of length 5**

The initial array element is age[0], the second is age[1] and so forth. If the array's length is n, then the final element is arrayName[n-1]. Now that 5 is the length of 'age' array, the last array element is 'age[4]' in the example above.

Zero is the default first value of elements of an array for the numeric types; for Boolean, it is 'false'. This can be demonstrated as:

275

```
class ArrayExample {
  public static void main(String[] args) {

    int[] age = new int[5];

    System.out.println(age[0]);
    System.out.println(age[1]);
    System.out.println(age[2]);
    System.out.println(age[3]);
    System.out.println(age[4]);
  }
}
```

Running the program gives the following output.

0

0

0

0

0

We have a better way of accessing elements of whichever array with the looping construct (the 'for loop' is generally used).

```
class ArrayExample {

  public static void main(String[] args) {

    int[] age = new int[5];

    for (int i = 0; i < 5; ++i) {
      System.out.println(age[i]);
    }
  }
}
```

How do you initialize Java arrays?

You can initialize arrays in Java during declaration or just initialize (changing values is also an option) later on in the program according to your need.

Initializing arrays during declaration

The following is how you can initialize arrays during declaration:

```
int[] age = {12, 4, 5, 2, 5};
```

This statement builds an array and then initializes it during declaration. An array's length is determined by the given number of values, which is divided by commas. In the example here, the age array's length is 5.

age[0]	age[1]	age[2]	age[3]	age[4]
12	4	5	2	5

We'll write a small program so that the elements of this array are printed.

```
class ArrayExample {
  public static void main(String[] args) {

    int[] age = {12, 4, 5, 2, 5};

    for (int i = 0; i < 5; ++i) {
      System.out.println("Element at index " + i +": " + age[i]);
    }
  }
}
```

Running the program will give the following output:

Element at index 0: 12

Element at index 1: 4

Element at index 2: 5

Element at index 3: 2

Element at index 4: 5

How can you access the array elements?

It is easy to access and change the array elements with its numeric index. Take the example below:

```java
class ArrayExample {
  public static void main(String[] args) {

    int[] age = new int[5];

    // insert 14 to third element
    age[2] = 14;

    // insert 34 to first element
    age[0] = 34;

    for (int i = 0; i < 5; ++i) {
      System.out.println("Element at index " + i +": " + age[i]);
    }
  }
}
```

Running the program will give you the following output:

Element at index 0: 34

Element at index 1: 0

Element at index 2: 14

Element at index 3: 0

Element at index 4: 0

An example of Java arrays

Below is a program that calculates the average and sum of values stowed in a type int array:

```java
class SumAverage {
  public static void main(String[] args) {

    int[] numbers = {2, -9, 0, 5, 12, -25, 22, 9, 8, 12};
    int sum = 0;
    Double average;

    for (int number: numbers) {
      sum += number;
    }

    int arrayLength = numbers.length;

    // Change sum and arrayLength to double as average is in double
    average = ((double)sum / (double)arrayLength);

    System.out.println("Sum = " + sum);
    System.out.println("Average = " + average);
  }
}
```

Running the program will give you the following output:

Sum = 36

Average = 3.6

There are a few things here:

The *int* values, *sum* as well as *arraylength* get converted into *double* to calculate the average because *average* is *double*. This is known as type casting (see glossary). Getting the length of an array uses the *length attribute*. In this case, *numbers.length* returns the array: length of *numbers*.

Multidimensional Arrays

So far, we've been talking about one-dimensional arrays. In Java though, you can declare arrays referred to as multidimensional arrays. The following is an example to declare/ initialize a multidimensional array

Double[][] matrix = {{1.2, 4.3, 4.0},

    {4.1, -1.1}

};

In this case, matrix is a 2-dimensional array. Let's talk a bit about multidimensional arrays in Java.

The following is a 2d (two-dimensional) array. This array can be able to hold up to 12 elements of *int* type.

	Column 1	Column 2	Column 3	Column 4
Row 1	a[0][0]	a[0][1]	a[0][2]	a[0][3]
Row 2	a[1][0]	a[1][1]	a[1][2]	a[1][3]
Row 3	a[2][0]	a[2][1]	a[2][2]	a[2][3]

Don't forget that Java utilizes zero-based indexing- that means that in Java, indexing of arrays begins with zero and 1 the same way you can declare a 3d (three dimensional) array. For instance,

String[][][] personalInfo = new String[3][4][2];

In this case, the *personalinfo* is a 3d array that's able to hold up to 24 (3*4*2) elements of *string* type.

The components of a multidimensional array in Java are also arrays. If you have some knowledge of C or C++ languages, you may have started thinking that Java's multidimensional arrays work the same way as those in C/C++. That is not the case though as Java's rows can vary in length. During initialization, you'll see the difference.

Initializing a 2d array in Java

Take the example below to initialize a 2d array:

```
int[][] a = {
    {1, 2, 3},
    {4, 5, 6, 9},
    {7},
};
```

Each one of the array component 'a' is actually an array itself, and the length of all rows differs as well. To prove that, we'll write a program.

```java
class MultidimensionalArray {
  public static void main(String[] args) {

    int[][] a = {
        {1, 2, 3},
        {4, 5, 6, 9},
        {7},
    };

    System.out.println("Length of row 1: " + a[0].length);
    System.out.println("Length of row 2: " + a[1].length);
    System.out.println("Length of row 3: " + a[2].length);
  }
}
```

You'll get the following output when you run the program:

Length of row 1: 3

Length of row 2: 4

Length of row 3: 1

Now that all the multidimensional array components are also arrays, it means that a[2], a[1] and (a[0] are arrays as well. You can find the length of the rows by using the 'length' attribute. Let's take a good example:

Printing all 2d array elements with Loop

```java
class MultidimensionalArray {
  public static void main(String[] args) {

    int[][] a = {
        {1, -2, 3},
        {-4, -5, 6, 9},
        {7},
    };

    for (int i = 0; i < a.length; ++i) {
      for(int j = 0; j < a[i].length; ++j) {
        System.out.println(a[i][j]);
      }
    }
  }
}
```

Note that it is better to utilize for...each loop when it comes to iterating through arrays when you get the chance. You can complete the same task with *for...loop* as:

```java
class MultidimensionalArray {
    public static void main(String[] args) {

        int[][] a = {
            {1, -2, 3},
            {-4, -5, 6, 9},
            {7},
        };

        for (int[] innerArray: a) {
            for(int data: innerArray) {
                System.out.println(data);
            }
        }
    }
}
```

You will get the following output when you run the program:

1

-2

3

-4

-5

6

9

7

Initializing 3d arrays in Java

Initializing a 3d array is the same as initializing the 2d array. Take a look at the example below:

```
// test is a 3d array
int[][][] test = {
        {
        {1, -2, 3},
        {2, 3, 4}
        },
        {
        {-4, -5, 6, 9},
        {1},
        {2, 3}
        }
};
```

A 3d array is basically an array of 2d arrays. Just like is the case with 2d arrays, 3d arrays can vary in length. Let's take an example:

A program to print 3d array elements using loop

```java
class ThreeArray {
  public static void main(String[] args) {


    // test is a 3d array
    int[][][] test = {
        {
        {1, -2, 3},
        {2, 3, 4}
        },
        {
        {-4, -5, 6, 9},
        {1},
        {2, 3}
        }
    };


    // for..each loop to iterate through elements of 3d array
    for (int[][] array2D: test) {
      for (int[] array1D: array2D) {
        for(int item: array1D) {
          System.out.println(item);
        }
      }
    }
}
```

You will get the following output when you run the program.

1

-2

3

2

3

4

-4

-5

6

9

1

2

3

Java Copy Arrays

We're now going to learn about the various ways copy arrays (that is one and two dimensional arrays) can be used in Java. We have a number of techniques we can use to achieve this as explained in this section:

Using the assignment operator to copy the arrays

Take a look at the following example:

```java
class CopyArray {
  public static void main(String[] args) {

    int [] numbers = {1, 2, 3, 4, 5, 6};
    int [] positiveNumbers = numbers;   // copying arrays

    for (int number: positiveNumbers) {
      System.out.print(number + ", ");
    }
  }
}
```

You'll get the following output when you run the program:
1, 2, 3, 4, 5, 6

Even though this particular method of copying arrays tends to work superbly, it tends to have a problem. The thing is, when you alter the elements of a single array in the above example, the other arrays' corresponding elements are also

```java
class AssignmentOperator {

    public static void main(String[] args) {

        int [] numbers = {1, 2, 3, 4, 5, 6};
        int [] positiveNumbers = numbers;   // copying arrays

        numbers[0] = -1;

        for (int number: positiveNumbers) {
            System.out.print(number + ", ");
        }
    }
}
```

altered.

You'll get the following output when you run the program:

-1, 2, 3, 4, 5, 6

When the initial element of the array 'numbers' becomes altered to -1, the initial element of the array 'positiveNumbers' likewise becomes -1. This is because the two arrays denote the same array object. This is known as shallow copy.

Nonetheless, we often require what's referred to as deep copy and not shallow copy. This (deep copy) copies the values to make a brand new array object.

Let's use looping construct to copy arrays

We'll begin with an example:

```java
import java.util.Arrays;


class ArraysCopy {

  public static void main(String[] args) {


    int [] source = {1, 2, 3, 4, 5, 6};
    int [] destination = new int[6];


    for (int i = 0; i < source.length; ++i) {
      destination[i] = source[i];
    }


    // converting array to string
    System.out.println(Arrays.toString(destination));
  }
}
```

Your output will be as follows after running the program:

> [1, 2, 3, 4, 5, 6]

In this case, the for loop is being used to iterate through each and every element of the 'source' array. In all iterations, the corresponding element of the 'source' array is copied to the 'destination' array.

The destination and source array do not share similar reference- that is deep copy. This means that id the elements of one array- either destination or source are altered, another array's corresponding elements are not changed.

The 'toString() method' basically works to change array to string - only for the output purposes. In Java, we have a better way of copying arrays (apart from using loops). This is by using the 'copyOfRange()' and 'arraycopy()' method.

How to use the arraycopy() method to copy arrays

The system class has the 'arraycopy()' method that let's you copy data from one particular array to another. The arraycopy() method is this efficient and also flexible. The method lets you copy a particular part of source array to destination array. Take a look:

public static void arraycopy(Object src, int srcPos,

Object dest, int destPos, int length)

In this case:
- Src is the array that you want to copy
- srcPos is the src array's starting position or index
- dest is the array which the the src elements will be copied to
- destPos is the dest array's starting position or index
- 'length' is the number of elements to be copied

We'll take an example:

```java
// To use Arrays.toString() method
import java.util.Arrays;


class ArraysCopy {
  public static void main(String[] args) {
    int[] n1 = {2, 3, 12, 4, 12, -2};


    int[] n3 = new int[5];


    // Creating n2 array of having length of n1 array
    int[] n2 = new int[n1.length];


    // copying entire n1 array to n2
    System.arraycopy(n1, 0, n2, 0, n1.length);
    System.out.println("n2 = " + Arrays.toString(n2));


    // copying elements from index 2 on n1 array
    // copying element to index 1 of n3 array
    // 2 elements will be copied
    System.arraycopy(n1, 2, n3, 1, 2);
    System.out.println("n3 = " + Arrays.toString(n3));
```

You'll get the following output when you run the program:

n2 = [2, 3, 12, 4, 12, -2]

n3 = [0, 12, 4, 0, 0]

You need to note that the default opening value of elements of the int type array is 0.

Using the copyOfrange() method to copy arrays

What's more, you can use this method that is defined in java.util.Arrays class to copy arrays. You don't necessarily have to build the destination array before this particular method is called. To learn more about this method, visit this page.

Let's see how you can do it:

```java
// To use toString() and copyOfRange() method
import java.util.Arrays;

class ArraysCopy {
  public static void main(String[] args) {

    int[] source = {2, 3, 12, 4, 12, -2};

    // copying entire source array to destination
    int[] destination1 = Arrays.copyOfRange(source, 0, source.length);
    System.out.println("destination1 = " +
Arrays.toString(destination1));

    // copying from index 2 to 5 (5 is not included)
    int[] destination2 = Arrays.copyOfRange(source, 2, 5);
    System.out.println("destination2 = " +
Arrays.toString(destination2));
  }
}
```

You'll get the following output when you run the program:

destination1 = [2, 3, 12, 4, 12, -2]

destination2 = [12, 4, 12]

Using loop to copy 2d arrays

Take the example below to copy irregular 2d arrays with loop:

import java.util.Arrays;

```java
class ArraysCopy {
public static void main(String[] args) {

    int[][] source = {
        {1, 2, 3, 4},
        {5, 6},
        {0, 2, 42, -4, 5}
        };

    int[][] destination = new int[source.length][];

    for (int i = 0; i < destination.length; ++i) {

        // allocating space for each row of destination array
        destination[i] = new int[source[i].length];

        for (int j = 0; j < destination[i].length; ++j) {
            destination[i][j] = source[i][j];
        }
    }
```

You will get the following output when you run the program:

[[1, 2, 3, 4], [5, 6], [0, 2, 42, -4, 5]]

As you can see, we've used the method 'deepToString()' for arrays here. This method better represents a multi-dimensional array as like in a 2 dimensional array. You can get more information about deepToString on this page.

You can use the System.arraycopy() or- in the case of one dimensional array- use Arrays.copyOf() array to replace the inner loop of the code above. Take a look at the example below that shows how to achieve the same thing with the arraycopy() method.

```java
import java.util.Arrays;

class AssignmentOperator {
public static void main(String[] args) {

    int[][] source = {
        {1, 2, 3, 4},
        {5, 6},
        {0, 2, 42, -4, 5}
        };

    int[][] destination = new int[source.length][];

    for (int i = 0; i < source.length; ++i) {

        // allocating space for each row of destination array
        destination[i] = new int[source[i].length];
        System.arraycopy(source[i], 0, destination[i], 0, destination[i].length);
    }

    // displaying destination array
    System.out.println(Arrays.deepToString(destination));
}
}
```

Arrays are, after all, not that complicated! The next topic is even more straightforward. Let's take a look at operators to ensure some of what we've learned so far makes more sense, as well as what's to come.

Java Operators

Simply put, operators are characters representing specific actions. For instance, +, as you know it, is an arithmetic operator that denotes addition. In Java, we have the following types of operators:

- Assignment operators
- Basic arithmetic operators
- Comparison or relational operators
- Auto-increment/decrement operators
- Bitwise operators
- Logical operators
- Ternary operators

Basic Arithmetic Operators

These include things like +, %, -, *, /

- Addition is represented by +
- Subtraction is represented by –
- Multiplication is represented by *
- Division is represented by /
- Modulo is represented by %

You have to note that modulo operator returns remainder- for instance 10 % 5 returns zero. Let's take a look at some of the arithmetic operators examples:

```
public class ArithmeticOperatorDemo {
  public static void main(String args[]) {
    int num1 = 100;
    int num2 = 20;

    System.out.println("num1 + num2: " + (num1 + num2) );
    System.out.println("num1 - num2: " + (num1 - num2) );
    System.out.println("num1 * num2: " + (num1 * num2) );
    System.out.println("num1 / num2: " + (num1 / num2) );
    System.out.println("num1 % num2: " + (num1 % num2) );
  }
}
```

The output will be as follows:

num1 + num2: 120

num1 - num2: 80

num1 * num2: 2000

num1 / num2: 5

num1 % num2: 0

Assignment Operators

The assignment operators include the following: =, %=, +=, -=, /=, *=

- The operator that would assign the num1 variable to the variable is num2=num1

- Num2 +=num1 is the same/equivalent to num2=num2+num1

- Again, num2-= num1 is equivalent to num2=num2-num1

- Num2 *=num1 is equivalent to num2 =num2 *num1

- Num2/ =num1 is equivalent to num2=num2/num1

- Num2% =num1 is equivalent to num2=num2%num1

Let's have an example of assignment operators:

```java
public class AssignmentOperatorDemo {
  public static void main(String args[]) {
    int num1 = 10;
    int num2 = 20;

    num2 = num1;
    System.out.println("= Output: "+num2);

    num2 += num1;
    System.out.println("+= Output: "+num2);

    num2 -= num1;
    System.out.println("-= Output: "+num2);

    num2 *= num1;
    System.out.println("*= Output: "+num2);

    num2 /= num1;
    System.out.println("/= Output: "+num2);

    num2 %= num1;
    System.out.println("%= Output: "+num2);
  }
}
```

The output you get by running the program is as follows:

```
= Output: 10
+= Output: 20
-= Output: 10
*= Output: 100
/= Output: 10
%= Output: 0
```

Auto-Increment And Decrement Operators

Here, we are dealing with -- and ++

Num ++ is equal to num+num+1 while num— is equal to num= num-1

Let's take an example of auto-increment/ auto decrement operators:

```java
public class AutoOperatorDemo {
  public static void main(String args[]){
    int num1=100;
    int num2=200;
    num1++;
    num2--;
    System.out.println("num1++ is: "+num1);
    System.out.println("num2-- is: "+num2);
  }
}
```

The output is as follows:

num1++ is: 101

num2-- is: 199

Logical Operators

A logical operator is used together with binary variables. They are mostly used in loops and conditional statements to evaluate a condition.

Essentially, Java's logical operators are ||, &&, !

Consider the case that we have two Boolean variables: b1 and b2. In this case, b1 && b2 will return true in the instance b1 as well as b2 are true; otherwise, it would definitely return false.

On the other hand, b1 || b2 returns false in the instance b1 as well as b2 are false, otherwise else would definitely return true.

!b1 would, on the other hand, return the opposite of b1, meaning that it would return true in the instance b1 is false and return false in case b1 is true.

Let's take an example of these logical operators:

```java
public class LogicalOperatorDemo {
  public static void main(String args[]) {
    boolean b1 = true;
    boolean b2 = false;

    System.out.println("b1 && b2: " + (b1&&b2));
    System.out.println("b1 || b2: " + (b1||b2));
    System.out.println("!(b1 && b2): " + !(b1&&b2));
  }
}
```

The output is as follows:

```
b1 && b2: false
b1 || b2: true
!(b1 && b2): true
```

Relational Or Comparison Operators

In Java, there are six relational operators which include: ==, >, >=, <, <=, ! =

- In the instance the left and right side are equal, == returns true
- In the instance the left side isn't equivalent to the operator's right side, != returns true
- In the instance the left side is more/greater than the right side, > returns true
- In the instance the left side is smaller/less than the right side, < returns true
- In the instance the left side is more/greater than the right side, or equal to it, >= returns true
- In the instance the left side is smaller/fewer/less than the right side, or equal to it, <= returns true

Let's take an example of these relational operators:

First of all, you need to note that the example below is using the if-else statement, which you need to be well conversant with before you continue. You can refer to what we discussed earlier on this statement before continuing.

```java
public class RelationalOperatorDemo {
  public static void main(String args[]) {
    int num1 = 10;
    int num2 = 50;
    if (num1==num2) {
        System.out.println("num1 and num2 are equal");
    }
    else{
        System.out.println("num1 and num2 are not equal");
    }

    if( num1 != num2 ){
        System.out.println("num1 and num2 are not equal");
    }
    else{
        System.out.println("num1 and num2 are equal");
    }

    if( num1 > num2 ){
        System.out.println("num1 is greater than num2");
    }
    else{
        System.out.println("num1 is not greater than num2");
    }

    if( num1 >= num2 ){
        System.out.println("num1 is greater than or equal to num2
    }
    else{
        System.out.println("num1 is less than num2");
    }

    if( num1 < num2 ){
        System.out.println("num1 is less than num2");
    }
    else{
        System.out.println("num1 is not less than num2");
    }

    if( num1 <= num2 ){
        System.out.println("num1 is less than or equal to num2");
    }
    else{
        System.out.println("num1 is greater than num2");
    }
  }
}
```

The output is as follows:

num1 and num2 are not equal
num1 and num2 are not equal
num1 is not greater than num2
num1 is less than num2
num1 is less than num2
num1 is less than or equal to num2

The Bitwise Operators
We basically have six bitwise operators which include:
>>, &, |, <<, ^, >>,~

num1 = 11; /* equal to 00001011*/
num2 = 22; /* equal to 00010110 */

I'm sure you've heard that bitwise operators perform processing bit by bit.

Num 1 & num 2 essentially compare their corresponding bits (of num1 and num2) before generating 1- if the two bits are equal, otherwise, else would return 0. In the case here, it would return: 2 which is just 00000010 since in num 1 and num 2 binary form, it's only the second last bits that are matching.

Num 1 | num 2 compares num 1 and num 2 bits and then generates 1, that is if either bit is 1, otherwise it returns zero. In the case here, it returns 31, which essentially is 00011111.

Num 1^ num 2 on the other hand compares the corresponding bits of num 2 and num 1 before generating a 1; that is if they are not equal, otherwise it returns 0. In our example here, it would return 29, which is equal to 00011101.-num1 happens to be a complement operator that only changes the bit from 0 to 1 and 1 to 0. In the example we have here, it returns -12. This one is signed 8 bit equal to 11110100.

Num 1 <<2 is a left shift operator, which is responsible for transferring the bits towards the left hand side and discards the bit that is far left, before assigning zeros to the rightmost bit. In the case here, the output is 44. This figure is equivalent to 00101100.

You need to note that in the example we have below, we are giving out 2 to the right hand side of the shift operator, which is the reason the bits are going 2 places towards the left hand side. You can change this number and the bits would have to be moved by the specified number of bits on the operator's right hand side. The same applies to the operator in the right side.

Num1 >> 2 is a right shift operator, which usually has a tendency of moving the bits to the right before discarding the far right bit, before then assigning the leftmost bit a value of 0. In the case here, the output is 2, which is equal to 00000010.

Let's take a look at an example of these operators:

```java
public class BitwiseOperatorDemo {
  public static void main(String args[]) {

    int num1 = 11;  /* 11 = 00001011 */
    int num2 = 22;  /* 22 = 00010110 */
    int result = 0;

    result = num1 & num2;
    System.out.println("num1 & num2: "+result);

    result = num1 | num2;
    System.out.println("num1 | num2: "+result);

    result = num1 ^ num2;
    System.out.println("num1 ^ num2: "+result);

    result = ~num1;
    System.out.println("~num1: "+result);

    result = num1 << 2;
    System.out.println("num1 << 2: "+result); result = num1 >> 2;
    System.out.println("num1 >> 2: "+result);
  }
}
```

The output is as follows:

num1 & num2: 2

num1 | num2: 31

num1 ^ num2: 29

~num1: -12

num1 << 2: 44 num1 >> 2: 2

That's pretty much what you need to know as regards to operators in Java. Before you continue though, you may want to cover ternary operator and Operator precedence in Java, which are not within the scope of this book, but are equally important.

Classes and Objects in Java

Some Basics Of Classes

Class or classification is a representation of an entity or something that is made up of behavior and state. The class' state is the data associated with it and the class behaviors are those actions the class can perform.

For instance, in classifying a simple vehicle, we can say that it has a model name, manufacturer name and a production year associated with it. You can also say that your simple car is able to accelerate and decelerate. In that case, you can define behavior and state with the rule below:

The class' state is simply what the class contains while the class' behavior is what the class is able to do. You can create a simple specification for your class using the example I've just given as follows:

```
class Vehicle:
    state:
        manufacturerName
        modelName
        productionYear
    behavior:
        accelerate
        decelerate
```

You need to note that nearly all the programming languages have a restriction on state entry names and behavior names from having spaces. For instance, *manufacturer name* isn't a valid state entry name, manufactuerName is. The latter name is written in what is known as the camel case, in which the first letter in lower case and the rest of the letters are capitalized.

We've achieved a basic description of a vehicle, even though it doesn't have enough detail to be deemed important. For instance, what action is done when you want to accelerate the vehicle? Here, our class' behaviors have been declared but are yet to be defined. A behavior declaration is a statement about the kind of behavior can be performed. The behavior definition is the statement about how the behavior is executed. For instance, adding a new state entry referred to as 'currentSpeed' enables you to define your behaviors *'accelerate'* and *'decelerate'*

```
class Vehicle:
  state:
    manufacturerName
    modelName
    productionYear
    currentSpeed
  behavior:
    accelerate:
      increase currenctSpeed by 1
    decelerate
      decrease currenctSpeed by 1
```

With the behavior definitions above, we are able to do some useful work with our class. As you would notice, the purpose of the behavior is altering the state of the class. This leads to a general rule concerning the class behavior: the purpose of the behavior allied with a class is either accessing or altering the class' state. This rule is very important – so much that there is a metric designed to measure it: *cohesion*. Cohesion refers to the extent to which the state of a class and behavior relate to each other and work towards a common goal.

Even though you know the way the vehicle accelerates and decelerates, you've only given a simplistic definition that does not account for an action that is unexpected. For instance, how about you begin with a current speed that is less than zero and decelerate? Generally, you should never be in a situation where the current speed is dropping below zero. This rule about the class state is known as an invariant. An invariant needs to stay true before a behavior is completed and afterwards as well. This logic can be supported by augmenting the current definition of deceleration like so:

```
class Vehicle:
  invariants:
    currentSpeed is greater than or equal to 0
  state:
    manufacturerName
    modelName
    productionYear
    currentSpeed
  behavior:
    accelerate:
      increase currenctSpeed by 1
    decelerate
      if currentSpeed is greater than 0:
        decrease currenctSpeed by 1
```

Types

We now have a more mature class specification, but don't have a major element. When you examine the current speed state entry, this deficiency becomes evident: what are the units for measuring the current speed? One kilometer per hour? One mile per hour? In this case, we've not even limited its value to be a measurement of distance per time. Given the specification, the vehicle's current speed could be in sloths units. We need to link a type with every state entry to be able to better specify our class.

Before supplying the types for the state entries, there has to be a connection that needs to be created: a class and type are one and the same. For instance, if you said that the current speed is a number, the number itself can be denoted by a class.

What exactly is a number?

Well, a number holds a value and has the ability to perform such actions as multiplying itself with another number or even adding another number to itself. You could essentially build a class specification for a number if you so wished.

```
class Number:
  state:
    value
  behavior:
    addWithAnotherNumber:
      update value to be value plus other number
```

Now that there is an understanding of the need for types, we can now update our vehicle class to have state entries that are properly typed (we'll use the 'type StateName' notation) where the name of the type precedes the state entry name.

```
class Vehicle:
  invariants:
    currentSpeed is greater than or equal to 0
  state:
    String manufacturerName
    String modelName
    Number productionYear
    Number currentSpeed
  behavior:
    accelerate:
      increase currentSpeed by 1
    decelerate:
      if currentSpeed is greater than 0:
        decrease currenctSpeed by 1
```

You need to note that a string is a sequence of characters and that we'll have to ignore the current speed units. It will, for the moment, suffice to limit the current speed to a number. As you go on to describe the types, you have run into two things that need to be addressed before continue adorning and maturing the vehicle class: the primitive and parameters to behavior.

Primitive Types

As you declare the state entries for the class in terms of other classes, we'll eventually come to a point where you can no longer reference another class without having a cyclical hierarchy. For instance, if you try assigning a type of 'number' to the state 'currentSpeed', how then do you define the class 'number'? If you try defining it in terms of other classes, how do you, therefore, define those classes? Since you cannot let a type system that accepts such infinite regression, you need to declare a value or values to exist. Such axiomatic types are known as primitive types.

Most programming languages have a basic set of primitive types which include decimal values (like single-precision floating point), integers, strings, characters and Boolean values (these could be true or false values). These types occur as a set of bits without the necessity to define a regressive structure of a class. Such primitive types can operate as building blocks to have more complex types in terms of classes created. For purposes of this discussion, we'll have to assume that the types 'string', 'number', 'Boolean' and 'character' exist.

Behavior Parameters

Another thing you have to look at is concerned with passing information to the class when you execute behaviors. For instance, when you want to accelerate to 80 kilometers per hour, you'd have to execute the accelerate behavior of the vehicle class successfully 80 times. That is definitely unruly for a real system. In place of that, you should try instructing the vehicle how much to accelerate by. For instance, when you execute 'accelerate by 30' and then 'accelerate by 15' gives you a speed of 45 kilometers per hour. To do this, you need to declare that your accelerate behavior can actually a value, which closely represents the increased speed as one of the parameters. For this, you'll border the parameter with a parenthesis before associating a type with the same notation as that for your class' state. As you would note, the parameter needs to be named, otherwise you would not be able to use or access the parameter inside your definition of the behavior. You also need to note that when a behavior fails to have any parameters, you'll use an empty set of parameters. For instance, if the 'drive' behavior doesn't take any parameters, its declaration will be 'drive ()'. As a result, you'll get the following class for your vehicle:

```
class Vehicle:
    invariants:
    currentSpeed is greater than or equal to 0
    state:
    String: manufacturerName
    String modelName
    Number productionYear
    Number currentSpeed
    behavior:
    accelerate(Number amount):
        increase currenctSpeed by amount
    decelerate(Number amount):
        if currentSpeed minus amount is greater or equal to 0:
        decrease currenctSpeed by amount
```

If right now you instruct the vehicle to accelerate by 30, you'd be able to increase the current speed of the vehicle by 30. Now that the value (30) is passed to your behavior at execution, it is referred to as an argument. Even though the argument and the terms parameter are closely related, you'll get a vital distinction: a parameter is a value referenced in the behavior definition. The argument on the other hand is the actual value passed to the behavior upon execution.

I deliberately selected the execution notation because it maps the arguments that are supplied to the declared parameters. For instance, 'accelerate(30)' maps the value (30) to *amount* (of the 'number' type) during execution. This parameters' notation can be extended for more than a single parameter by enumerating the multiple parameters in a list with comma-separation taking the form of 'doSomething (number valueOne, Number valueTwo)'. In instances when the arguments are positionally mapped, this very argument notation can come in handy- for instance 'doSomething (15, 37)' maps 37 to valueTwo.

Declaring Classes

Let's start with an example of a definition of classes:

```
class MyClass {
   // field, constructor, and
   // method declarations
}
```

This is a form of class declaration. The area in between the braces- or the class body- has all the code that offers for the life cycle of the objects made from the class- that is constructors to initialize new objects, the declarations for the fields providing the class' state and its objects, as well as methods to implement the behavior of both the class and its objects. The class declaration that precedes is a minimal one- it basically has all the required components of a class declaration. You can offer more information concerning the class, for instance, its super class' name, whether it implements any surfaces, and so forth, at the beginning of the class declaration. For instance:

```
class MyClass extends MySuperClass implements YourInterface {
   // field, constructor, and
   // method declarations
}
```

This means that 'MyClass' is MySuperClass' subclass which implements the interface 'YourInterface'. You can add such modifiers like 'private' or 'public' at the start- so you can see that the first line of a class declaration can get a bit complicated. Generally, class declarations can comprise the following components in order:

• Modifiers, like 'private' and 'public', as well as a couple of others that you'll come across later.

• The class name along with the initial letter conventionally capitalized

• The class' parent or superclass name, if any, with the keyword 'extends' preceding it. A class is only able to *extend* one parent.

• A list of interfaces separated by commas implemented by the class, if any which is preceded by the 'implements' keyword. A class can be able to implement more than one interface.

• The class body, bounded by braces {}

Declaring Member Variables

We have different kinds of variables:

• The member variables in a class known as fields

• The ones in a block of code or a method known as local variables and

• Those in method declarations known as parameters

The class 'bicycle' uses the lines of code below to define its fields:

```
public int cadence;
public int gear;
public int speed;
```

The field declarations are made up of three components, which include:

• The zero or more modifiers, for instance, the *private* or *public*

• The type of field

• The name of the field

314

The 'bicycle' fields have the name *cadence, gear* as well as *speed* and all of them are of data type integer known as *int*. the keyword 'bicycle' identifies these fields as public members, which are accessible by any object able to access the class.

The Access Modifiers

The first and left-most modifier that is used enables you control what the other classes can access a member field. At the moment, you can consider *private* and *public* modifiers.

The *public* modifier has the field that can be accessed from all classes.

The *private* modifier has the field that can only be accessed within its own class.

In light of encapsulation, you'll find it common to make fields private, which means that they can only be accessed *directly* from the class 'bicycle'. Nonetheless, you still require accessing these values- something that can be *indirectly* achieved by adding public methods, which obtain for you the field values:

```
public class Bicycle {

    private int cadence;
    private int gear;
    private int speed;

    public Bicycle(int startCadence, int startSpee
        gear = startGear;
        cadence = startCadence;
        speed = startSpeed;
    }

    public int getCadence() {
        return cadence;
    }

    public void setCadence(int newValue) {
        cadence = newValue;
    }

    public int getGear() {
        return gear;
    }

    public void setGear(int newValue) {
        gear = newValue;
    }

    public int getSpeed() {
        return speed;
    }

    public void applyBrake(int decrement) {
        speed -= decrement;
    }

    public void speedUp(int increment) {
        speed += increment;
    }
}
```

The Types

All the variables need to have a type. You can either use the primitive types mentioned earlier such as Boolean, float or int or just use the reference types such as objects, arrays or strings.

The variable names

All variables follow some conventions and naming rules, regardless of whether they were fields, parameters or fields. You need to keep in mind that the same conventions and naming rules are used for class names and method, except that:

- The first class name letter needs to be capitalized and
- The first word or only word in a method name has to be a verb.

Defining Methods

The following is an example of a typical method declaration:

```
public double calculateAnswer(double wingSpan, int numberOfEngines,
            double length, double grossTons) {
  //do the calculation here
}
```

The method declaration elements that are required include the return type, pair of parentheses (), name and a body in between the braces {} of the method. In general, the method declarations contain six components in order as follows:

- The modifiers like *private, public* among others.
- The return type, which is the data type of the value, which the method returned, or *void* if the method fails to return a value.
- The name of the method- the field name rules only apply to the names of the method as well but the convention is a bit different.
- The parenthesis-bound parameter list – a list of input parameters, which are delimited in commas that are preceded by their respective data types which are usually bound by parentheses. In case of no parameters, empty parentheses can be used.

- An exception list
- The method body that is enclosed between different braces- the code of the method, which includes the declaration of local variables comes here.

Two of the method declaration components contain the *method signature,* which is the name of the method and types of the parameter. The method declared above has the following signature:
calculateAnswer(double, int, double, double)

Naming A Method
Even though the method name can take the form of any legal identifier, the code conventions tend to restrict the method names. Conventionally, the method names need to be a lowercase verb or multi-word names that start with a verb in lowercase and then nouns, adjectives and so on. When it comes to multi-word names, the first letter of each of the second and following words needs to be capitalized. Take the examples below:

```
run
runFast
getBackground
getFinalData
compareTo
setX
isEmpty
```

A method typically has a special name within its class. Nonetheless, it's possible for a method to have the same name as the other methods, owing to method overloading discussed below:

Overloading Methods
Java supports overloading methods; the program can also differentiate between methods having dissimilar method signatures. This simply means that it is possible for the

318

methods in a class to have the same name if they contain different parameter lists.

Assume you have a class that is able to use calligraphy to draw various data types- this includes intergers, strings and so forth- and that which has a method for drawing every data type. It is stressful to use a new name for all methods. For instance, 'drawInteger', 'drawString', 'drawFloat' and so forth. In Java, you are allowed to use the same name for all the methods of drawing but then pass a different argument list to each one of these methods. Therefore, the data drawing class could declare four methods with the name 'draw', each of which contains a different list of parameters.

```
public class DataArtist {
  ...
  public void draw(String s) {
    ...
  }
  public void draw(int i) {
    ...
  }
  public void draw(double f) {
    ...
  }
  public void draw(int i, double f) {
    ...
  }
```

The type and number of arguments that are passed into the method helps differentiate overloaded methods. When you look at the code sample, the *draw (int i)* and *draw(string s)* are unique and distinct methods because they need different types of arguments.

You cannot declare more than one method that has the same name, the same type and number of arguments since the compiler is not able to tell them apart. The compiler doesn't typically consider the type when it is differentiating methods. This essentially means that you really cannot declare 2

319

methods using the same signature even if each uses a different return type.

Before you move to the next section below on creating objects, it would be great if you researched on these two sections as they are beyond the scope of this book:

- Providing Constructors for Your Classes
- Passing Information to a Method or a Constructor

Creating Objects

In java, objects are combinations of data and procedures working on the data available. An object contains a behavior and state. Both of these are kept in variables or fields while the functions or methods display the behavior of the object. The classes serve as templates to create objects. In Java, the keyword 'new' is used to create an object.

A class gives the blueprint for different objects. In this case, you make an object from class and each of the statements below from a program builds an object and assigns a variable to it.

Point originOne = new Point(23, 94);
Rectangle rectOne = new Rectangle(originOne, 100, 200);
Rectangle rectTwo = new Rectangle(50, 100);

The *point* class object is created in the first line; the second line and the third each create the rectangle class object. Each one of these statements is made up of three parts as described below:

Declaration- the code formatted to bold are variable declarations correlating a variable name with the object type.

Instantiation- like I mentioned, the keyword 'new' is an operator in Java that builds the object.

Initialization- a call to a constructor that initializes the new object follows the operator

How To Declare A Variable To Refer To An Object

You already know that declaring a variable requires you to write *type name:*

The compiler is this notified that you'll use 'name' in reference to the data whose type is 'type'. When dealing with a primitive variable, this declaration also tends to reserve the right amount of the variable memory. You are capable of declaring a reference variable on a line of its own- for instance: *point originOne;*

By declaring 'originOne' this way, its value remains undetermined until an object is created and assigned to it. The action of declaring a given reference variable doesn't stop at creating an object. To do that, you would need use the operator 'new' as I will describe shortly. You have to have an object assigned to 'originOne' before using it in your code lest you receive a compile error.

A variable in this state, which does not reference any object at the moment, can be illustrated in the following manner (the variable name and a reference not pointing to anything):

Class Instantiation

The operator 'new' allocates memory for a new object and then returns a reference to that particular memory to instantiate a class. You need to note that the phrase 'instantiation of a class' is no different from 'creation of an object'. By creating an object, you are building an instance of a class, thus, instantiating a class.

The operator 'new' needs one postfix argument – that is a call to a constructor, the constructor name gives the class name to instantiate. The operator 'new' returns a reference to the object it made. This reference is typically assigned to the appropriate type variable such as:

Point originOne = new Point(23, 94);

The reference that was returned by the operator 'new' doesn't require being assigned to a variable. You can also use it directly in whichever expression- take this example:

int height = new Rectangle().height;

This statement is discussed in a subsequent section.

Initialization of an object

Take a look at the code below for the *point* class:

```
public class Point {
    public int x = 0;
    public int y = 0;
    //constructor
    public Point(int a, int b) {
        x = a;
        y = b;
    }
}
```

This class has one constructor. You can recognize a constructor due to the fact that its declaration is using the same name as the class and it doesn't have any return type. The constructor that is in the class *point* takes two integer arguments as the code declares (int a, int b). The statement below gives values 23 and 94 as ones for those arguments:

Point originOne = new Point(23, 94);

When you execute this statement, the result is illustrated below:

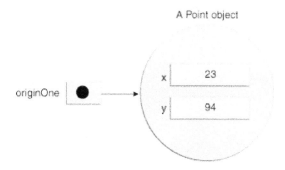

The code for the class 'rectangle', which entails four constructors is as follows:

```java
public class Rectangle {
    public int width = 0;
    public int height = 0;
    public Point origin;

    // four constructors
    public Rectangle() {
        origin = new Point(0, 0);
    }
    public Rectangle(Point p) {
        origin = p;
    }
    public Rectangle(int w, int h) {
        origin = new Point(0, 0);
        width = w;
        height = h;
    }
    public Rectangle(Point p, int w, int h) {
        origin = p;
        width = w;
        height = h;
    }

    // a method for moving the rectangle
    public void move(int x, int y) {
        origin.x = x;
        origin.y = y;
    }

    // a method for computing the area of the rectangle
    public int getArea() {
        return width * height;
    }
}
```

All the constructors allow you to give the initial values for the origin of the rectangle, its height, and width, with both reference and primitive types. In the instance a class has many constructors, they need to have unique (different) signatures. The Java compiler is able to differentiate the constructors according to the number of the arguments and their type. When this compiler comes across the code below, it knows to call the instructor in the class 'rectangle' that needs an argument 'point', which is followed by a double integer arguments.

Rectangle rectOne = new Rectangle(originOne, 100, 200);

This calls a rectangle's constructor, which then initializes 'origin' to 'originOne'. Moreover, a width is set by the constrictor to 100 and the height 200. You now have two references to the same *point object* – note that an object has the ability to contain many references to it, as you can see in the subsequent figure:

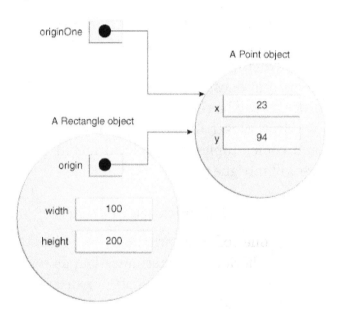

The constructor 'rectangle' is called by the line of code below- the constructor needs two integer arguments and they offer the initial values for the height and width. Inspecting the code inside the constructor enables you to see that it makes a new *point* object with x and y values that are initialized to 0:

Rectangle rectTwo = new Rectangle(50, 100);

The constructor 'rectangle' that is used in the statement below does not take any arguments, thus, it is known as a no-argument constructor:

Rectangle rect = new Rectangle();

All the classes don't have less than one constructor. In the instance a class is not declaring any, explicitly, the Java compiler will automatically give a no-argument constructor known as the default constructor. The default constructor usually calls the no-argument constructor of the class parent or the object constructor in case the class doesn't have another parent. If the parent doesn't have a constructor (the 'object' has one), the program will be rejected by the compiler.

As we draw closer to the end of the book, let's take a look at some cooler topics on object oriented programming that I'm sure will intrigue you!

Inheritance in Java

In Java, one of the principles of Object Oriented Programming is inheritance; inheritance lets us reuse existing code or extend a type that already exists or extend a type that is already existing. Put simply, Java allows a class to inherit another class and many interfaces, and interfaces are able to inherit other interfaces.

In our discussion today, we'll begin with looking at why you need inheritance and how it works with interfaces and classes. And then cover how the method or variable names and how the inherited members are affected by access modifiers, among other important things.

Why Inheritance?

Take a moment and imagine you are a car manufacturer offering multiple car models to your customers. While the different car models could provide features such as bulletproof windows or sunroof, they all have common features and components such as wheels and engine. It's only sensible to build a basic design and extend it to build their specialized versions instead of trying to design the car models individually, from scratch. Similarly, inheritance is here to assist you create a class that has simple features as well as behavior, and make its dedicated versions by building classes that inherit the base class. Similarly, interfaces are designed to extend the existing interfaces. You'll notice how multiple terms have been used to refer to a type which is under inheritance by another type: more specifically;

A base type is also known as a parent or super type

A derived type is known as a child or sub type, or an extended type

Inheritance With A Class
Extending a class

A class can inherit another class and define extra members. Let's begin by defining a base class known as Car:

```
1    public class Car {

2      int wheels;

3      String model;

4      void start() {

5        // Check essential parts

6      }

7    }
```

The 'ArmoredCar' class is able to inherit the 'Car' class members in its declaration with the keyword 'extends':

327

```
1    public class ArmoredCar extends Car {
2        int bulletProofWindows;
3        void remoteStartCar() {
4        // this vehicle can be started by using a remote control
5        }
6    }
```

In Java, the classes support single inheritance; the class 'ArmoredCar' cannot extend many classes. When the keyword 'extends' is not available, a class inherits the class 'java.lang.Object' implicitly.

What Is Being Inherited?

A derived class basically inherits (from the base class) the public and protected members –which are not static. Additionally, the members with package and default access get inherited in the instance the two classes are in one package.

A base class cannot allow its entire code to be accessed by the classes that are derived. A derived class static does not inherit the static and private members of a class. What's more, if the base class and derived classes become defined in isolated packages, the members who have package or default access in the base class don't get inherited within the derived class.

Access Parent Class Members -- From A Derived Class

Doing this is pretty simple; you only need to use them (you don't require a reference to the base class to be able to access its members). Take the brief example below:

```
public class ArmoredCar extends Car {
    public String registerModel() {
        return model;
    }
}
```

Members In The Hidden Base Class Instance

What if the base class and the derive class both define a method or variable that has a similar name? What happens? You should not worry in this case, as you can still be able to access the two. Nonetheless, you need to make your intent clear to Java, by prefixing the method or variable with the 'super' and 'this' keywords. The keyword 'this' refers to the instance which it is used in. The keywords 'this' refers to the instance which it is used in. The keyword 'super' denotes the parent class instance:

```
public class ArmoredCar extends Car {
    private String model;
    public String getAValue() {
        return super.model;   // returns value of model defined in base class Car
        // return this.model;   // will return value of model defined in ArmoredCar
        // return model;   // will return value of model defined in ArmoredCar
    }
}
```

Many developers use the keywords 'super' and 'this' keywords to state the variable or method that they are referring to explicitly. Nonetheless, using them with all the members can make your code appear cluttered.

Hidden Base Class Static Members

What if the derived classes as well as base class and derived classes actually define different static methods and variables with the same name? What happens? Is it possible to access a 'static' member from the base class within the derived class, as we often do in instance variables?

We'll find that out in the example below:

```
1    public class Car {
2        public static String msg() {
3            return "Car";
4        }
5    }
1    public class ArmoredCar extends Car {
2        public static String msg() {
3            return super.msg(); // this won't compile.
4        }
5    }
```

No, you cannot. The static members usually belong to a given class and not to the instances. This means that we cannot use the non-static keyword 'super' in 'msg()'.

Considering that static members are usually belonging to a specific class, you can amend the prior call in the following manner:

return Car.msg();

Consider the example below, in which the base class and the derived class both describe a static method:

'msg()' with a similar signature

```
1    public class Car {
2      public static String msg() {
3        return "Car";
4      }
5    }
1    public class ArmoredCar extends Car {
2      public static String msg() {
3        return "ArmoredCar";
4      }
5    }
```

The following is how you can call them:

```
1    Car first = new ArmoredCar();
2    ArmoredCar second = new ArmoredCar();
```

The preceding code 'first.msg()' outputs 'car' and the 'second.msg()' simply outputs 'ArmoredCar'. The static message called relies on the variable type used in referring the 'ArmoredCar' instance.

Inheritance With Interfaces
Implementing multiple interfaces

Try to imagine the 'ArmoredCar' we defined in the earlier section is needed for a super spy. Thus, the company manufacturing the 'Car' thought it best to add floating and flying functionality:

331

```
1   public interface Floatable {

2     void floatOnWater();

3   }

1   public interface Flyable {

2     void fly();

3   }

1   public class ArmoredCar extends Car implements Floatable, Flyable{

2     public void floatOnWater() {

3       System.out.println("I can float!");

4     }

5

6     public void fly() {

7       System.out.println("I can fly!");

8     }
```

In the above example, you've noticed that the 'implements' keyword has been used to inherit from an interface.

Problems With Multiple Inheritance

Java allows multiple inheritance with interfaces. This was not an issue until Java 7 as interfaces could only be able to define abstract methods (those methods that lack implementation). Therefore, if a class implemented multiple interfaces using the same method signature, it wasn't an issue; the implementing class eventually had only a single method to implement.

Let's now take a look at the way the simple equation changed when the 'default' methods in interfaces were introduced with Java 8.

Beginning with Java 8, the interfaces had an option of defining its methods' default implementation - that is an interface is still able to define the abstract methods. This means that when a class is implementing multiple interfaces that define methods having the same signature, the child class would actually inherit different implementations. This is not allowed just as it sounds complex.

Java doesn't allow multiple implementations' inheritance of the same methods that are defined in separate interfaces. Let me explain with an example:

```
1    public interface Floatable {

2        default void repair() {

3            System.out.println("Repairing Floatable object");

4        }

5    }
```

```
1    public interface Flyable {

2        default void repair() {

3            System.out.println("Repairing Flyable object");

4        }

5    }
```

```
1    public class ArmoredCar extends Car implements Floatable, Flyable {

2        // this won't compile

3    }
```

If you desire to implement the two interfaces, you'll have to override the method 'repair()'. If the interfaces in the earlier example are defining the variables with the same name- for instance, duration, you cannot be able to access them without having the interface name preceding the variable name:

```
1    public interface Floatable {
2        int duration = 10;
3    }
1    public interface Flyable {
2        int duration = 20;
3    }
1    public class ArmoredCar extends Car implements Floatable, Flyable {
2
3        public void aMethod() {
4          System.out.println(duration); // won't compile
5          System.out.println(Floatable.duration); // outputs 10
6          System.out.println(Flyable.duration); // outputs 20
7        }
8    }
```

Interfaces That Extend Other Interfaces

An interface can basically extend multiple interfaces as the example below explains

```
1    public interface Floatable {
2      void floatOnWater();
3    }
1    interface interface Flyable {
2      void fly();
3    }
1    public interface SpaceTraveller extends Floatable, Flyable {
2      void remoteControl();
3    }
```

An interface will inherit other interfaces by using the 'extends' keyword. The classes use the 'implements' keyword in inheriting an interface.

Inheriting Type

When a class inherits another one or interfaces, besides inheriting their members, it tends to inherit their type as well. This equally applies to an interface inheriting other interfaces. This is one very powerful concept that lets developers program to an interface- that is interface or base class- rather than programming to their implementations –either derived or concrete classes.

As an example, try to picture a condition in which an organizations is maintaining a list of the cars its employees own. All the employees definitely have different models. In this case, how can you refer to the different car instances? The solution lies in the example below:

```
1   public class Employee {
2       private String name;
3       private Car car;
4
5       // standard constructor
6   }
```

Since all the Car derived classes inherit the type 'Car', the class instances that are derived can be referred with a variable of class 'Car'.

```
1   Employee e1 = new Employee("Shreya", new ArmoredCar());
2   Employee e2 = new Employee("Paul", new SpaceCar());
3   Employee e3 = new Employee("Pavni", new BMW());
```

Encapsulation In Java

Encapsulation refers to the ability to package related behavior in an object bundle and control or restrict their access in both function and data from other objects. It essentially is all about packaging related stuff together and keeping them away from external elements. You will note that keywords encapsulation along with data hiding are used interchangeably all over. You should not misunderstand that encapsulation is only about data hiding. When you say encapsulation, you should emphasize on grouping, packaging or even bundling related data as well as behavior together.

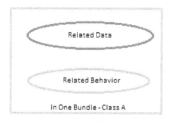

When you assign a class in object oriented programming, it is said that the first principle you should consider is encapsulation. Group the associated data and its behavior in a bucket. The main benefit of encapsulation is maintainability. Believe it all or not, that's pretty much it when it comes to encapsulation! You can leave it as simple as that with nothing more or less.

Java Encapsulation

Any Java class that is well defined in its context domain is a good example for Java encapsulation. Thus, the essence here is basically for bundling methods and data together only after this data hiding is highlighted. The term data hiding in this case relates to the access specifiers in Java. It is easier to hide an attribute or method from the outer word by using the access specifier 'private'. Therefore, hiding is quite plain and simple. But how about bundling method and data? This in particular is important. You have to understand well the business domain and design the class and group attributes, as well as its methods together based on that. This process is vital in encapsulation. Take the Java encapsulation outline example below. When you talk about an animal, you should have all its attributes listed as well as its behavior such as how it will run, mate, hunt and so forth. When you bundle all these behavior and data in one class, you are essentially following the principles of encapsulation.

```java
package com.javapapers.java;

public class Animal {
    private String animalName;
    private String animalType;
    private int height;
    private String color;

    public Animal(String animalName, String animalType) {
        this.animalName = animalName;
        this.animalType = animalType;
    }

    public void hunt() {
        // implementation of hunt
    }

    public void run() {
        // implementation of run
    }

    public void mate() {
        // implementation of mate
    }
    //encapsulation is not about having getter/setters
    public String getAnimalName() {

        return animalName;
    }

    public void setAnimalName(String animalName) {
        this.animalName = animalName;
    }

    public String getAnimalType() {
        return animalType;
    }

    public void setAnimalType(String animalType) {
        this.animalType = animalType;
    }
```

NOTE: there is a line of difference between encapsulation and abstraction. You'll understand that easily with a simple example and the next tutorial on abstraction will give you a better insight into that. Just make sure to practice encapsulation as you design the classes.

Abstraction In Java

Abstraction is the situation where you hide the implementation details and only show the functionality; in Java, abstraction is achieved by use of interface and abstract class. Interface will give you 100% abstraction and the abstract will offer you 0-100% abstraction.

When you are in the streets and spot a nice vehicle on the road, you only get to see the entire picture; the car is only a single unit. You don't see the core of it: the complex mechanical engineering behind it.

Now imagine yourself going to a showroom to purchase a car. What are you seeing now? You are seeing a powerful engine, four wheels, and the steering wheel and so on. You can now see the car for what it really is- at its high components. But even so, we have so much inside it that gives the car its completeness. Now imagine you are the mechanic who's going to service the vehicle, you'll get to see it one more level deeper with another level of information.

When you design software, you need to take the context. In the example above, you ask the question as to whether you are designing the software for casual onlookers, purchasers or mechanics. In this regard, the abstraction levels is applied accordingly on the design.

Abstraction in Object Oriented Programming

Generally speaking, the software language itself is a good example for the concept of abstraction. When you write a statement in the following way:

340

a=b+c

You are adding two values that are stored in 2 different locations then moving ahead to store the product in a brand new location. You just describe it in a form that easily understandable by human beings. What goes on beneath? We have instruction sets, registers, program counters, storage units and so forth involved. We have POP, PUSH taking place. High level language that we use tends to abstract these complex details.

When we talk of abstraction in Java, we mean abstraction in OOP and the way it's done in Java. Abstraction begins the moment a class begins getting conceived. I cannot really say that restricting the properties of a given object using Java access modifiers can be termed as abstraction, as there is a lot more to it. You will find abstraction being used often in object oriented programming and in software.

Abstraction And Encapsulation

When a class becomes conceptualized, what are the properties you can have in it based on the context? If you want to design a class called animal and the context is zoo, you need to have an attribute as animalType to define wild or domestic. This attribute may not make much sense when you are designing the class in another context.

In the same way, ask yourself what behavior you are going to have in the class. Abstraction is applied here as well. What is important to have is different from what will be an overdose. Cut off some of the information off from the class, and this process is using or applying abstraction.

When asked for the difference between encapsulation and abstraction, you can say that encapsulation applies abstraction just as a concept. Therefore, it is just encapsulation. But abstraction is a concept that is even applied as part of polymorphism (discussed later) and inheritance. You need to look at abstraction at a higher level among the other concepts of object oriented programming including polymorphism, inheritance and encapsulation.

Abstraction And Inheritance

Let's try to take inheritance in this discussion as well. When you are designing the hierarchy of classes, you apply abstraction and then create many layers between the hierarchies. Let's take a first level class cell as an example; next level will be LivingBeing and animal will be the next after that. The hierarchy you create here based on the context, which you are programming for uses abstraction itself. Now for each level, what exactly are the properties and behaviors that you are going to have? Abstraction also plays a very important role here in determining that. What are the common properties that can be exposed to a higher level in order for the lower level classes to inherit from it? Some properties don't need to be kept at higher level. This process of decision making is nothing but using abstraction to have different hierarchy layers.

Now that you read the short section, you should now have an idea about the way abstraction is done in Java.
- When you conceptualize classes
- When you write interfaces
- When you write abstract class methods
- When you write extends
- When you apply modifiers such as 'private', ...

You use abstraction as a concept in the areas identified above.

Polymorphism In Java

Polymorphism in its literal sense refers to a state of having many shapes or the ability to take on various forms. When it is used in an object oriented programming language such as Java, it describes the ability of the language to process objects of various classes and types through a uniform and single interface.

Polymorphism takes on two types: Runtime polymorphism and static binding (also known as compile time polymorphism). The former entails method overloading as an example while the latter is contained in dynamic polymorphism. Perhaps you need to note that polymorphism entails a very important example, which is how a parent class refers to a child class object. As a matter of fact, any object satisfying more than a single IS-A relationship is by nature polymorphic. As an example, we can consider the class *animal* and let one of its subclasses be *cat*. Therefore, any cat is an animal. The cat in this case satisfies the IS-A relationship for its own type and also its super class 'animal'. You also need to note that it is very legal to state that every object in Java is by nature polymorphic because each one of them passes the IS-A test for itself as well as that for the 'object' class.

Static Polymorphism

When it comes to Java language, we achieve static polymorphism through something called method overloading. Method overloading simply means that there are a number of methods available in a class that have the same name but different types or order or number of parameters.

Java knows, at compile time, the kind of method to invoke by looking at the method signatures. Therefore, this is known as static binding or the compile time polymorphism. Let the following example make this concept clearer for you:

```
class DemoOverload{

  public int add(int x, int y){ //method 1

  return x+y;

  }

  public int add(int x, int y, int z){ //method 2

  return x+y+z;

  }

  public int add(double x, int y){ //method 3

  return (int)x+y;

  }

  public int add(int x, double y){ //method 4

  return x+(int)y;

  }

}

class Test{

  public static void main(String[] args){

  DemoOverload demo=new DemoOverload();

  System.out.println(demo.add(2,3));     //method 1 called

  System.out.println(demo.add(2,3,4));   //method 2 called

  System.out.println(demo.add(2,3.4));   //method 4 called

  System.out.println(demo.add(2.5,3));   //method 3 called

  }

}
```

In the example above, we have four forms of 'add' methods. The first one takes two parameters and the second one takes three of them. The 3rd and 4th methods provide for a change of order of the parameters. The compiler usually checks the method signature after which it make a decision on which method to be invoked when compile time comes for a certain method call.

Dynamic Polymorphism

Imagine you have a sub class that is overriding a certain method of the super class. Imagine, you have, in the program, an object of the sub class created and have it assigned to the super class reference. In this case, if you call the overridden method on the reference of the super class, it means that the sub class version of the method will be called as a result. Take a look at the example below:

```
class Vehicle{

  public void move(){

  System.out.println("Vehicles can move!!");

  }

}

class MotorBike extends Vehicle{

  public void move(){

  System.out.println("MotorBike can move and accelerate too!!");

  }

}

class Test{

  public static void main(String[] args){

  Vehicle vh=new MotorBike();

  vh.move();   // prints MotorBike can move and accelerate too!!

  vh=new Vehicle();

  vh.move();   // prints Vehicles can move!!

  }

}
```

You need to note that in your first call to 'move()', the reference type is 'vehicle' while 'Motorbike' is the object being referenced. In this case, when you make a call to 'move()', the program will wait until it is runtime to determine the object that the reference is pointing to. In our case here, the object is of the 'MotorBike' class. Therefore the 'move()' method if the class 'MotorBike' will be called. The second call to 'move()' has the class 'vehicle' as its object. Therefore, the method 'move()' of the 'vehicle' will get called.

Note that at runtime, when the method to call is determined, this is referred to as late binding or dynamic binding.

As a recap, by now you should know that:

• In Java, an object that passes multiple IS-A tests is automatically polymorphic by nature

• In Java, all objects pass a minimum of two IS-A tests- that is one for the object class and one for itself

• In Java, static polymorphism is done through method overloading

• In Java, Dynamic polymorphism is attained through method overriding.

We discussed the concept of inheritance, which is undeniably a powerful mechanism when it comes to reusing code, improving the general organization of object oriented system and minimizing data redundancy. Inheritance is ideal when the classes are related to each other whereby the child class is essentially a parent class. For instance, a 'Car' is a 'vehicle' and as such, the class 'car' contains all the properties or features of the 'vehicle' class apart from its very own features. Nonetheless, you cannot always be having *is a* relationship in between object that are of different classes. Let's say with an example that 'a car isn't some kind of an engine'. You have an alternative referred to as composition to represent such a relationship. It is applied when the classes are related to each other in which the parent class is contained in the child class.

Composition basically makes a class reuse the functionality by making a reference to the class object that it wants to use- which is nothing like inheritance where a sub class extends the super class' functionality. For instance, a door has a button, a zoo has a lion, a car has an engine.

Composition is a special case of aggregation- this means that a restricted aggregation is known as composition. When an object has the other one (object) and the object that is contained does not exist without the other object, we can call that composition.

An example using a program

We'll consider a program that shows the concept of composition below. Follow the steps as indicated:

Step#1

We begin by creating a class 'Bike' which you can declare and define the data members and methods as follows:

```
class Bike
{

// declaring data members and methods

private String color;

private int wheels;

public void bikeFeatures()

{

  System.out.println("Bike Color= "+color + " wheels= " + wheels);

}

public void setColor(String color)

{

  this.color = color;

}

public void setwheels(int wheels)

{

  this.wheels = wheels;

}

}
```

Step#2

Now create a class called 'Honda' that extends the 'Bike' class above. In this case, 'Honda' class uses the 'HondaEngine' class, object 'start()' method via composition. You can now say that class 'Honda' has-a 'hondaEngine':

```
class Honda extends Bike
{
  //inherits all properties of bike class
  public void setStart()
  {
    HondaEngine e = new HondaEngine();
    e.start();
  }
}
```

Step# 3

Next, you have to create a class 'HondaEngine' through which we'll use the class object in the 'Honda' class above:

```
class HondaEngine
{
  public void start()
  {
    System.out.println("Engine has been started.");
  }
  public void stop()
  {
    System.out.println("Engine has been stopped.");
  }
}
```

Step#4

Now we have to build a class 'CompositionDemo' whereby we make a Honda class object and initialize it as follows:

```
class CompositionDemo

{

  public static void main(String[] args)

  {

    Honda h = new Honda();

    h.setColor("Black");

    h.setwheels(2);

    h.bikeFeatures();

    h.setStart();

  }

}
```

The output is as follows:

Bike color= Black   wheels= 2

Engine has been started

So what is the importance of composition?

You can be able to control other objects' visibility to client classes in composition and only reuse what you need.

Composition lets you create back-end class when it is required.

How Does Composition And Inheritance Compare?

My assumption is that you know how inheritance as well as composition compare, and want to know which one is the best to choose.

It is easier to change the back-end class' (or composition's) interface than a superclass (or inheritance). As illustrated in the previous example, changing the interface of a back-end class makes a change necessary to the front-end class interface provided that front-end interface stays the same. Conversely, changing the interface of a superclass can't just ripple down the hierarchy of inheritance to subclasses, but could as well ripple out to code, which only uses the interface of the subclass.

You'll also find it simpler to change the interface of the front-end composition/class compared to an inheritance or subclass. The same way superclasses are fragile, they can also be rigid. You cannot just change the interface of subclass without ensuring the new interface of the subclass is compatible with its super type. For instance, you cannot add a method that has the same signature to a subclass and yet it (the method) has a different return type as a method that is inherited from a superclass. On the other hand, composition lets you change the front-end-class' interface without affecting the back-end classes.

Composition lets you slow down the making of back-end objects unless and until they are required, and also altering the back-end objects throughout the front-end object's lifetime dynamically. Inheritance allows you to get the superclass' image in the object image of your subclass once the subclass is built, and it stays part of the subclass object throughout the subclass' lifetime.

You'd find it simpler to add a new subclass or inheritance that you'd find it to add new front-end classes or composition simply because inheritance has polymorphism. If you've got some code that depends on the interface of a superclass, the code can operate with a new subclass without changing. When it comes to composition, that is not true unless you are using composition with interfaces. When used together, composition and interfaces make very good design tools.

The explicit delegation or method-invocation forwarding composition approach will have a good performance cost often compared to the single invocation (in inheritance) of a superclass method implementation that has been inherited. Often here means that the performance entirely depends on many factors one of which includes how the Java virtual machine optimizes the program in the process of executing it. With both inheritance and composition, altering the implementation of any class (and not the interface) is simple. The implementation change's ripple effect stay within the same class.

Selecting Between Inheritance And Composition

How do the comparisons between inheritance and composition assist in your design? The following are a few guidelines reflecting how I typically choose between inheritance and composition.

Ensure the inheritance models the relationship 'is-a'

The main guiding philosophy is that you should only use inheritance when a subclass *is a* super class. For instance, an orange likely *is-a* fruit, thus, I would most likely go with inheritance.

A good question you need to ask yourself when you think you have 'is-a' relationship is definitely whether the 'is-a' relationship is constant throughout the application's lifetime and, perhaps when lucky, the code's lifecycle. For instance, you could think that 'employee' is a 'person' when essentially, the term 'employee' denotes a role a 'person' plays only during a given period of time. What if the person is fired? What if he is a 'supervisor' as well as an 'employee'? When dealing with impermanent is-a relationships like these, you should consider that they have to be modelled with composition.

Do not just use inheritance to get code reuse

If you want to reuse code and that's all, and also there is no 'is-a' that you can see, you can use composition.

Do not use inheritance if all you want is to get at polymorphism

When polymorphism is all you want, and there isn't any natural 'is-a' relationship, you just use composition with interfaces.

Now, let's see how we can implement all we've learned in a simple project of building a game in the next chapter:

Build A Simple Game With Java

The following guide will show you how you can make your own game in a simple step-by-step manner.

Before you begin, you need to install a program known as Java processing that is useful in building applications like the one we are going to build today. Just to explain a bit what it is, processing is open source and creates animations, interactive programs, drawings using basic syntax. It also includes the basic IDE that works as the interface for your programming. With Processing, you are able to create an extra abstraction to sort of mask particular Java's programmatic elements that an average beginner would deem difficult.

NOTE: abstraction lets you perform stuff with more ease especially when you don't have much background knowledge on the subject. If you were to build or process images in plain Java, you'd have a really painful headache.

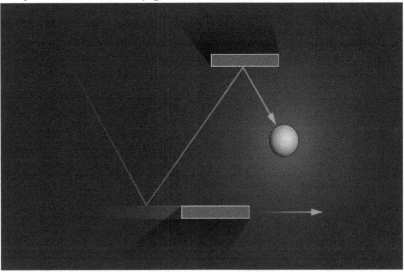

The game we are about to build in this section is some kind of combination of Pong, Flappy bird and brick breaker. I picked this game particularly because it entails simple concepts and works to bring sense to others, which have been giving beginners a problem with regards to game development. You need to note that it is very difficult, first of all, to make complex games like platform games that have multiple levels, entities, players and so on. As we continue, you will see the way the code gets complicated really fast but the good thing is that it is generally well organized and simple. Just follow the piece slowly, making reference to areas in the book for concepts that need clarity, grab the entire code and play with it on your own as you begin pondering about your game soonest possible, and begin to implement it. Let's begin with the basics.

How To Build Flappy Pong
Initialize the different screens

We'll begin by initializing the project. First of all, we'll write the setup and draw blocks as anybody would normally do- so nothing new or fancy here! After that, we'll handle the various screens- these include the game screen, initial screen, game over screen and so forth. The question may arise though: how do you ensure the right page is shown at the right time?

It is quite simple to accomplish this task. We'll have a global variable storing the information of the screen that is active at the current time. We'll then draw contents of the right screen- this however depends on the variable. In the draw block, we'll include an 'if statement' which basically checks the variable and then presents the screen contents accordingly. Each time you want to change the screen, we'll change the variable to the screen you'll have to change the variable to the identifier you want displayed. That said, let's have an overview of how your skeleton code is:

```
/********* VARIABLES *********/

// We control which screen is active by settings / updating
// gameScreen variable. We display the correct screen according
// to the value of this variable.
//
// 0: Initial Screen
// 1: Game Screen
// 2: Game-over Screen

int gameScreen = 0;

/********* SETUP BLOCK *********/

void setup() {
  size(500, 500);
}



/********* DRAW BLOCK *********/

void draw() {
  // Display the contents of the current screen
  if (gameScreen == 0) {
    initScreen();
  } else if (gameScreen == 1) {
    gameScreen();
  } else if (gameScreen == 2) {
    gameOverScreen();
  }
}


/********* SCREEN CONTENTS *********/

void initScreen() {
```

Indeed, that may appear scary in the beginning but all I've done is create the basic structure and separate the different sections with comment blocks. As you can see, for every screen to display, we define a distinct method. In your draw block, you simply check the value of your variable 'gameScreen' before calling the corresponding method. When it comes to the part 'void mousepressed() {...}', you are basically listening to mouse clicks and in case the active screen is 0- the initial screen- you call the method 'startGame ()' which then begins the game as you would expect. This method's initial line changes the variable 'gameScreen' to 1—the game screen. When you understand this, the next thing you have to do is implement your initial screen. You will be editing the method 'initScreen ()' to do that. It goes like this:

```
void initScreen() {

  background(0);

  textAlign(CENTER);

  text("Click to start", height/2, width/2);

}
```

The initial screen now has a black background and a simple text reading 'click to start' that is right in the middle and aligned to the center. Nonetheless, when you click, nothing happens. You have not yet specified any yet for your game screen, the 'gameScreen ()' method does not have anything in it- which means that you are not covering the earlier contents drawn from the previous screen – which is the text- by having the first line of draw being 'background ()'. This is exactly why the text is still there, even though the line 'text ()' is no longer being called. For the same reason, the background is still black. We'll go ahead and start implementing the game screen.

```
void gameScreen() {

background(255);

}
```

Once you complete this change, you'll notice the background turning white and the text disappearing.

Create the ball and implement gravity

We'll now begin operating on the game screen. We'll start by creating our ball. Right now, you have to define variables for its color, coordinates and size since you might want to change these values sometime later. For example, if you want to increase the ball's size as the player scores more so that the game is more difficult, you'll need to alter its size, so it has to be a variable. You'll define the ball's speed as well, once you implement gravity. Begin by adding the code below:

```
...
int ballX, ballY;
int ballSize = 20;
int ballColor = color(0);
...
void setup() {
...
ballX=width/4;
ballY=height/5;
}
...
void gameScreen() {
...
drawBall();
}
...
void drawBall() {
fill(ballColor);
ellipse(ballX, ballY, ballSize, ballSize);
}
```

We have the coordinates defined as global variables, built a method that draw the ball, caked from the method 'gameScreen' but we had them defined in 'setup()'. The main reason for doing that is so that the ball starts from the left by one fourth and from the top by one fifth. I cannot give a particular reason as to why I want that but generally, that is a great point for the ball to start. Therefore, we needed to have the 'height' and 'width' dynamically on the sketch. 'setup ()' defined the size of the sketch, right after the first line. The 'height' and 'width' aren't set before the running of 'setup ()' and that is why you could not do this if you defined the variables on top. **Gravity.** On to the easy part: let's use a few tricks to implement the gravity- the following comprises the implementation first.

```
...
float gravity = 1;
float ballSpeedVert = 0;
...
void gameScreen() {
  ...
  applyGravity();
  keepInScreen();
}
...
void applyGravity() {
  ballSpeedVert += gravity;
  ballY += ballSpeedVert;
}
void makeBounceBottom(float surface) {
  ballY = surface-(ballSize/2);
  ballSpeedVert*=-1;
}
void makeBounceTop(float surface) {
  ballY = surface+(ballSize/2);
  ballSpeedVert*=-1;
}
// keep ball in the screen
void keepInScreen() {
  // ball hits floor
  if (ballY+(ballSize/2) > height) {
    makeBounceBottom(height);
  }
  // ball hits ceiling
  if (ballY-(ballSize/2) < 0) {
    makeBounceTop(0);
  }
}
```

Click here to see the expected result.

I'm sure you might be wondering whether your understanding of physics is being threatened. I know in real life, that's not how gravity works. Consider this to be simply an animation process. "Gravity", the variable, is only a numeric value- just a 'float' which makes it possible to use decimal values and not only integers- which, on every loop, we add to 'ballSpeedVert'. Actually, ballSpeedVert refers to the ball's vertical speed, which goes to the ball's Y coordinate (bally) on all the loops. You watch the ball's coordinates to ensure it remains in the screen and that if you don't (as you may know already), the ball will only fall to infinity. For now though, the ball is moving in a vertical direction only. This means that we watch the boundaries of the floor and ceiling in the screen. With method 'keepInScreen ()', we check whether 'bally' or + the radius is less than 'height' and in the same way, 'bally' or – the radius is higher than 0. In case the conditions don't meet, you get the ball to bounce (right from the bottom or top) using the methods: 'makeBounceTop ()' and 'makeBounceBottom ()'. We can have the ball move to the very location where it had to bounce and then get the product of vertical speed or 'ballSpeedVert' and -1 (note that the sign changes when you multiply with -1). when the speed value gets a – sign, it means that when you add the Y coordinate, the speed will then become bally–ballSpeedVert that's obtained from bally+(-ballSpeedVert). In this case, the ball changes its direction with that same speed immediately. Now, as you include 'gravity' to 'ballSpeedVert' and it has a negative value, it will begin getting close to 0, and eventually becoming 0 and then beginning to increase once more. This will make the ball to rise, then rise slower, stop and then begin falling.

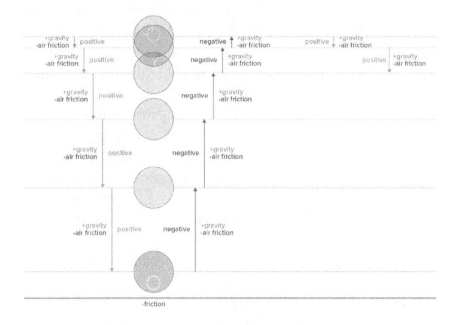

If you are keen enough, you'd notice that our animation process has a problem- the ball does not stop bouncing. If we used a real-world scenario to look at it, we'd say that the ball would face friction and air resistance each time it came into contact with a surface. That is exactly the behavior we want the animation process to have. Implementing that is pretty easy. Just add the code below:

```
...
float airfriction = 0.0001;
float friction = 0.1;
...
void applyGravity() {
  ...
  ballSpeedVert -= (ballSpeedVert * airfriction);
}
void makeBounceBottom(int surface) {
  ...
  ballSpeedVert -= (ballSpeedVert * friction);
}
void makeBounceTop(int surface) {
  ...
  ballSpeedVert -= (ballSpeedVert * friction);
}
```

The animation process will produce something like this.

'Friction', as the name suggests, refers to the surface friction; 'airfriction' on the other hand refers to friction of air. Obviously therefore, 'friction' needs to apply each time the ball comes in contact with any surface. Therefore, that is exactly what we did. The method 'applygravity ()' runs on every loop, you thus take away 0.0001 percent of its present value from ballSpeedVert on all loops. The methods 'makeBounceTop ()' and makeBounceBottom () run when the ball comes in contact with any surface. Therefore, we did the same thing in those method, only that we used 'friction' this time.

Now create the racket

You'll now require a racket which the ball will bounce on. You should also be able to control the racket. We'll make it controllable with a mouse. The code for that is as follows:

```
...
color racketColor = color(o);
float racketWidth = 100;
float racketHeight = 10;
...
void gameScreen() {
  ...
  drawRacket();
  ...
}
...
void drawRacket(){
  fill(racketColor);
  rectMode(CENTER);
  rect(mouseX, mouseY, racketWidth, racketHeight);
}
```

We defined the racket's width, height and color as a global variable. You might want to see them change during the game. We implemented the 'drawRacket ()' method, which does exactly what its name suggests. You have to set 'rectMode' to center so that the racket gets aligned to your cursor's center. Having created the racket, the next thing is making the ball bounce on it.

```
...
int racketBounceRate = 20;

...
void gameScreen() {

  ...
  watchRacketBounce();

  ...
}

...
void watchRacketBounce() {
  float overhead = mouseY - pmouseY;
  if ((ballX+(ballSize/2) > mouseX-(racketWidth/2)) && (ballX-(ballSize/2) <
  mouseX+(racketWidth/2))) {
    if (dist(ballX, ballY, ballX, mouseY)<=(ballSize/2)+abs(overhead)) {
      makeBounceBottom(mouseY);
      // racket moving up
      if (overhead<0) {
        ballY+=overhead;
        ballSpeedVert+=overhead;
      }
    }
  }
}
```

Click here for the result:

So, 'watchRacketBounce ()' ensures the racket and the ball collide. You need to check whether the ball and racket lined up horizontally and vertically. The initial if statement checks to see whether the X coordinate on the ball's right side is more than that on its left and vice versa. In case it is, the second statement will check whether the distance between the ball and the racket is equal or smaller than the ball's radius. If this conditions therefore meet, the method 'makeBounceBottom ()' is called and the ball bounces on the racket.

The variables 'pmouseY' and 'pmouseX' store the mouse coordinates at the previous frame. Since the mouse is able to move really fast, it is possible you might not detect the distance between the racket and the ball right between the frames in case the mouse is moving quickly enough towards the ball. Therefore, we take the difference of the coordinates of the mouse between the frames and consider that while detecting the distance. The quicker the mouse moves, the more distance is tolerable.

You also have to use 'overhead' for some other reason. We detect the path the mouse is moving my looking at the 'overhead' sign. If it's negative, it means the mouse was underneath in the last frame, which means the racket is going upwards. You want to increase the ball speed and a bit further than the regular bounce in order to stimulate the impact of hitting the ball using the racket. In case 'overhead' is below 0, you've got to add it to bally and also ballSpeedVert to have the ball move faster, higher. Thus, the faster the ball is hit by the racket the faster and higher it moves.

Moving horizontally and controlling the ball
We'll add horizontal movement to the ball here and then make it possible to control it horizontally using the racket.

```
...
// we will start with 0, but for we give 10 just for testing
float ballSpeedHorizon = 10;
...
void gameScreen() {
  ...
  applyHorizontalSpeed();
  ...
}
...
void applyHorizontalSpeed(){
  ballX += ballSpeedHorizon;
  ballSpeedHorizon -= (ballSpeedHorizon * airfriction);
}
void makeBounceLeft(float surface){
  ballX = surface+(ballSize/2);
  ballSpeedHorizon*=-1;
  ballSpeedHorizon -= (ballSpeedHorizon * friction);
}
void makeBounceRight(float surface){
  ballX = surface-(ballSize/2);
  ballSpeedHorizon*=-1;
  ballSpeedHorizon -= (ballSpeedHorizon * friction);
}
...
void keepInScreen() {
  ...
  if (ballX-(ballSize/2) < 0){
    makeBounceLeft(0);
  }
  if (ballX+(ballSize/2) > width){
    makeBounceRight(width);
  }
```

Check the result here.

The idea is the same as that in the vertical movement. We created 'ballSpeedHorizon', a horizontal speed variable. We then created ballSpeedHorizon, a horizontal speed variable and also made a method that applies the horizontal speed to the ballx while removing air friction. Also, we added another two if statements to the method 'keepInScreen ()' that is meant to watch the ball for hitting the right and left screen edges. Lastly, we made sure the bounces from left to right are handled with methods 'makeBounceRight ()' and 'makeBounceLeft ()'.

Having added horizontal space to the game, the next thing is controlling the ball using the racket. The ball needs to move right based on the point on the racket that it hits. The racket edges should give it more horizontal speed:

```
void watchRacketBounce() {

  ...

  if ((ballX+(ballSize/2) > mouseX-(racketWidth/2)) && (ballX-(ballSize/2) <
  mouseX+(racketWidth/2))) {
    if (dist(ballX, ballY, ballX, mouseY)<=(ballSize/2)+abs(overhead)) {

      ...

      ballSpeedHorizon = (ballX - mouseX)/5;

      ...

    }
  }
}
```

Here's the result.

What you did is determine the distance of the point the ball hits from the racket's middle using 'ballX-mouseX'. We then make it the horizontal speed. The difference isn't that much- I figured one tenth of the value is ideally natural.

Create the walls

We'll now add walls that move towards the left.

```
...
int wallSpeed = 5;
int wallInterval = 1000;
float lastAddTime = 0;
int minGapHeight = 200;
int maxGapHeight = 300;
int wallWidth = 80;
color wallColors = color(0);
// This arraylist stores data of the gaps between the walls. Actuals walls are draw
accordingly.
// [gapWallX, gapWallY, gapWallWidth, gapWallHeight]
ArrayList<int[]> walls = new ArrayList<int[]>();
...
void gameScreen() {
  ...
 wallAdder();
 wallHandler();
}
...
void wallAdder() {
 if (millis()-lastAddTime > wallInterval) {
   int randHeight = round(random(minGapHeight, maxGapHeight));
   int randY = round(random(0, height-randHeight));
   // {gapWallX, gapWallY, gapWallWidth, gapWallHeight}
   int[] randWall = {width, randY, wallWidth, randHeight};
   walls.add(randWall);
   lastAddTime = millis();
 }
}
```

```
void wallHandler() {
  for (int i = 0; i < walls.size(); i++) {
    wallRemover(i);
    wallMover(i);
    wallDrawer(i);
  }
}
void wallDrawer(int index) {
  int[] wall = walls.get(index);
  // get gap wall settings
  int gapWallX = wall[0];
  int gapWallY = wall[1];
  int gapWallWidth = wall[2];
  int gapWallHeight = wall[3];
  // draw actual walls
  rectMode(CORNER);
  fill(wallColors);
  rect(gapWallX, 0, gapWallWidth, gapWallY);
  rect(gapWallX, gapWallY+gapWallHeight, gapWallWidth, height-
  (gapWallY+gapWallHeight));
}
void wallMover(int index) {
  int[] wall = walls.get(index);
  wall[0] -= wallSpeed;
}
void wallRemover(int index) {
  int[] wall = walls.get(index);
  if (wall[0]+wall[2] <= 0) {
    walls.remove(index);
  }
}
```

This is the result.

The first thing you need to note is the 'ArrayList', which is simply an implementation of the list and behaves like an Array. It however is resizable and contains great methods such as list.remove (index), list.add (index) and list.get (index). We store the wall data as arrays of integers inside the arraylist. The data we store in the arrays is meant for the gap in between 2 walls. Our arrays have these values:

[gap wall X, gap wall Y, gap wall width, gap wall height]

The actual walls are drawn according to the values of the gap wall. You need to note that these can be handled cleaner and better with classes. This is however how we'll handle it: we've got two base methods for management of the walls: wallHandler and wallHandler (). The latter adds to the arraylist new walls per wallInterval millisecond. We've got a global variable 'lastAddTime' that stores the last wall you added. In case the present millisecond millis () deducting the last millisecond added —lastAddTime- is bigger than the interval value —wallInterval- this essentially means that you have to add a new wall. Random gap variables then get generated according to the global variables defined at the top. A mew wall is then added into the arraylist and 'lastAddTime' set to the current millis (). The wallHandler () loops through the current walls that's in the arraylist and calls wallRemover (i), wallDrawer (i) and wallMover (i) for each item by the index value of the arraylist.

The wallDrawer draws the walls according to the gap wall data. The wallDrawer will usually grab the wall data array from arraylist before it can call the method 'rect ()' for drawing the walls to where they need to be. The wallMover takes the element right from the arraylist and alters its X location according to the 'wallSpeed' global variable. The wallRemover gets the walls off the arraylist, which are out of the screen.

371

When a wall is thus removed from arraylist, this eliminates it from being drawn in all the following loops. We now have to detect any collisions between the walls and the balls:

```java
void wallHandler() {
  for (int i = 0; i < walls.size(); i++) {
    ...
    watchWallCollision(i);
  }
}
...
void watchWallCollision(int index) {
  int[] wall = walls.get(index);
  // get gap wall settings
  int gapWallX = wall[0];
  int gapWallY = wall[1];
  int gapWallWidth = wall[2];
  int gapWallHeight = wall[3];
  int wallTopX = gapWallX;
  int wallTopY = 0;
  int wallTopWidth = gapWallWidth;
  int wallTopHeight = gapWallY;
  int wallBottomX = gapWallX;
  int wallBottomY = gapWallY+gapWallHeight;
  int wallBottomWidth = gapWallWidth;
  int wallBottomHeight = height-(gapWallY+gapWallHeight);

  if (
    (ballX+(ballSize/2)>wallTopX) &&
    (ballX-(ballSize/2)<wallTopX+wallTopWidth) &&
    (ballY+(ballSize/2)>wallTopY) &&
    (ballY-(ballSize/2)<wallTopY+wallTopHeight)
  ) {
    // collides with upper wall
  }

  if (
    (ballX+(ballSize/2)>wallBottomX) &&
```

The method 'hWallCollision ()' is called for every wall on all the loops. You get the coordinates of the gap wall and calculate the actual walls' coordinates (from top to bottom) and then check whether the ball's coordinates are colliding with the walls.

Health and score

I don't know about you but I think we should have a health bar on top. When the ball touches the walls, it should lose health. This logic however doesn't make sense to have the ball bouncing back from the walls. When the health is 0, the game should end.

```
int maxHealth = 100;
float health = 100;
float healthDecrease = 1;
int healthBarWidth = 60;
...
void gameScreen() {
  ...
  drawHealthBar();
  ...
}
...
void drawHealthBar() {
  // Make it borderless:
  noStroke();
  fill(236, 240, 241);
  rectMode(CORNER);
  rect(ballX-(healthBarWidth/2), ballY - 30, healthBarWidth, 5);
  if (health > 60) {
    fill(46, 204, 113);
  } else if (health > 30) {
    fill(230, 126, 34);
  } else {
    fill(231, 76, 60);
  }
  rectMode(CORNER);
  rect(ballX-(healthBarWidth/2), ballY - 30, healthBarWidth*(health/maxHealth), 5);
}
void decreaseHealth(){
  health -= healthDecrease;
  if (health <= 0){
    gameOver();
  }
}
```

The simple run is right here.

We made 'health', a global variable and then the method 'drawHealthBar ()' to draw two rectangles over the ball. The first one is the base health bar and the other one is the active one that displays the current health. The width of the second one is pretty dynamic and the formula healthBarWidth*(health/maxHealth) calculates it, the current health's ratio with respect to the health bar's width. The fill colors are now set based on the value of the health. Now for the scores:

```
...
void gameOverScreen() {
  background(0);
  textAlign(CENTER);
  fill(255);
  textSize(30);
  text("Game Over", height/2, width/2 - 20);
  textSize(15);
  text("Click to Restart", height/2, width/2 + 10);
}
...
void wallAdder() {
  if (millis()-lastAddTime > wallInterval) {
    ...
    // added another value at the end of the array
    int[] randWall = {width, randY, wallWidth, randHeight, 0};
    ...
  }
}
void watchWallCollision(int index) {
  ...
  int wallScored = wall[4];
  ...
```

```
if (ballX > gapWallX+(gapWallWidth/2) && wallScored==0) {
  wallScored=1;
  wall[4]=1;
  score();
 }
}
void score() {
  score++;
}
void printScore(){
  textAlign(CENTER);
  fill(0);
  textSize(30);
  text(score, height/2, 50);
}
```

We need to score whenever our ball passes through the wall. We also need to create a maximum of 1 score per wall. This means that in case the ball passes a wall and then goes back to pass it again, there shouldn't be another added score. To do that, we included another variable to the gap wall array inside the arraylist. The new variable will store 0 in case the ball did not pass that wall yet and a 1 in case it did. Then, we made a modification to the method 'watchWallCollision ()'. We included a condition which fires method 'score ()' and marks the wall as having been passed in the instance the ball passes a wall which it hadn't passed earlier.

The last thing we now have to do is have 'click to restart' implemented over the screen. We have to have all variables we used to their first value, and then restart the game:

```
...
public void mousePressed() {

  ...
 if(gameScreen==2){
   restart();
 }
}
 ...
void restart() {
   score = 0;
   health = maxHealth;
   ballX=width/4;
   ballY=height/5;
   lastAddTime = 0;
   walls.clear();
   gameScreen = 0;
 }
```

We'll <u>now add a few colors.</u>

Success! We now have our very own flappy pong.

<u>Conclusion</u>

We have come to the end of the book. Thank you for reading and congratulations for reading until the end.

I truly hope you now have enough information about Java that you can use as a stepping stone for more learning.

If you found the book valuable, can you recommend it to others? One way to do that is to post a review on Amazon.

Thank you and good luck!

Excel 2016

A Comprehensive Beginner's Guide
to Microsoft Excel 2016

By *Timothy C. Needham*

Table of Contents

Introduction

Microsoft Excel is the spreadsheet application of the MS Office suite. It is widely used for storing, organizing, and analyzing data or information.

Every Excel file is equivalent to a workbook that is comprised of one or more worksheets. Each worksheet represents your work space which gives you further access to Excel's wide range of functions. These include data input and storage, data organization and formatting, and data analysis through calculations, table and chart plotting tools, and statistical operations, among many others.

Whether it involves tasks as simple as creating a project timeline or tracking a budget, to more complicated ones such as organizing process maps for flowcharts or even analyzing business cashflows, Excel can surely get the job done.

This e-book features a comprehensive beginner's guide to Microsoft Excel 2016, in which basic and frequently used features and functions are discussed in detail. Plus, hands-on examples are illustrated with guide photos and step-by-step procedures.

Here is a brief overview of what is in store for you:

In Chapter 1: Excel Essentials, you will be introduced to the main framework and structure of Excel—the Excel Interface and the Excel Environment, in which you will be given a general idea of what Excel can do for you. Basically, this chapter is your Excel starter pack.

Moving on, Chapter 2: The Cell will let you know more about the building blocks of an Excel worksheet—the Cell. Here, you will be taught about the basics of a cell and different cell content types. Performing fundamental functions such as inserting, cutting, copying, pasting, deleting, and formatting cell content will also be discussed.

In Chapter 3: Formulas, you will be presented with various mathematical operations that can be surprisingly performed in Excel. Gone are the days when you would still need an actual calculator to help you perform both simple and complex mathematical operations. You will be likewise taught how to incorporate these formulas into your worksheet.

Meanwhile, you will learn more of Excel's predefined formulas, known as Functions, in Chapter 4: Functions. In this chapter, you will be taught of what constitutes a function, how to formulate one, and multiple ways to insert a function into a worksheet. We have also listed some of the most common functions that you may find helpful for your daily Excel activities.

In Chapter 5: Managing Data, you will be taught how to effectively organize your data through sorting, filtering, or grouping them. You will also be presented ways on how to format your data into a table.

Lastly, you will also be instructed on how to present your data visually and graphically through charts in Chapter 6: Charts. You will also be introduced to different chart types that are readily available in Excel, to help you identify which types of charts are applicable to a given set of data.

We have also included a bonus list of common Excel keyboard shortcuts that every beginner must know. By the end of this e-book, you may have already memorized some of these shortcut keys with the help of our hands-on exercises.

Get ready to accomplish more data storing, organizing, and analyzing tasks done whether in school or at work, with these helpful Microsoft Excel 2016 lessons.

Enjoy!

Chapter 1:

Excel Essentials

The Excel Interface

By the time you already have Microsoft Excel 2016 installed into your computer, the first step is to get to know and become familiar with the Excel Interface. If you have encountered using Excel 2010 or Excel 2013 in the past, then transitioning to Excel 2016 should not be a big problem.

Similar to other MS Office applications, Excel is a comprehensive program that consists of extensive features and functions. But unlike other applications, Excel involves dealing with much intricate data such as formulas, functions, and other computations. As such, its structure and interface may seem a bit overwhelming at first.

As such, if you totally do not have any experience of using Excel, you have to first familiarize yourself with its interface, and navigate it extensively to know the specific descriptions and functions of its parts.

Upon opening Excel 2016, the Start or Welcome Screen will be displayed. Here, you are given the options to create an entirely new workbook, create a workbook based on a preset template, or access a workbook that you have recently worked on.

To start off our hands-on exercise:

Select the Blank workbook option to open and create a new Excel file.

In the future, you may also choose from any of the available templates, depending on the output you wish to generate. Some of Excel's common templates include calendars, meal planners, to-do lists, process maps, and expense logs.

After selecting **Blank workbook,** a new workbook will open, with a default "Book1" filename. You can now start navigating the Excel Interface and start familiarizing yourself with its several parts.

Here are the parts of the Excel Interface:

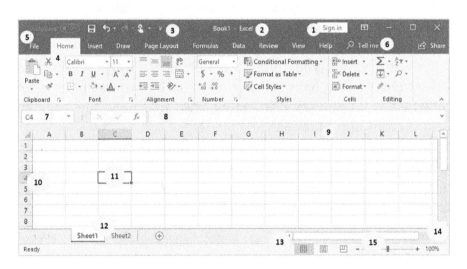

1. **Microsoft Account** – you may optionally sign in with your Microsoft ID to easily access your account and MS Office subscription information, or check your profile. If you are sharing your computer with a family member or a friend, he may also switch to his account if he wishes.

2. **Title Bar** – horizontal bar located at the top of a window. As its name denotes, this displays the filename and the application name of an open or active file.

3. **Quick Access Toolbar** – enables you to access frequently used commands that are independent of the ribbon tab currently selected. You can customize the toolbar with commands that you usually use, and change or move its location based on your work area preference.

4. **Ribbon** – set of toolbars that includes all the necessary commands in performing typical tasks in Excel. The Ribbon comprises of several tabs. Each tab is further divided into groups that contain specific commands.

5. **Backstage View** – allows you to use Excel's file management features—including, but not limited to, creating, opening, saving, and printing a new or existing document.

6. **Tell Me** – a text field wherein you can easily key in words or phrases on what you want to do next, or which commands you wish to perform.

7. **Name Box** – shows the cell address or cell name (combined column letter and row number) of an active or selected cell.

8. **Formula Bar** – here, you can enter or edit the data, formula, or function of an active or selected cell.

9. **Column** – a range of cells extending vertically on a worksheet. Columns are classified by uppercase letters. (Trivia: Excel has a 16,384-column limit).

10. **Rows** – a range of cells extending horizontally on a worksheet. Rows are classified by numbers. (Trivia: Excel has a 1,048,576-row limit).

11. **Cell** – appears as a box-like structure in a workbook. Essentially, a cell is the intersection of a row and a column in a worksheet. You may click on a cell to select it, and double-click on it to edit its data or content. An active or selected cell is enclosed in green borders.

12. **Worksheets** – represents your work space in a given Excel file. Default name for worksheets starts with "Sheet1", and so on. You may double-click the sheet name if you wish to rename it. You may also right-click the sheet name to view more options and commands.

13. **Horizontal and Vertical Scroll Bars** – enable you to navigate the worksheet from top to bottom, and from side to side. To do this, just click on the scroll bars and drag them depending on the location or destination in the worksheet that you wish to view or display.

14. **Workbook Views** – provides a shortcut access to view the worksheet in the following modes: Normal, Page Layout, or Page Break Preview.

15. **Zoom Bar/Slider** – allows you to zoom in and out of the worksheet conveniently. You may also click on the zoom percentage level to manually set or adjust your worksheet's magnification level.

The Excel Environment

Now that you are familiar with the Excel Interface, it is time to know how Excel really works, identify the various functions it can perform, and determine ways in which it can help you accomplish your tasks.

Let's start with the elements of the Excel work environment, namely: Quick Access Toolbar, Ribbon, and Backstage View.

Quick Access Toolbar

The Quick Access Toolbar provides easy and fast access to the tools or commands that you often use in an Excel session. It is located on the left side of the Title Bar, and above the Ribbon. By default, it consists of the Save, Undo, and Redo commands.

Nonetheless, you can customize this toolbar by adding or removing commands. Likewise, you can change its location by moving it below the Ribbon if you wish to make it closer to your work area.

a. Adding a Command to the Quick Access Toolbar

• Locate the Quick Access Toolbar using your mouse pointer and click the drop-down arrow found at the rightmost part of the toolbar.

• From the drop-down list, choose and click on the command you want to add to the toolbar. In this example, we have selected Open. You may click More Commands if the command you wish to add is not found in the list.

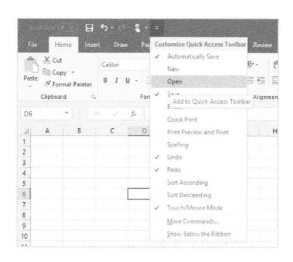

• The command (Open) will then be added to the toolbar.

b. Removing a Command from the Quick Access Toolbar

- Choose and right-click on the command (Open) you want to remove from the toolbar.
- Click Remove from Quick **Access Toolbar.**

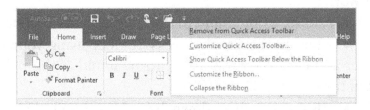

Tip: In adding or removing commands to and from the Quick Access Toolbar, you may also simply right-click anywhere on the toolbar, and click Customize **Quick Access Toolbar.**

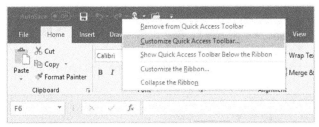

Upon clicking **Customize Quick Access Toolbar**, the **Excel Options** dialog box will appear. From here, you may select the command(s) (from the left column list) you wish to add to the toolbar, then click **Add**. Meanwhile, you may also select the command(s) (from the right column list) you wish to remove from the toolbar, then click **Remove**. Lastly, click **OK** to apply your changes.

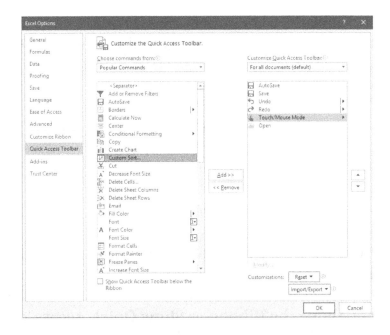

c. Moving the Quick Access Toolbar below the Ribbon

- Locate the **Quick Access Toolbar** using your mouse pointer and click the drop-down arrow found at the rightmost part of the toolbar.
- Click **Show Below the Ribbon**.

- Similarly, you can right-click anywhere on the toolbar, and click **Show Quick Access Toolbar Below the Ribbon**.

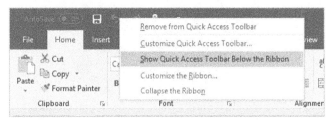

- The Quick Access Toolbar will then be moved below the Ribbon.

To move it back to its default position, repeat the step of clicking the drop-down arrow located at the rightmost part of the toolbar or right-clicking anywhere on the toolbar, then click **Show Above the Ribbon** or **Show Quick Access Toolbar Above the Ribbon**, respectively.

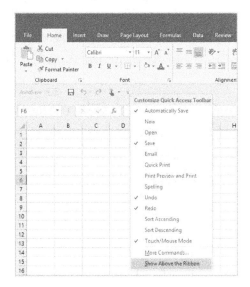

Ribbon

Majority of the tools and functions that you will use while working on a worksheet are found in the Ribbon. The Ribbon is composed of a series of command tabs. Each tab is then further divided into command groups containing specific commands that perform distinct tasks.

a. Exploring the Ribbon and its Tabs

By default, the Ribbon displays the following tabs: **Home**, **Insert**, **Draw**, **Page Layout**, **Formulas**, **Data**, **Review**, **View**, and **Help**. The Tell Me text field is also found in the Ribbon.

Each tab may contain one or more command groups. For example, the **Home** tab consists of seven (7) command groups: Clipboard, Font, Alignment, Number, Styles, Cells, and Editing. Each group further includes several commands that are designed to perform specific functions. More of these will be discussed in the succeeding chapters.

Some command groups have an expand arrow icon that you can click on, to view more options and settings.

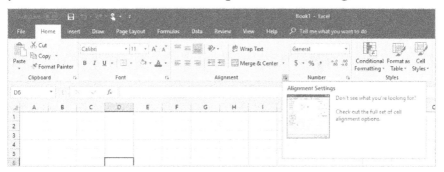

You may click on each tab to view more of the commands it includes.

Tip: You can hover your mouse pointer over any command to show the **ScreenTips.** These are small dialog boxes that briefly describe the function of a command, and/or how to perform a certain command. ScreenTips also display the keyboard shortcut keys of some commands. For starters, you may use these as guides, to further familiarize yourself with the wide selection of commands in Excel.

b. Adjusting the Ribbon Display

Just like the Quick Access Toolbar, you may also adjust the Ribbon display. To do so:

- Locate the **Ribbon Display Options** icon, found at the right side of the window, and to the left of the Minimize icon. This icon is represented by a small box with an upwards arrow inside it. Click on it to access more options.

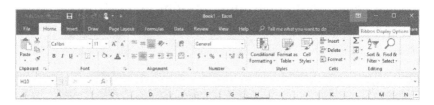

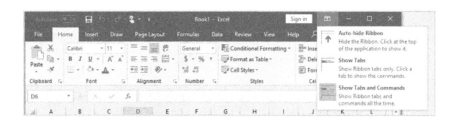

- Choose your desired display mode from the three (3) options:

  o **Auto-hide Ribbon** – presents the worksheet in a full-screen view, while hiding both the Quick Access Toolbar and the Ribbon entirely.

  o **Show Tabs** – displays the tabs only. You may click on a tab to view and display the commands under it.

Tip: You can also activate the **Show Tabs** mode by right-clicking anywhere on the Ribbon and selecting **Collapse the Ribbon**.

  o **Show Tabs and Commands** – this is the default Excel display mode, which shows all the tabs and the commands under them.

c. Customizing the Ribbon

- Right-click anywhere on the Ribbon and select **Customize the Ribbon**.

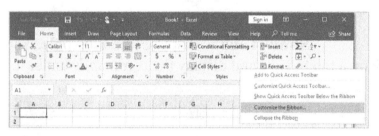

- Similar to customizing the Quick Access Toolbar, customizing the Ribbon may be done through the **Excel Options** dialog box. From here, select the command(s) (from the left column list) you wish to add to a Ribbon tab, then click **Add**. Meanwhile, select the command(s) (from the right column list) you wish to remove from a Ribbon tab, then click **Remove**. Lastly, click **OK** to apply your changes.

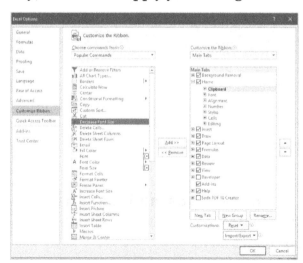

Backstage View

The Ribbon provides various commands that you can do "in" a file, such as changing font, formatting data, and inserting tables, to name a few. On the other hand, the Backstage View provides more of the commands that you can do "to" a file, including, but not limited to, creating, opening, saving, and printing a new or existing document. Essentially, the Backstage View grants you access to Excel's file management features.

The Backstage View is accessed through the **File** tab located on the upper leftmost corner of the Ribbon.

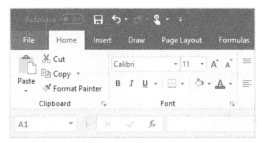

Now that you have successfully accessed the Backstage View, here are the following commands (located in the left-side navigation pane) that can help you further manage your Excel workbooks and files:

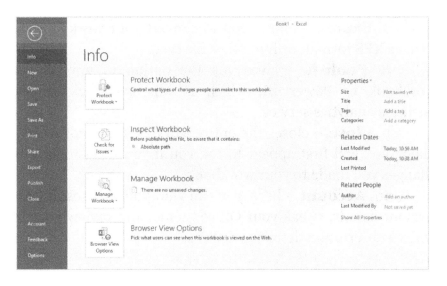

1. **Info** – displays details about the active workbook, such as file properties, related dates on when the file was created or last modified, and by whom. This pane also gives you the option to protect your workbook, inspect it for issues, further manage it, and view it in browser mode.

2. **New** – allows you to create an entirely new workbook and select from a wide range of available worksheet templates.

3. **Open** – enables you to access recent or existing workbooks from any location in your computer. You may optionally open files from your OneDrive account.

4. **Save or Save As** – saves your file to any location in your computer. You may optionally save your workbooks to your OneDrive account. You may also use the **Save As** function when saving a copy of the file with a different file name.

5. **Print** – here, you can modify the printer properties and print settings based on your requirements. A print preview will also be available for you to see if you have set the correct print area.

6. **Share** – lets you share your Excel file online via your OneDrive account. You can either attach and share your file as an Excel workbook or convert it into PDF format.

7. **Export** – allows you to convert your workbook into PDF or XPS format, or into other file types.

8. **Publish** – gives you the option to publish your workbook to Power BI, which is Microsoft's cloud-based business analytics service.

9. **Close** – closes the entire workbook. Do not worry, a dialog box will first appear to ask you if you want to save the changes you made to your workbook.

10. **Account** – here, you can view your Microsoft Office account details, tweak your Office theme, and review your MS Office subscription details and status.

11. **Feedback** – enables you to give either a positive or a negative feedback based on your user experience. You may also send a suggestion through the Feedback pane.

12. **Options** – prompts the Excel Options dialog box open, where you can customize the general settings, proofing options, language preferences, along with the Quick Access Toolbar and the Ribbon.

After having familiarized yourself with the Excel framework and its work environment, the next step is to get down to business and start working on an actual workbook.

In the succeeding chapter, you will learn about the building blocks of an Excel worksheet—the **Cell**, and all its other integral components.

Try This Out!

Discover the unique functions of the Tell Me text field and be amazed of what it can do! To start off, follow these simple steps:

1. Open **Excel 2016**.

2. Choose **Blank workbook**.

3. Select cell **G2** (take note: an active or selected cell is enclosed in green borders).

4. Click on the **Tell Me** text field.

5. Key in **Fill Color**.

6. Excel will then suggest a function or a command that best matches the keywords that you have entered. It will also provide a list of related actions based on the keywords you have entered.

7. Click **Fill Color** and select the color yellow.

8. The active cell would then look like this:

Feel free to explore other commands that you can key in to the Tell Me field.

Chapter 2

The Cell

Data, content, or any information in a workbook or a worksheet is inputted and stored through the **Cells**. These are the box-like structures found in each worksheet. To effectively store, organize, and analyze data in an Excel file, it is necessary to first know the fundamentals of cells.

Basically, the cell represents the intersection of a column and a row. As mentioned previously, **Columns** consist of groups of cells that run vertically on a worksheet. Every column is marked by an uppercase letter. On the other hand, **Rows** consist of groups of cells that run horizontally on a worksheet. Every row is marked by a numerical character.

As such, the first cell in an open new worksheet is known as **A1**. Notice that the cell name or address of an active or selected cell appears on the worksheet's Name Box. At the same time, the active or selected cell is enclosed in bold green borders.

It is also possible to select multiple cells or a group of cells all at once. This is known as a **cell range**. Instead of having a single cell name, a cell range's name is determined using the names of the first and last cells in the range, separated by a colon (:).

For instance, a cell range that is comprised of cells A1, A2, A3, A4, A5, A6, and A7, would be collectively known as cell range **A1:A7**.

Here are other examples of cell ranges:
Cell range **B2:G2**

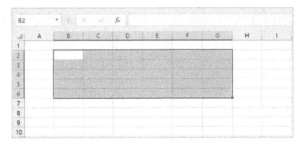

Cell range **B2:G6**

Cell Content

There are three (3) basic types of data that you can enter into an Excel worksheet cell:

1. **Text (Labels)** – generally consist of words that are used for worksheet headings, data names, and other content labels. Text data contain letters, numbers, and special characters.

2. **Numbers (Values)** – series of digits that are used in calculations. Hence, these may have specific number formatting. Numbers may be in the form of currency, date, time, percentage, and fraction, to name a few.

3. **Formulas** – involve mathematical equations and can also contain references to other cells. Formulas include simple arithmetic operations such as the MDAS (multiplication, division, addition, and subtraction), advanced equations, and other predefined formulas, known as functions. Formulas always begin with the equals (=) sign.

a. Entering Data into a Cell

- Click on the cell where you want to enter your data. We have selected cell *A1* in this example.
- Key in *Expenses*, and press **Enter**.

Tip: By pressing the **Enter** key, the cell selection moves to the cell below the previously selected cell. Cell *A2*, in this example.

- Click cell A1 again. Notice that the formula bar also displays *Expenses*.

With this, you may enter a cell content by either clicking on a cell to directly key in your data into it, or click on the formula bar to enter the data there.

b. Deleting or Clearing Data from a Cell

- Select the cell(s) with the content you want to delete. In this example, we have selected cell range B2:H2.

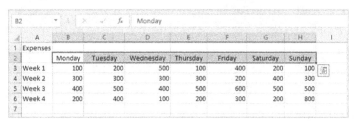

- On the **Home** tab, click the drop-down arrow of the **Clear** command from the **Editing** command group.
- Click **Clear Contents**.

Tip: On the ScreenTip, the shortcut key **(Del)** appears to the right of **Clear Contents**. This means that alternatively, you may also press the **Delete** key to clear the contents of the selected cell(s). Meanwhile, you may also use the **Backspace** key to delete content from one cell at a time.

- The contents of the selected cells will then be deleted.

Aside from inserting and deleting content to and from a cell, Excel also allows you to cut, copy, and paste content from one cell to another. This enables you to easily transfer data and content—without manually typing or retyping them, and to rearrange data in your worksheet and make them easier to understand and analyze.

In addition, you may choose specific contents or attributes to copy from one cell to another. For instance, you can copy a cell as it is. You can also copy just the cell format without copying its cell value, and vice versa. Likewise, you can copy the resulting value of a formula without copying the formula itself.

There are several ways to perform cut, copy, and paste functions in Excel:

1. Using the Office Clipboard pane

2. Using the mouse

3. Using keyboard shortcut keys such as **Ctrl+C** for copy, **Ctrl+X** for cut, and **Ctrl+V** for paste.

c. Copying and Pasting Data

• Select the cell(s) you want to copy. We have selected cell range G2:H6 in this example.

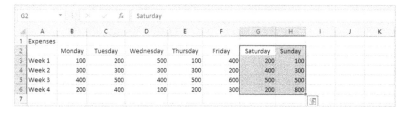

• Click **Copy** from the Clipboard pane on the upper left side of the Ribbon or simply press **Ctrl+C** on your keyboard.

405

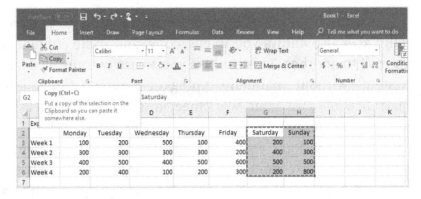

- The selected copied cells will then be enclosed in dashed borders.

Tip: You may also access the **Copy as Picture** option by clicking the drop-down arrow found to the right of the **Copy** command:

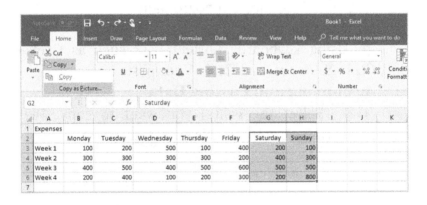

- Select the cells where you want your copied content to be pasted. In this example, we have selected cell K2. But since you copied cell range G2:H6, expect that it will be pasted on cell range K2:L6. In Excel, the copy area and paste area must be of the same size and shape.

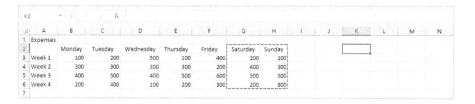

Tip: Make sure that there are no other data in the cells where you want to paste your content. Otherwise, these will be overwritten, or a dialog box will appear, to confirm if you want to replace the existing data in the cell.

- Click **Paste** or simply press **Ctrl+V** on your keyboard to paste the copied content.

- The copied content will then be pasted into the selected empty cells.

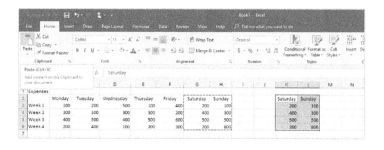

d. Cutting and Pasting Data

Copying and pasting allows you to duplicate content. On the other hand, cutting and pasting enables you to move content from one cell to the other. To cut and paste data from a cell:

- Select the cell(s) you want to cut. For this example, we will select cell range G2:H6 once again.

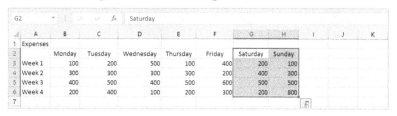

- Click **Cut** from the Clipboard pane on the upper left side of the Ribbon or simply press **Ctrl+X** on your keyboard.

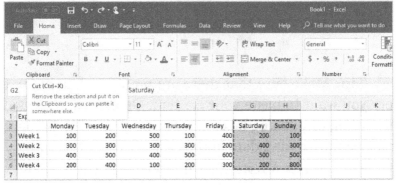

- Select the cells where you want your cut content to be pasted. In this example, we have selected cell K2 once more. Again, since you cut the content in cell range G2:H6, expect that it will be pasted on cell range K2:L6. Similar to copying content, the cut area and paste area must be of the same size and shape.

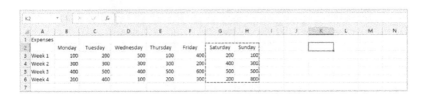

- Click **Paste** or simply press **Ctrl+V** on your keyboard to paste the cut content.
- The cut content will then be pasted into the selected empty cells.

Tip: In cutting, copying, and pasting content, you may also simply right-click on your selected content, and choose among the three functions.

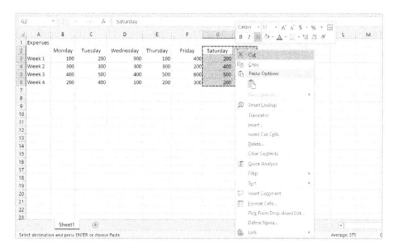

e. Other Paste Options

You can also make use of the additional paste options, especially when working with cells with formulas or special formatting.

- To access these options, click on the drop-down arrow below the **Paste** command.

- Hover your mouse over the icons to see the detailed paste options. Options include, but do not limit to, pasting formulas, values, number formatting, source formatting, and so on.

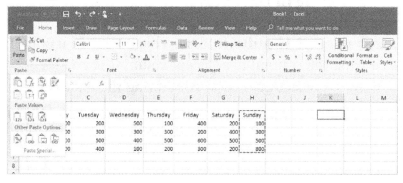

f. Dragging and Dropping Cells

Instead of cutting and pasting content, **dragging and dropping** cells also work to move them from one location to another.

    • Select the cells you want to move. In this example, we have selected cell range E3:F6.

    • Hover your mouse over one side of the border of the selected cells. Wait for an arrow with four pointers to appear.

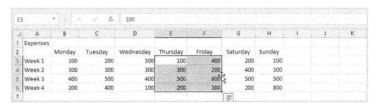

    • This time, move the cells to cell range K3:L6. To do this, click the cells and drag them to their next location.

    • Afterwards, release the mouse. The cells will then be dropped in the selected location.

g. Filling in Data Series

Another time-saving option for filling in a series of data is through the **Fill Handle** feature. This comes in handy if you are copying cell content to adjacent columns or rows.

    • Select the cell(s) containing the data you want to copy or the data series you want to continue. Then, hover your mouse pointer over the lower right corner of the cell, until the fill handle appears. The fill handle is characterized by a small cross icon.

- For this example, we have selected *Week 4* in cell A6.

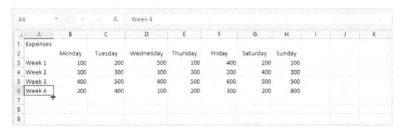

- Click and drag the cell down to cell A12.
- Pay close attention to the **Auto Fill Options** icon. You may click the drop-down arrow to its right to view more of its options.

There are various ways to fill in a data series. The Auto Fill feature allows you to Copy Cells, Fill Series, Fill Formatting Only, Fill Without Formatting, and Flash Fill.

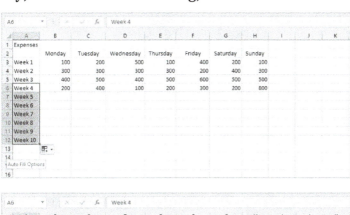

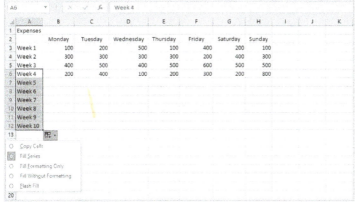

Notice that by default, **Fill Series** is selected, since *Week 4* contains a numerical value, which is 4. As a result, upon clicking and dragging the fill handle down, the cell will then be followed by *Week 5*, *Week 6*, and so on. Nonetheless, you may choose **Copy Cells** if you only wish to duplicate or multiply the cell. **Fill Series** works with data that usually follow a sequential order, such as numbers, days of the week, and months.

After learning how to insert, delete, cut, copy, and paste cell content, the next step is to know how to format them. Contrary to popular belief, worksheets are not meant to be plain and boring. In the next section, you will learn that Excel worksheets can also be customized and even personalized. Formatting your content not only enhances the look and feel of your worksheet, it also helps make your content easier to read and understand.

Formatting Cells

The **Home** tab displays various formatting and editing commands to help you enhance the appearance of your worksheet. In school or at work, Excel worksheets are usually printed or shared with others. Thus, your worksheets must be pleasing to the eyes and understandable, as much as possible.

Aside from giving your worksheet your own personal touch, formatting can also help you emphasize or highlight the important details of the worksheet. In turn, this enables you and your readers to view and understand your content easier and more convenient.

While working on a worksheet, you may find the need to add more data or delete unnecessary content along the way. In addition to inserting and deleting cell content, Excel also allows you to insert or delete cells, depending on your requirement.

a. Inserting Cells

Inserting cells into a column or a row entails shifting the other cells down or to the right, respectively. To insert a cell, follow these steps:

- Click on the cell where the inserted cell should precede.
- In this example, *April* comes after *February*. So, you would need to insert *March* in between. Thus, click on cell D1.

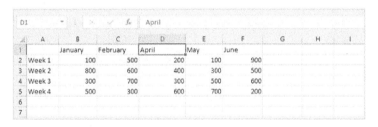

- Click the drop-down arrow below the **Insert** command. The **Insert** command allows you to insert cells, sheet rows, sheet columns, and an entirely new sheet.
- Click the **Insert Cells** option. Alternatively, you may press **Ctrl+Shift+=** on your keyboard.

- Upon clicking **Insert Cells**, a dialog box will prompt open to let you choose the shift orientation of the remaining cells, as well as options to insert an entirely new row or an entirely new column.

- By choosing **Shift cells down**, the selected cell and the cells below it in the same column will shift down, to make room for the inserted cell:

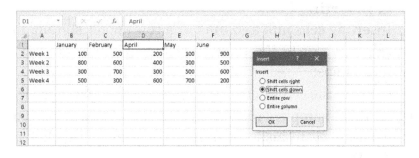

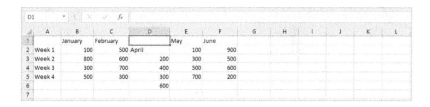

- By choosing **Shift cells right**, the selected cell and the cells to its right in the same row will shift to the right, to make room for the inserted cell:

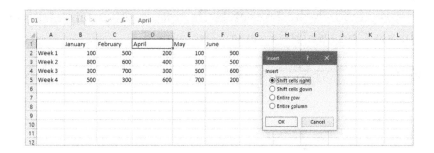

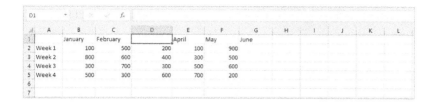

- Do note that the initial data inputted under *April* stay the same. To avoid confusion, you may select the entire cell range under *April* (D1:D5), and click **Shift cells right**, or just consider inserting an entirely new column. As such, click **Entire Column**. Then, click **OK**.

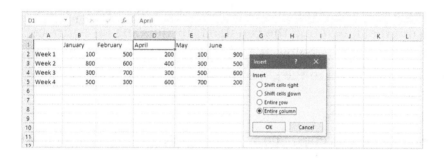

- Now, you can add the data for *March*.

Tip: Upon selecting the cells where you want the inserted cells to precede, you may also simply right-click, then choose **Insert**. The same dialog box will prompt open.

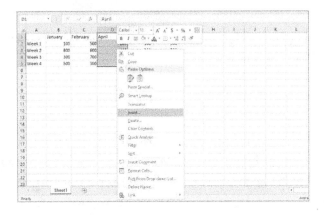

While you have learned to delete a cell's content in the previous section, keep in mind that deleting a cell's content does not mean deleting the cell itself. By deleting an entire cell, the cells beside or below it will either shift to the left or up, respectively, to fill in the gaps and replace the deleted cells.

b. Deleting Cells

- Select the cell(s) you want to delete. In this example, we have selected cell F1.

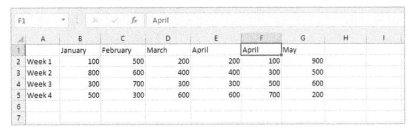

- Click the drop-down arrow below the **Delete** command. Conversely to the Insert options, you may delete cells, sheet rows, sheet columns, or even the entire sheet.
- Click **Delete Cells**. Alternatively, you may press **Ctrl+-** on your keyboard.

- Upon clicking **Delete Cells**, a dialog box will prompt open to let you choose the shift orientation of the remaining cells, as well as options to delete the entire row or the entire column.

- By choosing **Shift cells up**, the selected cell will be deleted, and the cells below it

  in the same column will shift up, to replace the deleted cell:

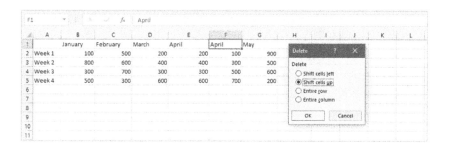

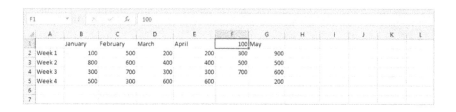

417

- By choosing **Shift cells left**, the selected cell will be deleted, and the cells to its right will shift to the left, to replace the deleted cell:

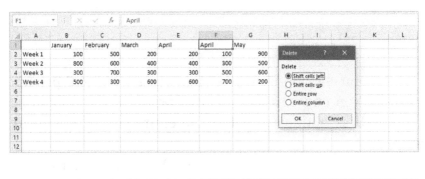

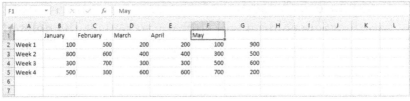

- Choosing **Entire row** will delete the entire row where your selected cell is located, and all its content:

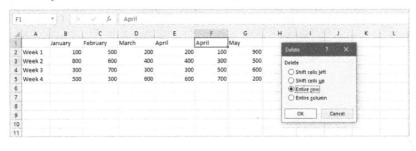

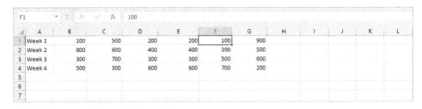

- Choosing **Entire column** will delete the entire column where your selected cell is located, and all its content:

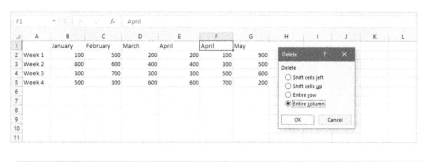

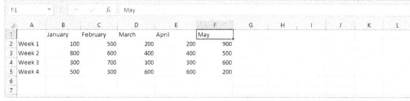

Tip: Upon selecting the cell(s) you want to delete, you may also right-click, then choose **Delete**. The same dialog box will prompt open.

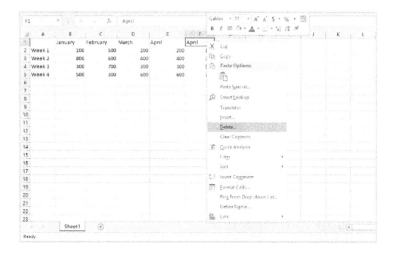

c. Formatting Cells

In Excel, there are countless ways to format a cell. You may click the drop-down arrow below the **Format** command to discover multiple methods of modifying a cell. Each method will also be further discussed in this section:

1. **Cell Size** – Excel gives you the option to either manually set the row and/or column height and/or width, or automatically adjust them to fit the cell content.

It is inevitable to encounter instances when some content in certain cells become unreadable, especially if the data is longer than the default Excel column width, and another cell with content follows it.

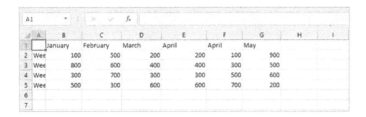

To adjust the width of a specific cell:

- Select the cell with unreadable content. In this example, we have selected cell A2.

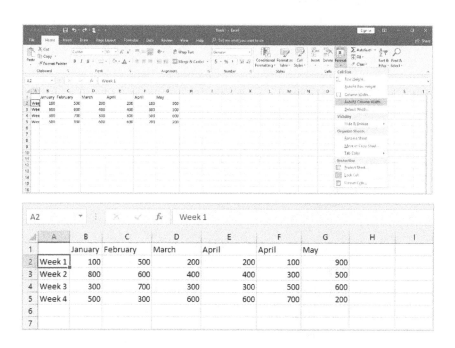

A2				fx	Week 1			
	A	B	C	D	E	F	G	H	I
1		January	February	March	April	April	May		
2	Wee	100	500	200	200	100	900		
3	Wee	800	600	400	400	300	500		
4	Wee	300	700	300	300	500	600		
5	Wee	500	300	600	600	700	200		
6									
7									

- Click **Format** and choose **AutoFit Column Width**.

A2				fx	Week 1			
	A	B	C	D	E	F	G	H	I
1		January	February	March	April	April	May		
2	Week 1	100	500	200	200	100	900		
3	Week 2	800	600	400	400	300	500		
4	Week 3	300	700	300	300	500	600		
5	Week 4	500	300	600	600	700	200		
6									
7									

- The cell will automatically adjust its width to display the content completely.

Tip: You can also position the mouse pointer over the top column line, until it becomes a cross icon with arrows pointing left and right.

421

A2 | Week 1

	A	B	C	D	E	F	G	H	I
1		January	February	March	April	April	May		
2	Wee	100	500	200	200	100	900		
3	Wee	800	600	400	400	300	500		
4	Wee	300	700	300	300	500	600		
5	Wee	500	300	600	600	700	200		
6									
7									

- Click the cross icon and drag it to the right, depending on your desired width.
- You may also double-click the column line to automatically adjust the width based on the cell content.

A2 | Week 1

	A	B	C	D	E	F	G	H	I
1		January	February	March	April	April	May		
2	Week 1	100	500	200	200	100	900		
3	Week 2	800	600	400	400	300	500		
4	Week 3	300	700	300	300	500	600		
5	Week 4	500	300	600	600	700	200		
6									
7									

To adjust the height of a specific cell:
- Select the cell with unreadable content. In this example, we have selected cell A3.
- Position the mouse pointer over the row line, until it becomes a cross icon with arrows pointing up and down.

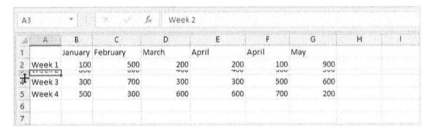

- Click the cross icon and drag it down, depending on the desired height.

- You may also simply double-click the row line to automatically adjust the height based on the cell content.

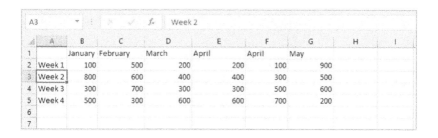

2. **Visibility** – rows, columns, and even an entire sheet may also be shown or hidden, depending on your preference or requirement. To do this:
- Select the row or column you want to hide. In this example, we have selected row 5.
- Click **Format** and hover your mouse over **Hide & Unhide** to see more options.
- Click **Hide Rows**.

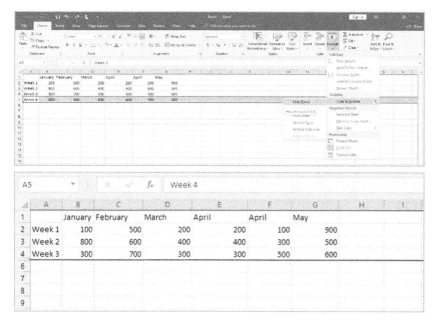

- The entire row 5 is now hidden.

Tip: To hide a row or a column faster, right-click on the selected row or column you want to hide, then click **Hide**.

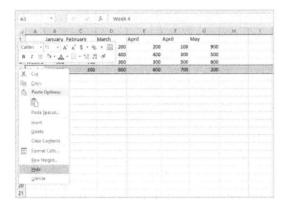

Meanwhile, to unhide the same row:

- Select the rows on both sides of the hidden row.

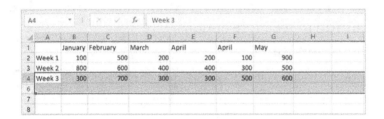

- Click **Format** and hover your mouse over **Hide & Unhide** to see more options.
- Click **Unhide Rows**.

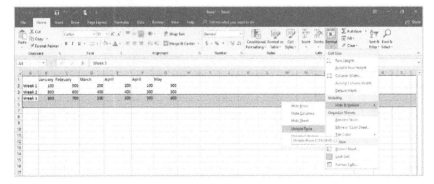

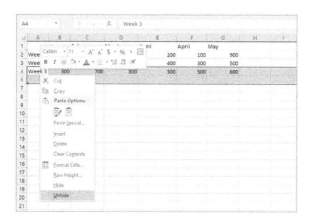

A4			f_x	Week 3				
	A	B	C	D	E	F	G	H	I
1		January	February	March	April		April	May	
2	Week 1	100	500	200	200	100	900	
3	Week 2	800	600	400	400	300	500	
4	Week 3	300	700	300	300	500	600	
5	Week 4	500	300	600	600	700	200	
6								
7								
8								

- Row 5 is now unhidden.

Tip: There are two more alternative ways to unhide a row or a column:

(1) Right-click on the selected rows or columns on both sides of the hidden row or column, then click **Unhide**.

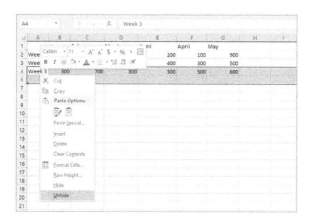

(2) Position the mouse pointer over the row line where the hidden row is located, until it becomes a double-line icon with arrows pointing up and down. Double-click it to unhide or show the hidden row.

I10			f_x					
	A	B	C	D	E	F	G	H	I	J
1		January	February	March	April		April	May	
2	Week 1	100	500	200	200	100	900	
3	Week 2	800	600	400	400	300	500	
4	Week 3	300	700	300	300	500	600	
7								
8								

425

3. **Sheet Organization** – under the **Format** command, it is also possible to rename the sheet, move or copy it to another location in the same workbook or into another workbook, and change the tab colors of the sheets to organize them better.

To rename a sheet:

- Click the drop-down arrow below **Format**. Choose **Rename Sheet**.

- After which, the sheet name, **Sheet1** by default, will be selected. This means that you can now edit or change it.

Tip: Another way to do this is by simply double-clicking the sheet name to select it. Proceed to editing it afterwards.

To move or copy sheet to another location in the same workbook, there must be at least two (2) sheets in it first. To add a new sheet:

- Click on the **plus sign** to the right of the last sheet in the workbook.

- As mentioned previously, the second sheet will be named as "Sheet2" by default.

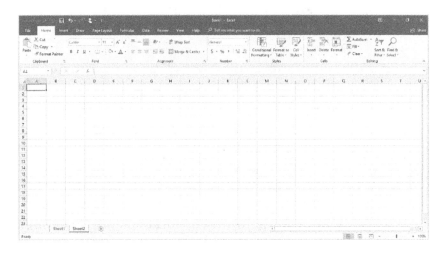

Now that you have created a new sheet, we can illustrate moving a sheet to another location in the same workbook better:

- To move or copy a worksheet, click **Format**, then choose **Move or Copy Sheet**.

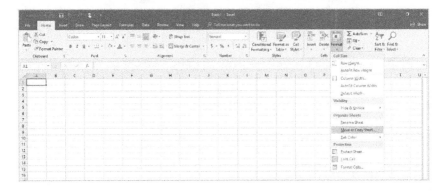

- A dialog box will prompt open to let you choose where to move the sheet.

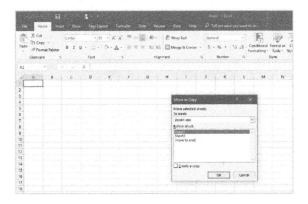

- First, choose to which workbook are you going to move the sheet.
- Then, choose the location of the sheet in the said workbook. You can move it either before another sheet, or to the end of the workbook.
- You may also click on the **Create a copy** checkbox, to create a copy of the sheet and preserve it in its original location.

Tip: Alternatively, you may also right-click the tab of the sheet you wish to move or copy. Then click **Move or Copy**. A similar dialog will prompt open.

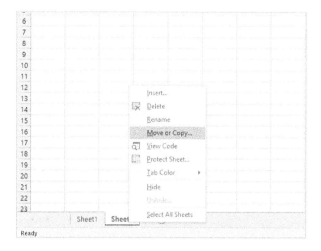

To easily distinguish one sheet from another, you may also consider changing the tab color of the sheet. To do this:

• Select the sheet tab with the color you wish to change. Click **Format**, then position your mouse pointer over **Tab Color** to see the color options.

• For this example, select **Sheet2**, and change its tab color into orange.

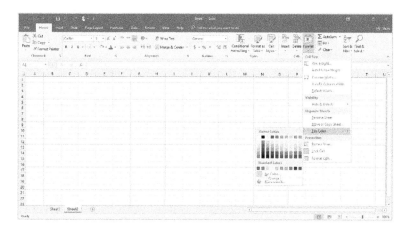

• Click on **Sheet1** to see the tab color change on Sheet2.

Tip: You can also do this by right-clicking the sheet tab with the color that you want to change. Once again, position your mouse pointer over **Tab Color** to see the color options.

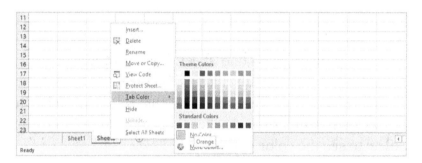

4. **Protection** – Excel has also set a few protection features to keep your worksheets free from unwanted changes by limiting other people's ability to edit or modify them. You may choose to **protect the entire sheet** or **simply lock specific cells**.

To protect a worksheet:

- Click **Format**, then choose **Protect Sheet**.

• A dialog box will prompt open, allowing you to create a password to unprotect or unlock the sheet, and to choose which features will be available to the users of the worksheet. Features include, but do not limit to, formatting, inserting, and deleting columns and rows.

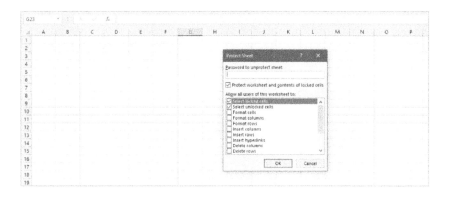

You can also select specific cells to lock to keep people from making unwanted changes to them. But first, **Protect Sheet** must be enabled for this feature to work:

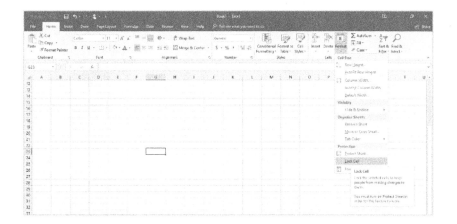

- In this example, we will protect **Sheet1**.
- Key in your preferred password to unprotect or unlock the sheet. In this example, we have set *12345* as the password.
- Uncheck all the features to make them unavailable to other users without the password.
- Click **OK**.

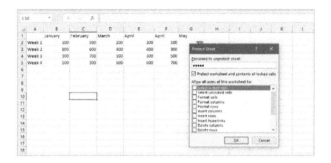

- You will be asked to re-enter your password for confirmation purposes. Never forget your password, as it is impossible to recover it.
- Afterwards, click **OK**.

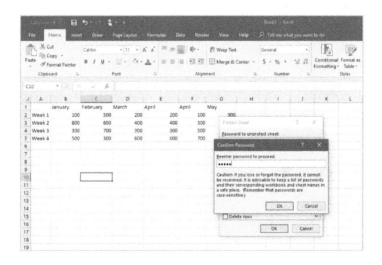

- By the time another person opens your workbook and tries to modify the data in a certain cell, a dialog box will appear, stating that the cell is on a protected sheet. Thus, a password is required to unlock it.

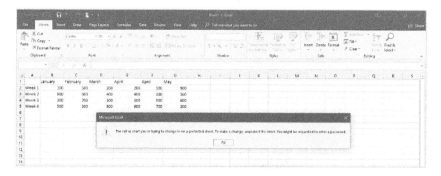

To unlock the sheet:
- Click **Format** and choose **Unprotect Sheet**.
- You will then be asked to provide the password.

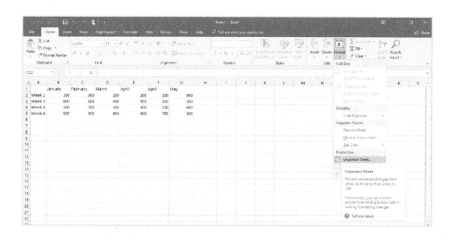

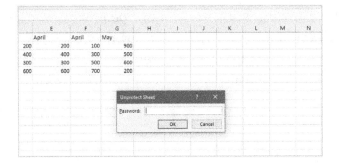

- Enter the password. For this example, key in *12345*. Then, click **OK**.

- You may now click on any of the cell in the sheet and start editing its content.

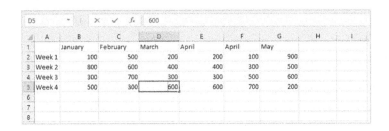

5. **Font** – working on a worksheet means dealing with a lot of data. Hence, content readability is a major factor to consider when preparing a worksheet.

Similar to other MS Office programs, Excel allows you to customize data text through changing its font, size, font face, and color. Moreover, you can add various kinds of borders to a cell and even change its fill color.

All these features can be accessed through the **Font** command group in the **Home** tab:

• You may click on the drop-down arrow to the right of certain icons in the Font group to view more command options.

• You may also click on the expand arrow icon on the lower left corner of the command group to view more font effects such as strikethrough, superscript, and subscript:

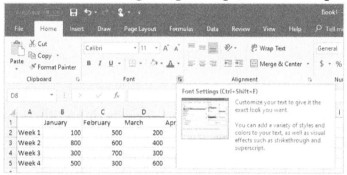

• Upon clicking on the expand arrow icon, the **Format Cells** dialog box will appear.

- Here, you will find the full lists of fonts, font styles, font effects, and sizes that you can apply to your data.
- You may also explore the **Border** and the **Fill** tabs to view more cell border styles, fill colors, and fill patterns.

 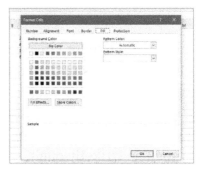

6. **Alignment** – by default, any text entered into a worksheet will be left-aligned to the bottom of a cell, while any number entered will be right-aligned to the bottom of a cell. Imagine having both text and number contents—with different alignments in a single worksheet. That is definitely going to be a big eyesore.

Adjusting your cell contents' alignment enables you to design how your content is going to be showcased in your worksheet. Just like fonts, alignment is a major factor that greatly affects a worksheet's readability.

The **Alignment** command group is also found under the **Home** tab, beside the **Font** command group:

It consists of the following commands:
- o Top Align
- o Middle Align
- o Bottom Align

o   Align Left

o   Align Center

o   Align Right

o   Orientation – allows you to rotate text diagonally or vertically. This comes in handy when labelling narrow columns.

o   Decrease Indent – moves content closer to the left cell border

o   Increase Indent – moves content farther from the left cell border

o   Wrap Text – displays an extra-long data into multiple lines to make it completely visible and readable.

o   Merge & Center – combines two or more cells, and aligns the content to the center. However, keep in mind that this feature only keeps the data of the upper leftmost cell, and discards the contents of the other cells.

•   You may also click on the drop-down arrow to the right of certain Alignment icons to view more command options.

•   You may also click on the expand arrow icon on the lower left corner of the command group to view more alignment settings:

•   Upon clicking on the expand arrow icon, the **Format Cells** dialog box will appear. This is also the same dialog box that pops up for the additional Font settings, as discussed previously.

- For more alignment settings, just click on the **Alignment** tab. Here, you can set the text alignment horizontally or vertically, adjust the text control based on your content, and even change the direction of the text.

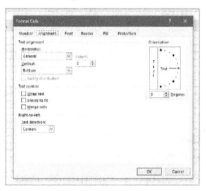

7. **Number Format** – by default, all data entered into a cell are classified as **General**, since they do not have a specific number format. However, when working with a spreadsheet, it is important to use appropriate number formats to easily classify the type of your data, and apply necessary formulas or functions to them.

Number formats may be in the form of currency, date, time, percentage, fraction, and even plain text, to name a few.

The **Number** command group in the Home tab provides easy access to selecting number format, setting accounting number format, formatting data as percentage, inserting comma for thousands separator, and adjusting decimal places:

- You may also click on the expand arrow icon on the lower left corner to view more number format settings:

• Again, the **Format Cells** dialog box will appear where you will see all the available number format categories and a brief description of each category.

• Click on each category to see more format options.

8. **Styles** – Excel also offers various formatting style options to save you time from manually formatting the cells. These include **Conditional Formatting**, **Format as Table**, and other **Cell Styles**.

Conditional Formatting works best when dealing with cell rules and much complicated data that require special formatting. This will be additionally discussed in Chapter 6: Charts.

Format as Table allows you to easily convert your inputted data into a table. This will be further discussed in Chapter 5: Managing Data.

Cell Styles provide quick yet professional formatting options for distinct parts of your workbook, such as titles and headings. You may choose from a wide variety of themed cell styles, and even create your own style.

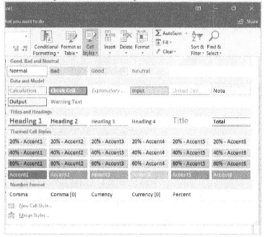

Try This Out!

Formulate a personal monthly expense sheet based on the various cell formatting features and functions that you have learned:

- Explore different font styles, colors, and sizes.
- Add cell borders and fill colors to highlight important parts of your worksheet.
- Adjust alignment based on your content requirement.
- Make use of the Wrap Text and Merge & Center features, particularly for headings and other content labels.
- Apply appropriate number formats when necessary.

We have created a simple sample for your reference:

CATEGORY	JANUARY	FEBRUARY	MARCH	APRIL	MAY	JUNE	JULY	AUGUST	SEPTEMBER	OCTOBER	NOVEMBER	DECEMBER
MONTHLY LIVING EXPENSES												
Phone	$ 28.50	$ 30.60	$ 35.58	$ 30.23	$ 40.89	$ 50.50	$ -	$ -	$ -	$ -	$ -	$ -
Electricity	$ 100.34	$ 250.90	$ 200.89	$ 210.45	$ 350.23	$ 400.89	$ -	$ -	$ -	$ -	$ -	$ -
Gas	$ 34.09	$ 45.95	$ 50.00	$ 55.23	$ 45.75	$ 40.75	$ -	$ -	$ -	$ -	$ -	$ -
Water	$ 65.90	$ 70.35	$ 50.95	$ 60.93	$ 70.85	$ 80.45	$ -	$ -	$ -	$ -	$ -	$ -
Taxes	$ 120.85	$ 200.87	$ 150.95	$ 100.95	$ 120.45	$ 250.98	$ -	$ -	$ -	$ -	$ -	$ -
House Rental	$ 520.12	$ 520.12	$ 520.12	$ 520.12	$ 520.12	$ 520.12	$ -	$ -	$ -	$ -	$ -	$ -
Car Rental	$ 400.00	$ 400.00	$ 400.00	$ 400.00	$ 400.00	$ 400.00	$ -	$ -	$ -	$ -	$ -	$ -
Internet	$ 60.50	$ 70.55	$ 60.93	$ 100.00	$ 124.68	$ 200.98	$ -	$ -	$ -	$ -	$ -	$ -
Cable	$ 45.00	$ 50.67	$ 80.94	$ 45.00	$ 50.00	$ 50.00	$ -	$ -	$ -	$ -	$ -	$ -

440

Chapter 3: Formulas

Creating Formulas

Excel is widely known and used for its ability to calculate numerical operations using formulas. Formulas allow you to perform simple arithmetic operations such as addition, subtraction, multiplication, and division, to complex equations.

In Excel, formulas always begin with the equals (=) sign, since these contain values to be calculated. Otherwise, formulas inputted without the equals sign will be deemed invalid or be considered merely as text.

Excel also uses the standard mathematical symbols for formulas such as, plus sign (+) for addition, minus sign (-) for subtraction, asterisk (*) for multiplication, forward slash (/) for division, and caret (^) for exponents.

To start off, try this simple example in performing addition in Excel:

- Enter =4+5 in cell A1.
- Notice that the cell only displays the result, while the formula bar displays the entire formula.

Tip: You may also double-click on the cell to view the formula and edit it directly on the cell.

- Try removing the equals sign (=) in the formula. Without the equals sign, Excel will only treat the formula as plain text.

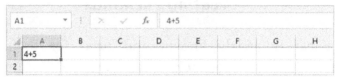

Aside from creating simple formulas using numbers, you can also make use of cell addresses to create a formula, which you will do most of the time in Excel. Using cell addresses involves making **cell references**. With this, there is no need to key in the numbers one by one. As such, there is a better assurance that your results are accurate because you only update the value of referenced cells, without altering or retyping the entire formula.

To work with cell references, use this example as a guide:

- Enter *4* and *5* in cells A1 and B1, respectively.

- To add these values, make a cell reference. In cell C1, enter the formula *=A1+B1*, with reference to the cell addresses of the values.

Instead of manually typing the cell addresses of the values you want to calculate, you may also use your mouse to click on the cells to automatically display their cell addresses:

- Key in the equals sign (=).

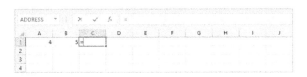

- Click on cell A1.

- Enter the plus (+) sign.

- Lastly, click on cell B1, and press Enter.

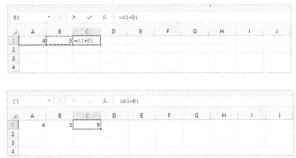

Keep in mind that when you edit or change the values of the referenced cells, the formula will automatically recalculate the result.

Feel free to try other mathematical operations such as subtraction, multiplication, and division, to know more of Excel's extensive calculating abilities.

Tip: Cell references need not be adjacent to each other. In addition, a cell reference may also be used as reference for multiple sets of formulas. Lastly, formulas may also be a combination of numbers and cell references.

Try This Out!

Assign your own values to the following cells and try out these few sample formulas:

- =D3*G9 (cell D3 multiplied by cell G9)
- =250/J7 (250 divided by cell J7)
- =L26^5 (cell L26 raised to the 5th power)
- =B12 − 100 (cell B12 minus 100)
- =1.25*F4 (1.25 multiplied by cell F4)

Copying Formulas

Just like any other cell content, formulas can also be copied in Excel. This is particularly useful when you are dealing with the same formula or calculation for several times in a worksheet.

Instead of manually retyping a formula to copy it from one cell to another, you can simply copy and paste a formula to save time and effort. Moreover, copy and pasting formulas makes them less susceptible to typographical errors and other mistakes.

There are two ways to copy and paste a formula:

1. **Using the standard "copy & paste" method**

Keep in mind to paste only the formula, which can be done through accessing other paste options in the Clipboard pane.

For this example, we will get the subtotal of the 1st Quarter (Q1) expense for each category. Thus, we will need to add the values under January, February, and March.

CATEGORY	JANUARY	FEBRUARY	MARCH	Q1 SUBTOTAL	APRIL	MAY	JUNE	Q2 SUBTOTAL
				H1 LIVING EXPENSES				
Phone	$ 28.50	$ 30.60	$ 35.58	=B3+C3+D3	$ 30.23	$ 40.89	$ 50.50	
Electricity	$ 100.34	$ 250.90	$ 200.89		$ 210.45	$ 350.23	$ 400.89	
Gas	$ 34.89	$ 45.95	$ 50.00		$ 55.23	$ 45.75	$ 40.75	
Water	$ 65.98	$ 70.35	$ 50.95		$ 60.93	$ 70.85	$ 80.45	
Taxes	$ 120.65	$ 200.67	$ 150.95		$ 100.95	$ 120.45	$ 250.98	
House Rental	$ 520.12	$ 520.12	$ 520.12		$ 520.12	$ 520.12	$ 520.12	
Car Rental	$ 400.00	$ 400.00	$ 400.00		$ 400.00	$ 400.00	$ 400.00	
Internet	$ 60.50	$ 70.55	$ 80.93		$ 100.00	$ 124.68	$ 200.98	
Cable	$ 45.00	$ 50.67	$ 80.94		$ 45.00	$ 50.00	$ 50.00	

To copy the same formula used in cell E3 to the succeeding cells below it:

- Right-click on cell E3 and click **Copy**. Alternatively, you may also click on cell E3 and press Ctrl+C on your keyboard.
- Click on cell E4 and choose **Formulas** under the Paste command in the Clipboard pane.

CATEGORY	JANUARY	FEBRUARY	MARCH	Q1 SUBTOTAL	APRIL	MAY	JUNE	Q2 SUBTOTAL
				H1 LIVING EXPENSES				
	$ 28.50	$ 30.60	$ 35.58	$ 94.68	$ 30.23	$ 40.89	$ 50.50	
	$ 100.34	$ 250.90	$ 200.89	$ 552.13	$ 210.45	$ 350.23	$ 400.89	
	$ 34.89	$ 45.95	$ 50.00		$ 55.23	$ 45.75	$ 40.75	
Water	$ 65.98	$ 70.35	$ 50.95		$ 60.93	$ 70.85	$ 80.45	
Taxes	$ 120.65	$ 200.67	$ 150.95		$ 100.95	$ 120.45	$ 250.98	
House Rental	$ 520.12	$ 520.12	$ 520.12		$ 520.12	$ 520.12	$ 520.12	
Car Rental	$ 400.00	$ 400.00	$ 400.00		$ 400.00	$ 400.00	$ 400.00	
Internet	$ 60.50	$ 70.55	$ 80.93		$ 100.00	$ 124.68	$ 200.98	
Cable	$ 45.00	$ 50.67	$ 80.94		$ 45.00	$ 50.00	$ 50.00	

2. **Using the Fill Handle**

This comes in handy if you are copying formulas to adjacent cells, either horizontally or vertically. As discussed previously, the Fill Handle is characterized by a small cross icon at the bottom right corner of the selected cell.

Using the same example, getting the subtotals for each category will require using the same formula. Thus, using the Fill Handle feature is highly applicable here.

Since we have already copied the formula to cell E4, we may begin here for the Fill Handle feature:

- Click on cell E4 and hover your mouse pointer over the bottom right corner of the cell, until it becomes a small cross icon.

E4				f_x	=B4+C4+D4				
	A	B	C	D	E	F	G	H	I
1					**H1 LIVING EXPENSES**				
2	CATEGORY	JANUARY	FEBRUARY	MARCH	Q1 SUBTOTAL	APRIL	MAY	JUNE	Q2 SUBTOTAL
3	Phone	$ 28.50	$ 30.60	$ 35.58	$ 94.68	$ 30.23	$ 40.89	$ 50.50	
4	Electricity	$ 100.34	$ 250.90	$ 200.89	$ 552.13	$ 210.45	$ 350.23	$ 400.89	
5	Gas	$ 34.89	$ 45.95	$ 50.00		$ 56.23	$ 45.75	$ 40.76	
6	Water	$ 65.98	$ 70.35	$ 50.95		$ 60.93	$ 70.85	$ 80.45	
7	Taxes	$ 120.65	$ 200.87	$ 160.95		$ 100.95	$ 120.45	$ 250.98	
8	House Rental	$ 520.12	$ 520.12	$ 520.12		$ 520.12	$ 520.12	$ 520.12	
9	Car Rental	$ 400.00	$ 400.00	$ 400.00		$ 400.00	$ 400.00	$ 400.00	
10	Internet	$ 60.50	$ 70.55	$ 80.93		$ 100.00	$ 124.68	$ 200.98	
11	Cable	$ 45.00	$ 50.67	$ 80.94		$ 45.00	$ 50.00	$ 50.00	
12									

- Click the fill handle icon and drag it down to cell E11, to copy the formula to all the selected cells.

E4				f_x	=B4+C4+D4				
	A	B	C	D	E	F	G	H	I
1					**H1 LIVING EXPENSES**				
2	CATEGORY	JANUARY	FEBRUARY	MARCH	Q1 SUBTOTAL	APRIL	MAY	JUNE	Q2 SUBTOTAL
3	Phone	$ 28.50	$ 30.60	$ 35.58	$ 94.68	$ 30.23	$ 40.89	$ 50.50	
4	Electricity	$ 100.34	$ 250.90	$ 200.89	$ 552.13	$ 210.45	$ 350.23	$ 400.89	
5	Gas	$ 34.89	$ 45.95	$ 50.00		$ 55.23	$ 45.75	$ 40.75	
6	Water	$ 65.98	$ 70.35	$ 50.95		$ 60.93	$ 70.85	$ 80.45	
7	Taxes	$ 120.65	$ 200.67	$ 150.95		$ 100.95	$ 120.45	$ 250.98	
8	House Rental	$ 520.12	$ 520.12	$ 520.12		$ 520.12	$ 520.12	$ 520.12	
9	Car Rental	$ 400.00	$ 400.00	$ 400.00		$ 400.00	$ 400.00	$ 400.00	
10	Internet	$ 60.50	$ 70.55	$ 80.93		$ 100.00	$ 124.68	$ 200.98	
11	Cable	$ 45.00	$ 50.67	$ 80.94		$ 45.00	$ 50.00	$ 50.00	
12									

- Release the mouse. The formula will then be copied to the selected cells.

446

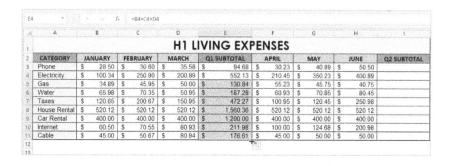

Editing Formulas

There are times when you may need to edit or modify an existing formula, especially when you have mistakenly entered a wrong cell address. To do so:

- Select the cell with the formula you wish to edit. In this example, we have entered the wrong formula for cell E11. It should be *=B11+C11+D11*, instead of *=B11+C11+D10*. So, click on cell E11.

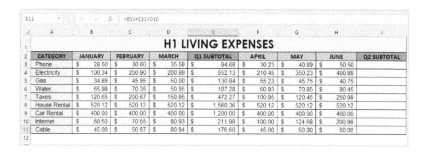

- Click on the formula bar to edit the formula.

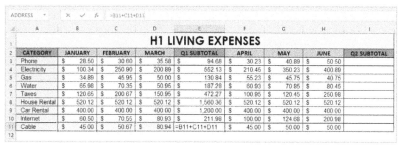

- Or, you may also double-click on the cell to directly edit the formula there.

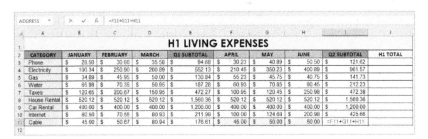

Tip: Notice how the formula changes color, depending on where you choose to edit it.

- Repeat the same process to calculate the 2nd Quarter (Q2) expense for each category. Keep in mind that Q2 expenses consist of values from April, May, and June.

CATEGORY	JANUARY	FEBRUARY	MARCH	Q1 SUBTOTAL	APRIL	MAY	JUNE	Q2 SUBTOTAL	H1 TOTAL
Phone	$ 28.50	$ 30.60	$ 35.58	$ 94.68	$ 30.23	$ 40.89	$ 50.50	$ 121.62	
Electricity	$ 100.34	$ 250.90	$ 200.89	$ 552.13	$ 210.46	$ 350.23	$ 400.89	$ 961.57	
Gas	$ 34.89	$ 45.95	$ 50.00	$ 130.84	$ 55.23	$ 45.75	$ 40.75	$ 141.73	
Water	$ 65.98	$ 70.35	$ 50.95	$ 187.28	$ 60.93	$ 70.85	$ 80.45	$ 212.23	
Taxes	$ 120.65	$ 200.67	$ 150.95	$ 472.27	$ 100.95	$ 120.45	$ 250.98	$ 472.38	
House Rental	$ 520.12	$ 520.12	$ 520.12	$ 1,560.36	$ 520.12	$ 520.12	$ 520.12	$ 1,560.36	
Car Rental	$ 400.00	$ 400.00	$ 400.00	$ 1,200.00	$ 400.00	$ 400.00	$ 400.00	$ 1,200.00	
Internet	$ 60.50	$ 70.55	$ 80.93	$ 211.98	$ 100.00	$ 124.68	$ 200.98	$ 425.66	
Cable	$ 45.00	$ 50.67	$ 80.94	$ 176.61	$ 45.00	$ 50.00	$ 50.00	=F11+G11+H11	

- Lastly, to compute for the total 1st Half (H1) expense for each category, simply add the Q1 subtotal and Q2 subtotal of each.

CATEGORY	JANUARY	FEBRUARY	MARCH	Q1 SUBTOTAL	APRIL	MAY	JUNE	Q2 SUBTOTAL	H1 TOTAL
Phone	$ 28.50	$ 30.60	$ 35.58	$ 94.68	$ 30.23	$ 40.89	$ 50.50	$ 121.62	$ 216.30
Electricity	$ 100.34	$ 250.90	$ 200.89	$ 552.13	$ 210.45	$ 350.23	$ 400.89	$ 961.57	$ 1,513.70
Gas	$ 34.89	$ 45.95	$ 50.00	$ 130.84	$ 55.23	$ 45.75	$ 40.75	$ 141.73	$ 272.57
Water	$ 65.98	$ 70.35	$ 50.95	$ 187.28	$ 60.93	$ 70.85	$ 80.45	$ 212.23	$ 399.51
Taxes	$ 120.65	$ 200.67	$ 150.95	$ 472.27	$ 100.95	$ 120.45	$ 250.98	$ 472.38	$ 944.65
House Rental	$ 520.12	$ 520.12	$ 520.12	$ 1,560.36	$ 520.12	$ 520.12	$ 520.12	$ 1,560.36	$ 3,120.72
Car Rental	$ 400.00	$ 400.00	$ 400.00	$ 1,200.00	$ 400.00	$ 400.00	$ 400.00	$ 1,200.00	$ 2,400.00
Internet	$ 60.50	$ 70.55	$ 80.93	$ 211.98	$ 100.00	$ 124.68	$ 200.98	$ 425.66	$ 637.64
Cable	$ 45.00	$ 50.67	$ 80.94	$ 176.61	$ 45.00	$ 50.00	$ 50.00	$ 145.00	=E11+I11

Excel's computing abilities do not limit to a single mathematical operation per formula. In fact, you may also perform complex formulas that contain multiple operations, such as addition and multiplication combined. When there is more than one operation involved, reviewing the **Order of Operations**, taught back in school, may help you recall some guidelines.

In addition, Excel is programmed to calculate multiple operations based on this principle. Thus, it is necessary to equip yourself with adequate knowledge regarding the order of operations. To get the correct result, entering the right formula is a must.

Here is a simple mnemonic that can help you remember the order of operations that Excel follows:

Parenthesis

Exponent

Multiplication

Division

Addition

Subtraction

Tip: Multiplication and Division are on the same rank, so are **Addition and Subtraction**. This means that these are interchangeable, respectively, depending on which operation comes first (from left to right) in a formula.

For instance, to solve for the answer to 150/3-(5*1)^2+5-1:

- First, solve the operation enclosed in a parenthesis, that is 5*1 = 5
- Next, solve the exponential operation: 5^2 = 25
- Then, solve the multiplication and division operations: 150/3 = 50
- Lastly, solve the addition and subtraction operations: 50-25+5-1 = 29

Likewise, should you input the same formula in a cell, Excel will also come up with the same answer:

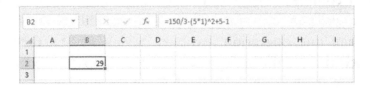

B2		✗	✓	f_x	=150/3-(5*1)^2+5-1			
◢	A	B	C	D	E	F	G	H	I
1								
2		29						
3								

PEMDAS is also applicable to formulas with cell references. Just remember to enclose the operations you want to be solved first in a parenthesis.

In this example, we will compute for the growth rate of each fruit's sales volume from 2016 to 2017. The formula for computing growth rate is (Present Value − Past Value)/Past Value x 100%.

To compute for the growth rate in Excel:

- Enter the equal sign (=) in cell D3.
- Key in the open parenthesis icon (( ).
- Click on cell C3 because it contains the 2017 value.
- Key in the minus sign (-).
- Click on cell B3 because it contains the 2016 value.
- Key in the close parenthesis icon ( )). This is to indicate that *C3-B3* is the operation to be solved first.
- Enter the forward slash symbol (/) for division.
- Click on cell B3 again.
- Press **Enter.**

ADDRESS	▾	✗	✓	f_x	=(C3-B3)/B3			
◢	A	B	C	D	E	F	G
1							
2	FRUIT	2016	2017	GROWTH RATE			
3	Lemons	5,346	8,237	=(C3-B3)/B3			
4	Apples	7,903	10,902				
5	Oranges	6,745	8,957				
6							
7							

D4		fx					
A	B	C	D	E	F	G

	A	B	C	D	E	F	G
1							
2	FRUIT	2016	2017	GROWTH RATE			
3	Lemons	5,346	8,237	0.540778152			
4	Apples	7,903	10,902				
5	Oranges	6,745	8,957				
6							
7							

- By default, the result will be in decimal form. Since this is a growth rate, click on the **Percentage Style** in the Number command group, to format the result as a percent.

D3		fx	=(C3-B3)/B3				
A	B	C	D	E	F	G

	A	B	C	D	E	F	G
1							
2	FRUIT	2016	2017	GROWTH RATE			
3	Lemons	5,346	8,237	54%			
4	Apples	7,903	10,902				
5	Oranges	6,745	8,957				
6							
7							

- To solve for the growth rates of Apples and Oranges, simply copy the formula throughout the remaining cells using the Fill Handle. Through the Fill Handle feature, not only will the formula be copied, but also the number formatting.

D3		fx	=(C3-B3)/B3				
A	B	C	D	E	F	G

	A	B	C	D	E	F	G
1							
2	FRUIT	2016	2017	GROWTH RATE			
3	Lemons	5,346	8,237	54%			
4	Apples	7,903	10,902	38%			
5	Oranges	6,745	8,957	33%			
6							
7							

Tip: You can also add parentheses to any formula, to make it easier to decipher, and for your personal convenience as well.

While adding parentheses do not necessarily change the result of the formula, it can be used to group the operations and emphasize which need to be solved first:

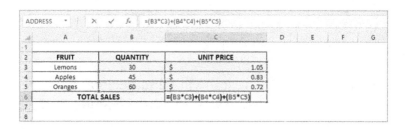

Chapter 4: Functions

Understanding Functions

While you have learned to enter formulas manually and use cell references, another easier and more convenient way to solve common mathematical operations is through Functions.

Functions are predefined formulas that are usually used to perform calculations on a range of cells, quickly and conveniently. Basic Functions in Excel can be used to easily determine the sum, average, count, minimum value, and maximum value of a cell range.

Understanding and knowing the use of each function can help you save a great amount of time and effort, especially when working with large amounts of data in your worksheet. While you may still end up with the same results through manually entering formulas, using functions is certainly more effective and efficient.

In this section, you will learn which operations may be alternatively solved through functions, and other simple yet powerful functions that can be used in daily Excel activities.

To access Excel's wide variety of functions, click on the **Formulas** tab in the ribbon.

Here, you can find the **Function Library** where functions are classified into several categories: Financial, Logical, Text, Date & Time, Lookup & Reference, and Math & Trig. You can also access the **More Functions** option for other functions used in Statistics, Engineering, and other fields.

The number of functions in Excel may be quite overwhelming, but once you get the grasp of the basic functions, understanding the more complicated ones becomes easier.

First, you have to understand the different parts of a function, and how arguments are created to calculate specific values.

Functions are written in a unique and specific way, known as **syntax**. Basically, a function consists of the **equals sign** (=), a **function name** (SUM, for example), and one or more **arguments**. Arguments contain the information you want to calculate. These may be in the form of numbers, cell addresses, or cell ranges.

It is important to note that arguments must always be enclosed in a parenthesis. In addition, when entering multiple arguments, each must be separated by a comma in between.

For example, in getting the sum of a cell range, the SUM function may be used, instead of entering the cell addresses of each cell in the formula.

Meanwhile, to get the sum of multiple cells that are not adjacent to each other, separate each cell address using a comma.

F1			×	✓	fx	=sum(A7,F1)		
	A	B	C	D	E	F	G	H
1	10	23	55	89	34	211		
2	14							
3	32							
4	57							
5	90							
6	34							
7	237					=sum(A7,F1)		
8								
9								

F7			×	✓	fx	=sum(A1:A7,F1,F7)				
	A	B	C	D	E	F	G	H	I	J
1	10	23	55	89	34	211				
2	14									
3	32									
4	57									
5	90									
6	34									
7	237					448	=sum(A1:A7,F1,F7)			
8										
9										

Basic Functions

As previously discussed, there are tons of Excel functions to choose from. Perhaps, in reality, only a few people know exactly what each function does. Or possibly, they only master those that are relevant to their fields. As a beginner, it is alright to start with the basics first. These may be the basic functions, but these are among the most frequently used functions in daily Excel activities.

Here are the 15 basic functions you need to know:

1. **SUM** – adds all the numbers in a cell range or any given argument. This is probably the most frequently used function in Excel. Everyone definitely encounters having to add a few values each day.

455

2. **AVERAGE** – determines the mean or central value in a given set of numbers. This function is commonly used in analyzing and evaluating performances.

3. **COUNT** – counts the number of cells that contain **numeric values** in a given range. Zero (0) also counts as a numeric value.

4. **COUNTA** – while the **COUNT** function is used to determine the number of cells that contain numeric values, **COUNTA** counts all the cells that are **not blank**, regardless of their content type, in a given range.

5. **MIN** – identifies the least numerical value in a given set of numbers.

6. **MAX** – identifies the greatest numerical value in a given set of numbers.

7. **SQRT** – computes for the square root of any given number.

8. **DAYS** – calculates the number of days between two given dates in a spreadsheet. This function may be particularly helpful in managing project timelines and deadlines.

9. **NETWORKDAYS** – calculates the number of (net) work days between two given dates in a spreadsheet. This function automatically excludes weekends (Saturdays and Sundays) in its calculation. Holidays may optionally be inputted to be excluded from the calculation. Similar to DAYS, this may also be helpful in managing project timelines and deadlines. Likewise, both functions play crucial roles especially for human resources and payroll management purposes.

10. **NOW** – displays the current date and time, and refreshes by the time the worksheet is opened or updated. In some cases, this may be used in displaying the print date and time of a particular worksheet needed for a report or presentation.

11. **ROUND** – provides an approximate number that is somehow close to the original value, depending on your

desired level of accuracy. In Excel, you may round a value up or down, or set specific rounding parameters. This function comes handy in simplifying numbers and making them easier to work with.

12. **TRIM** – removes all the extra spaces from text, leaving only a single space in between words. This function may be used to conveniently clean text formats from another source or application that may have irregular spacing.

13. **LEN** – calculates the length of a given text string through its number of characters. Spaces and numbers also count as characters.

14. **RANK** – generates the rank of a number in a list of numbers. This function is used to rank values from ascending or descending order, based on a given order argument.

15. **IF** – allows you to perform logical tests to evaluate a certain condition, and to return one value if that condition is met, and another value if that condition is not met. Essentially, the IF function is among the most popular functions in Excel as it can simplify data evaluation process, through laying specific criteria.

Inserting Functions

Now that you have learned the basic functions, pretty much, you would be able to remember most of them as you go on, especially those that you would need in your daily activities. Similar to formulas, functions may also be entered manually into a cell. As such, memorizing a few of your frequently used functions is also a great time-saver, especially when working with a lot of data.

However, if you are not the kind who likes to memorize formulas, keeping your own personal list of frequently used functions may also help. Or you could just simply resort to the good old Function Library under the Formulas tab.

As discussed in the previous section, the Function Library houses more or less 400 Excel functions, that are grouped into several categories.

Some basic functions may also be easily accessed through the AutoSum command found both in the Home tab and Formulas tab.

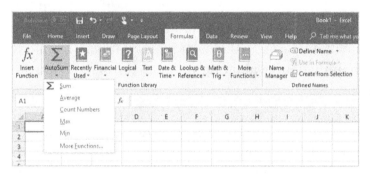

In this section, we will provide simple examples on how each of the basic function previously mentioned is used in an actual worksheet.

There are four ways that you can explore in inserting a function into a cell: (1) inserting a function **manually**—this is applicable for functions that you have probably memorized due to frequent use; (2) commonly used functions such as Sum and Average, may be easily accessed through the **AutoSum** command; (3) familiar functions may be searched from the

Function Library; lastly, (4) unfamiliar functions may also be searched through the **Insert Function** command using keywords and brief descriptions.

Accessing Functions Using the AutoSum Command

The **AutoSum** command is found both in the **Editing** group under the **Home** tab, and in the **Formulas** tab. For every user's convenience, commonly used functions such as Sum, Average, Count, Max, and Min may be easily accessed through the **AutoSum** command.

a. **SUM**

To find the sum of the values in cell range B3:B12:

• Click on the cell where you want the sum to be displayed. In this example, we have selected cell B13.

• Click on the **Formulas** tab.

• Click on the drop-down arrow under the **AutoSum** command, and choose **Sum**.

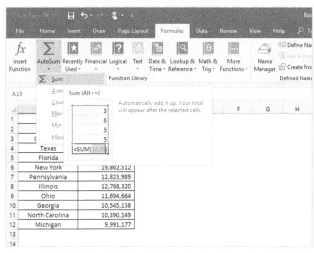

• Notice how Excel automatically inserts the function into the cell, and selects a cell range for the argument.

If by any chance, Excel selects the wrong cells, you can just manually enter your desired cells into the argument.

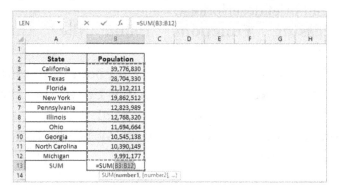

- Press **Enter** to show the result. Now, you have the sum of the values in cell range B3:B12, which is **177,869,320**.

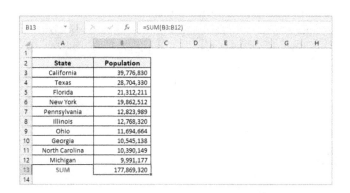

Tip: The Sum function may also be used for values with number formatting such as currency and percentage.

b. **AVERAGE**

To compute the average of the values in cell range B3:B12:

- Click on the cell where you want the average to be displayed. In this example, we have selected cell B14.

- Click on the **Formulas** tab.

- Click on the drop-down arrow under the **AutoSum** command, and choose **Average**.

- Excel has automatically selected cell range B3:B13. In this case, we have to change the argument to B3:B12, instead of B3:B13.

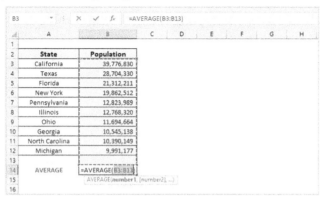

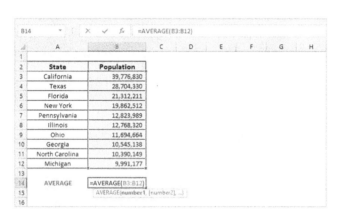

- Press **Enter** to show the result. Now, you have the average of the values in cell range B3:B12, which is **17,786,932**.

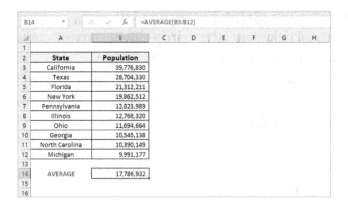

c. **COUNT**

To determine the number of cells in cell range B3:B12 with numerical values:

• Click on the cell where you want the result to be displayed. In this example, we have selected cell B13.

• Click on the **Formulas** tab.

• Click on the drop-down arrow under the **AutoSum** command, and choose **Count Numbers**.

• See to it that Excel selected the correct cell range. If not, apply the necessary changes.

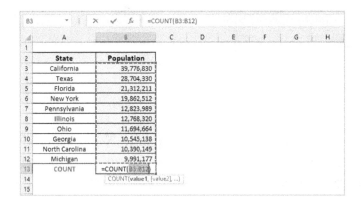

- Press **Enter** to show the result. The number of cells in cell range B3:B12 with numerical values is **10**.

B13				f_x	=COUNT(B3:B12)				
	A	B	C	D	E	F	G	H
1								
2	**State**	**Population**						
3	California	39,776,830						
4	Texas	28,704,330						
5	Florida	21,312,211						
6	New York	19,862,512						
7	Pennsylvania	12,823,989						
8	Illinois	12,768,320						
9	Ohio	11,694,664						
10	Georgia	10,545,138						
11	North Carolina	10,390,149						
12	Michigan	9,991,177						
13	COUNT	10						
14								
15								
16								

Tip: There is another convenient way to find the sum, average, and count of specific cells, without using any formula or function:

- Select the cells or cell range containing the values you wish to find the sum, average, and count of.
- Pay close attention to the lower left corner of the Excel interface.
- Notice that the Average, Count, and Sum are all readily indicated beside the Workbook Views icons.
- There you have it! You now know the Average, Count, and Sum of your selected cells with no formulas or functions involved. However, keep in mind that Count here stands for the COUNTA function, which counts the non-empty cells in a given range.

463

d. **MIN**

To identify the minimum or least numerical value in cell range B3:B12:

• Click on the cell where you want the value to be displayed. In this example, we have selected cell B13.

• Click on the **Formulas** tab.

• Click on the drop-down arrow under the **AutoSum** command, and choose **Min**.

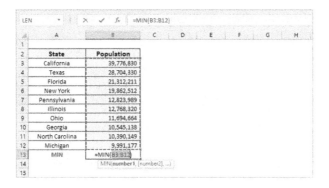

• Make sure that the selected range is correct. Then, press **Enter** to show the result. The minimum or least numerical value in cell range B3:B12 is **9,991,177**.

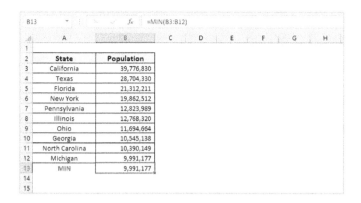

e. **MAX**

To identify the maximum or greatest numerical value in cell range B3:B12:

- Click on the cell where you want the value to be displayed. In this example, we have selected cell B13.
- Click on the **Formulas** tab.
- Click on the drop-down arrow under the **AutoSum** command, and choose **Max**.

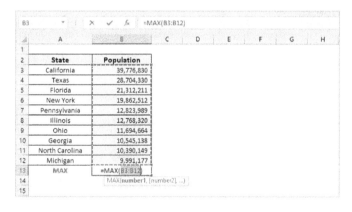

Make sure that the selected range is correct. Then, press **Enter** to show the result. The maximum or greatest numerical value in cell range B3:B12 is **39,776,830**.

B13		×	✓	f_x	=MAX(B3:B12)				

⊿	A	B	C	D	E	F	G	H
1								
2	**State**	**Population**						
3	California	39,776,830						
4	Texas	28,704,330						
5	Florida	21,312,211						
6	New York	19,862,512						
7	Pennsylvania	12,823,989						
8	Illinois	12,768,320						
9	Ohio	11,694,664						
10	Georgia	10,545,138						
11	North Carolina	10,390,149						
12	Michigan	9,991,177						
13	MAX	39,776,830						
14								
15								

Accessing Functions from the Function Library

For functions that seem familiar to you, you may simply look for them in the Function Library. Here, functions are classified into several categories based on the results that they produce. In addition, you may also retrieve your recently used functions here to help you save time and effort.

a. COUNTA

To determine the number of cells in cell range A3:A12 that are not empty:

- Click on the cell where you want the result to be displayed. In this example, we have selected cell A14.
- Click on the **Formulas** tab.
- Click on the drop-down arrow below **More Functions** and hover your mouse pointer over **Statistical** to view more functions.
- Choose **COUNTA**.

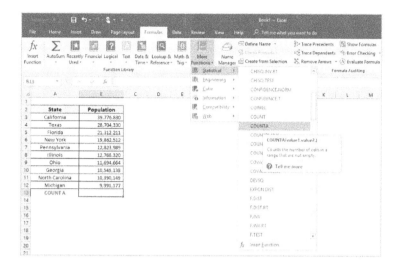

- A dialog box will prompt open to ask you to enter the values for the argument. A brief description of the function is also displayed to guide you. Likewise, the formula result is also instantly shown.

- Click on the **Value1** text field.

- Instead of entering each cell address that comprises cell range A3:A12, simply click and drag the cell range to select the cells.

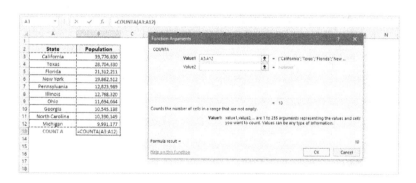

- Click **OK** to show the result. The number of cells in cell range A3:A12 that are not empty is **10**.

| B13 | | ▼ | × | ✓ | *fx* | =COUNTA(A3:A12) |

⊿	A	B	C	D	E	F	G	H
1								
2	**State**	**Population**						
3	California	39,776,830						
4	Texas	28,704,330						
5	Florida	21,312,211						
6	New York	19,862,512						
7	Pennsylvania	12,823,989						
8	Illinois	12,768,320						
9	Ohio	11,694,664						
10	Georgia	10,545,138						
11	North Carolina	10,390,149						
12	Michigan	9,991,177						
13	COUNT A	10						
14								

Tip: Technically, both **COUNT** and **COUNTA** functions fall under the **Statistical** category since these are used for data collection, organization, and analysis. Likewise, the AVERAGE, MIN, and MAX functions can also be found in the same category.

b. **SQRT**

To compute the square root of the value in cell B7:

• Click on the cell where you want the result to be displayed. In this example, we have selected cell D7.

• Click on the **Formulas** tab.

• Click the drop-down arrow below the **Math & Trig** category and look for the **SQRT** function.

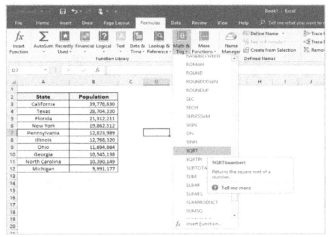

- A dialog box will prompt open to ask you to enter the values for the argument.

- Click on the **Number** text field.

- You may enter the value in the text field manually, or simply click on the cell containing the value to register its cell address automatically on the text field.

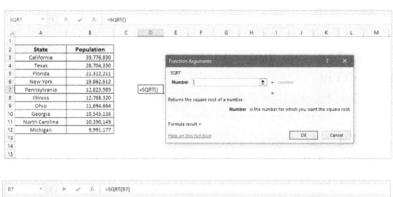

- Click **OK** to show the result. The square root of the value in cell B7 (12,823,989) is **3,581**.

- By default, the result will be a whole number, and not in decimal form. You may adjust its number formatting based on your requirement.

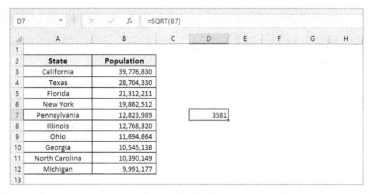

Tip: You can also find the SUM function under the **Math & Trig** category, along with functions for other mathematical terms like PRODUCT, and QUOTIENT, to name a few.

c. ROUND

To round the value in cell B3 to the nearest hundreds place:

•   Click on the cell where you want the result to be displayed. In this example, we have selected cell C3.

•   Click on the **Formulas** tab.

•   Click the drop-down arrow below the **Math & Trig** category and look for the **ROUND** function.

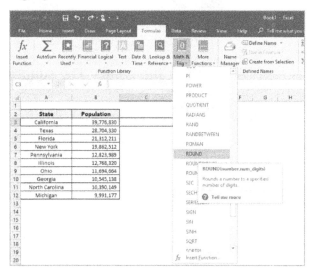

- A dialog box will prompt open to ask you to enter the values for the argument.

Here, you will also be asked to fill in two text fields—first is for **Number** which refers to the value that you want to round, second is for **Num_digits** which refers to the number of digits to which you want to round. Entering the arguments for the Num_digits field may be a bit tricky. So, keep in mind these few reminders: a negative value for the Num_digits rounds to the left of the decimal point; a positive value rounds to the right of the decimal point; and lastly, zero rounds to the nearest integer.

- In this example, we will round the value in cell B3 to the nearest hundred. Click on cell B3 to register its cell address on the **Number** text field.

- To round a value to the nearest hundreds, you will have to round it to **2 digits to the left of the decimal point**. Thus, the argument for **Num_digits** is -2.

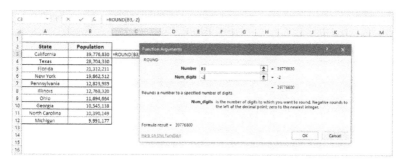

- The formula result is initially displayed in the dialog box, so you may instantly check if it is correct.
- Upon getting your desired result, proceed to clicking **OK** to show the result in the cell. The value in cell B3 (39,776,830) rounded to the nearest hundreds is equal to **39,776,800**.

	A	B	C	D	E	F
			C3 fx =ROUND(B3,-2)			
1						
2	**State**	**Population**				
3	California	39,776,830	39,776,800			
4	Texas	28,704,330				
5	Florida	21,312,211				
6	New York	19,862,512				
7	Pennsylvania	12,823,989				
8	Illinois	12,768,320				
9	Ohio	11,694,664				
10	Georgia	10,545,138				
11	North Carolina	10,390,149				
12	Michigan	9,991,177				
13						

Tip: Just like formulas, Functions may also be copied through the **Fill Handle** option.

To round the other values below cell B3 to the same place value,

- Click on cell C3.
- Hover your mouse pointer over the bottom left corner of the cell, until the fill handle icon appears. As discussed previously, the fill handle feature is characterized by a small cross icon.

	A	B	C	D	E	F	G
			C3 fx =ROUND(B3,-2)				
1							
2	**State**	**Population**					
3	California	39,776,830	39,776,800				
4	Texas	28,704,330					
5	Florida	21,312,211					
6	New York	19,862,512					
7	Pennsylvania	12,823,989					
8	Illinois	12,768,320					
9	Ohio	11,694,664					
10	Georgia	10,545,138					
11	North Carolina	10,390,149					
12	Michigan	9,991,177					
13							
14							

- Drag it down to cell C12, to apply the same function to the selected cells.

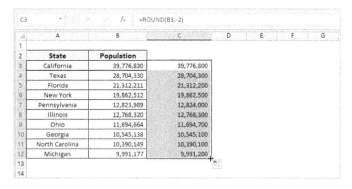

- Now, you have rounded all the values in cell range B3:B12.

d. NOW

To display the current date and time on a worksheet:

- Click on the cell where you want the result to be displayed. In this example, we have selected cell D1.

- Click on the **Formulas** tab.

- Click the drop-down arrow below the **Date & Time** category and look for the **NOW** function.

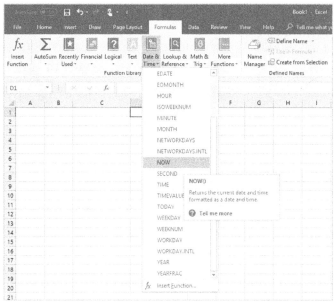

- A dialog box will prompt open to inform that the NOW function takes no arguments.

- Click **OK**. The current date and time will now be displayed.

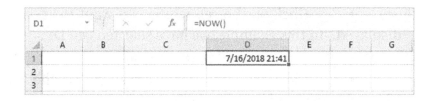

e. DAYS

To calculate the number of days between two given dates—**January 1, 2017** and **July 16, 2018**, in this example:

- Click on the cell where you want the result to be displayed. In this example, we have selected cell E1.
- Click on the **Formulas** tab.
- Click the drop-down arrow below the **Date & Time** category and look for the **DAYS** function.

- A dialog box will prompt open to let you fill in the **End_date** and the **Start_date** fields. These signify the two dates between which you want to know the number of days.

- You may manually enter the dates in the text fields, or simply click on the cell(s) containing the dates to automatically register their cell address(es) in the text fields.

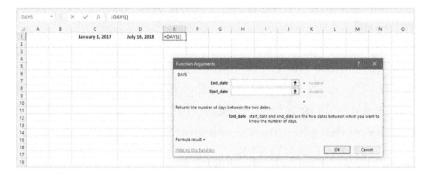

- For the **Start_date** field, click on cell C1 because it contains January 1, 2017. Meanwhile for the **End_date** field, click on cell D1 because it contains July 16, 2018.

- Click **OK** to show the result. There are are **561** days between January 1, 2017 and July 16, 2018.

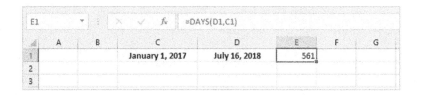

Accessing Functions Using the Insert Function Command

The **Insert Function** command comes in handy when you do not know the exact name of the function you wish to perform. Through this command, you will be asked to enter related keywords or a brief description of what you want to do, so that Excel can recommend relevant functions to you.

a. **NETWORKDAYS**

In this example, we will use the same given dates— January 1, 2017 and July 16, 2018, but this time, to compute the working days between them.

- Click on the cell where you want the result to be displayed. In this example, we have selected cell E1 again.
- Click on the **Formulas** tab, Then, click **Insert Function**.

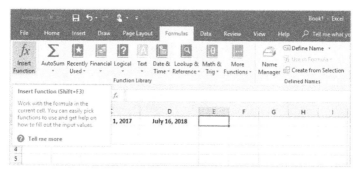

- A dialog box will prompt open to ask you to key in a brief description of what you want to do.

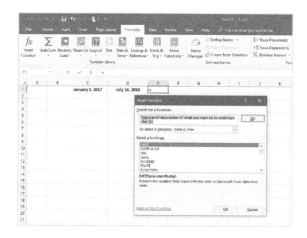

- Since we are computing for the number of work days between two given dates, you may enter *working days* in the search field. Then, click **Go**.
- Excel will then recommend possible and relevant functions to help you with the task you wish to perform.

- In addition, a brief description of each function is also displayed to further guide you in choosing the appropriate function for your task.

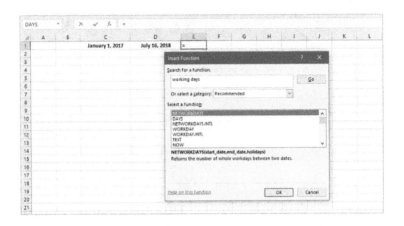

- For this example, choose **NETWORKDAYS**. Then, click **OK**.
- A dialog box will prompt open to ask you to fill in the necessary fields, such as the **Start_date, End_date**, and **Holidays**.

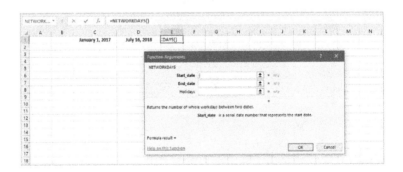

- Click on cell C1 for the Start_date, and cell D1 for the End_date, respectively. Filling in the Holidays field is optional. For this example, we will enter January 1, 2018 as a holiday.

- Lastly, click **OK**.

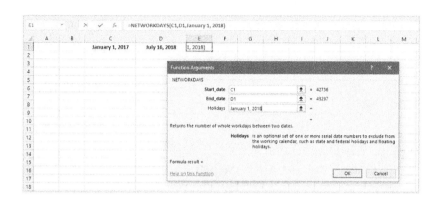

- Overall, there are **400** working days between January 1, 2017 and July 16, 2018, excluding one holiday.

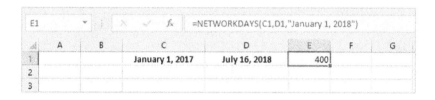

- Should you remove the Holiday argument, the number of days will be increased to **401**.

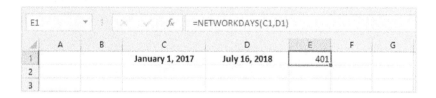

Tip: NETWORKDAYS automatically excludes weekends (Saturdays and Sundays) in its calculation. For cases where you need to custom weekends (e.g. Sunday only), you will have to switch to the **NETWORKDAYS.INTL** function which allows you to set parameters to indicate which and how many days are weekend days.

b. **TRIM**

To clean text data by removing unnecessary spaces in between words:

- Click on the cell where you want the result to be displayed. In this example, we have selected cell B2.
- Click on the **Formulas** tab, Then, click **Insert Function**.
- A dialog box will prompt open to ask you to key in a brief description of what you want to do.
- You may simply enter *remove spaces* or *remove spaces between texts* in the search field. Then, click **Go**.
- Select **TRIM** from the list of recommended functions, as this is the most appropriate function for your required task. Then, click **OK**.

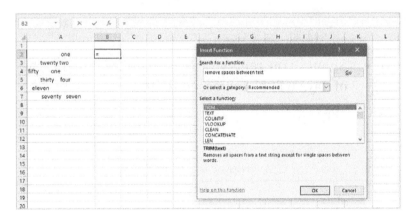

- Another dialog box will prompt open for you to enter your function arguments. Click on cell A2 as this cell contains the text you want to be formatted. Then, click **OK**.

- Notice how the text is now stripped off of unnecessary spaces, and is adjusted based on Excel's default text format—aligned left to the bottom of the cell.

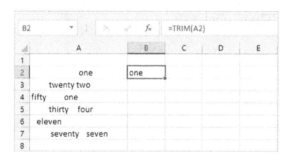

- Apply the same function to the remaining cells using Fill Handle.

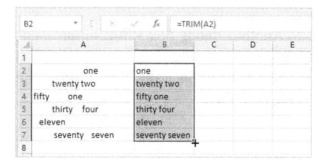

c. **LEN**

To determine the number of characters in a given text string:

• Click on the cell where you want the result to be displayed. In this example, we have selected cell B2.

• Click on the **Formulas** tab, Then, click **Insert Function**.

• A dialog box will prompt open to ask you to key in a brief description of what you want to do.

• You may simply enter *text length* or *character length* in the search field. Then, click **Go**.

• Select **LEN** from the list of recommended functions, as this is the most appropriate function for your required task. Then, click **OK**.

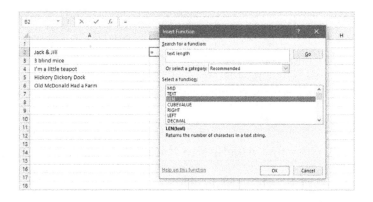

• Another dialog box will prompt open for you to enter your function arguments. Click on cell A2 as this cell contains the text which you want to determine the character count of. Then, click **OK**.

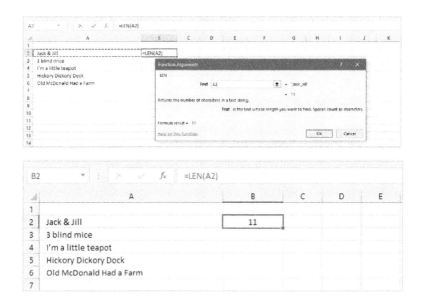

Tip: Spaces count as characters, along with numbers and special characters.

- Apply the same function to the remaining cells using Fill Handle.

- Now, you have the text length and character counts each given text string.

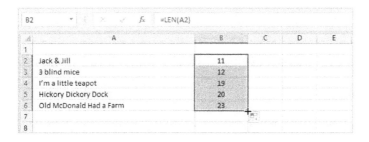

d. RANK

To rank the values in cell range B3:B12, in an ascending order:

- Click on the cell where you want the result to be displayed. In this example, we have selected cell C3.

- Click on the **Formulas** tab, Then, click **Insert Function**.

- A dialog box will prompt open to ask you to key in a brief description of what you want to do.

- You may simply enter *rank* in the search field. Then, click **Go**.

- Select **RANK** from the list of recommended functions. Then, click **OK**.

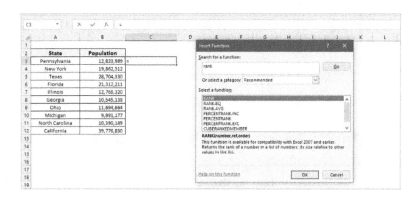

A dialog box will prompt open for you to enter your function arguments: **Number** refers to the value which you want to rank; **Ref** stands for reference to a list of numbers; lastly, **Order** is a number that will be used to specify how the values will be ranked—0 or omitted for descending order, while any nonzero value for ascending order.

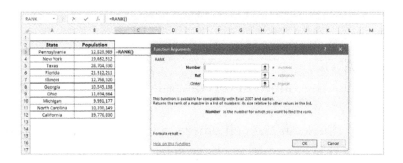

- For the **Number** field argument, click on cell B3 because it contains the value you wish to rank.
- For the **Ref** field argument, select cell range B3:B12, to serve as the reference in ranking the values.
- For the **Order** field argument, key in *1* or any nonzero value since we are to rank the values in an ascending order.
- Then, click **OK**.

- Cell B3's rank with reference to the values in cell range B3:B12 is **6**.

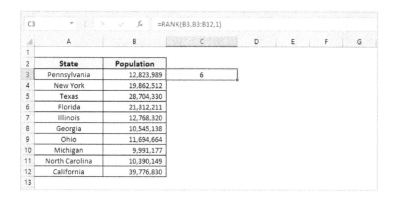

To generate the ranks of the other values in cells below cell B3, we may also use the Fill Handle. However, we must keep in mind to make the cell reference, an **absolute** reference.

An absolute cell reference is used when several formulas need to consistently refer to a particular cell. An absolute reference remains as it is and does not change when it is copied or filled to other cells. As such, it is used to keep a row, a column, or both, constant.

The difference between a relative reference and an absolute reference lies in the addition of a dollar sign ($) in the cell address. The dollar sign can precede the column reference, the row reference, or both, depending on which values you want to keep constant.

For instance, in ranking the values in cell range B3:B12, cell range B3:B12 as the reference, must be an absolute reference. Thus, in the function, we have to add the dollar signs ($) in the **Ref** argument, to make it constant when copied across the other cells.

From B3:B12, we will update it into *$B$3:$B$12*.

RANK	▼	⁝	×	✓	*fx*	=RANK(B3,$B$3:$B$12,1)

◢	A	B	C	D
1				
2	**State**	**Population**		
3	Pennsylvania	12,823,989	=RANK(B3,$B$3:$B$12,1)	
4	New York	19,862,512	RANK(number, ref, [order])	
5	Texas	28,704,330		
6	Florida	21,312,211		
7	Illinois	12,768,320		
8	Georgia	10,545,138		
9	Ohio	11,694,664		
10	Michigan	9,991,177		
11	North Carolina	10,390,149		
12	California	39,776,830		
13				

- We can now use the Fill Handle in copying the function to the remaining cells.

- Notice how the **Ref** argument $B$3:$B$12 remains constant across all the cells, despite using the Fill Handle.

- We now have the ranks of each value in cell range B3:B12.

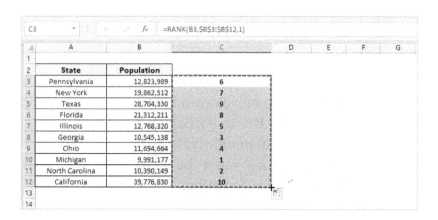

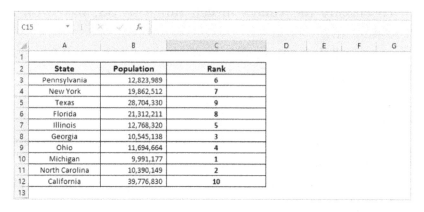

On the other hand, if you do not convert the reference into an absolute reference, and simply proceed with the Fill Handle feature, the cell references will just update, or change based on the relative position of rows and columns.

	RANK		×	✓	fx	=RANK(B4,B4:B13,1)			

	A	B	C	D	E	F	G
1							
2	State	Population	Rank				
3	Pennsylvania	12,823,989	6				
4	New York	19,862,512	=RANK(B4,B4:B13,1)				
5	Texas	28,704,330	7				
6	Florida	21,312,211	6				
7	Illinois	12,768,320	5				
8	Georgia	10,545,138	3				
9	Ohio	11,694,664	3				
10	Michigan	9,991,177	1				
11	North Carolina	10,390,149	1				
12	California	39,776,830	1				
13							
14							

For example, as you move down to cell B4, the reference also moved down from B3:B12 to B4:B13, and so on.

Thus, in using the fill handle feature, it also important to note which cells or values must be kept constant across multiple cells, to avoid miscalculations and misinterpretations of data.

e. **IF**

To classify the values in cell range B1:B8, based on a given condition:

• Click on the cell where you want the result to be displayed. In this example, we have selected cell C1.

• Click on the **Formulas** tab, then, click **Insert Function**.

• A dialog box will prompt open to ask you to key in a brief description of what you want to do.

• You may simply enter *condition* in the search field. Then, click **Go**.

• Select **IF** from the list of recommended functions. Then, click **OK**.

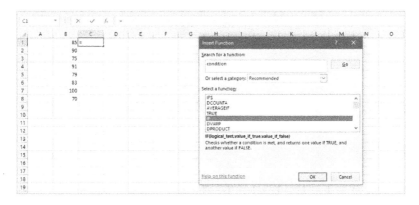

Tip: You can also use the IFS function if you are dealing with two or more conditions.

- Another dialog box will prompt open to ask you to enter the necessary function arguments: **Logical_test** refers to an expression or condition that can be evaluated to be TRUE or FALSE; **Value_if_true** is the returned value when the Logical_test is met or is true; **Value_if_false** is the returned value when the Logical_test is not met or is false.

- In this example, we will set the **Logical_test** argument to $B1>=80$, **Value_if_true** argument to "Good", and **Value_if_false** argument to "Bad", respectively.
- Then, click **OK**.

489

This means that if the condition of a certain value in a cell being greater than or equal to (>=) 80 is met, the value will be classified as "Good." However, if the condition is not met, the value will be classified as "Bad."

- The value in cell B1 is 85. As a result, the condition of being greater than or equal to 80 is met. Thus, the value is classified as Good.

C1				f_x	=IF(B1>=80,"Good","Bad")			
	A	B	C	D	E	F	G	H
1		85	Good					
2		90						
3		75						
4		91						
5		79						
6		83						
7		100						
8		70						
9								

- Use the Fill Handle to apply the same function to the remaining cells, and see whether the other values meet the condition or not.

C1				f_x	=IF(B1>=80,"Good","Bad")			
	A	B	C	D	E	F	G	H
1		85	Good					
2		90						
3		75						
4		91						
5		79						
6		83						
7		100						
8		70						
9								

C8		▼	:	⋋	✓	ƒₓ	=IF(B8>=80,"Good","Bad")			
◢	A	B	C	D	E	F	G	H		
1		85	Good							
2		90	Good							
3		75	Bad							
4		91	Good							
5		79	Bad							
6		83	Good							
7		100	Good							
8		70	Bad							
9										
10										

- Consequently, all values greater than or equal to 80 are classified as Good, while values less than 80 are classified as Bad.

Chapter 5:

Managing Data

If cells are the building blocks of a worksheet, then data constitute the heart of a worksheet. Without data, there would be nothing to store, organize, and analyze. Now that you have learned the types of data—text, numbers, and formulas—and how to input them into worksheets, the next step is to learn how to manage them.

Excel offers several features to help you effectively organize data. These features are especially useful when you are working with a lot of data. In addition, an organized worksheet makes it easier and more convenient for you to find the information that you need, and to generate analysis.

Sorting Data

Excel allows you to instantly reorganize your worksheet through sorting the data in it. In line with this, data can be sorted alphabetically, numerically, and based on cell color, font color, or assigned conditional formatting icon.

In this example, we will sort the following states alphabetically and numerically based on population.

A2	f_x	State	
	A	B	C	D
1				
2	State	Population	Rank	
3	Pennsylvania	12,823,989	6	
4	New York	19,862,512	7	
5	Texas	28,704,330	9	
6	Florida	21,312,211	8	
7	Illinois	12,768,320	5	
8	Georgia	10,545,138	3	
9	Ohio	11,694,664	4	
10	Michigan	9,991,177	1	
11	North Carolina	10,390,149	2	
12	California	39,776,830	10	
13				

To sort data alphabetically:

- Click on the **header cell** of the range you want to sort. In this example, we have selected cell A2.

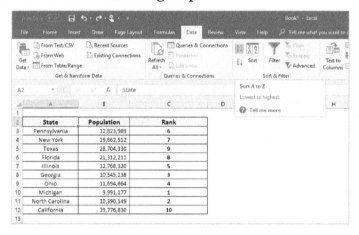

- Under the **Data** tab, click **Sort A to Z**, in the **Sort & Filter** command group.

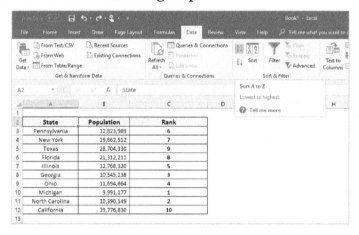

- The cells under the **State** header are now arranged alphabetically, from A to Z.

- Notice how the values under the **Population** and **Rank** headers are also automatically rearranged relatively to the order of its respective state.

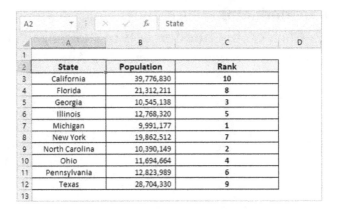

To sort data numerically:

- Click on the **header cell** of the range you want to sort. In this example, we have selected cell B2.

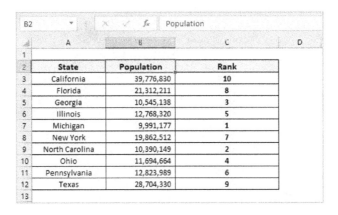

- Under the **Data** tab, click **Sort**, in the **Sort & Filter** command group.

- A dialog box will prompt open to ask you on how to sort the data.

- Also, notice how the entire cell range A3:C12 is automatically selected.

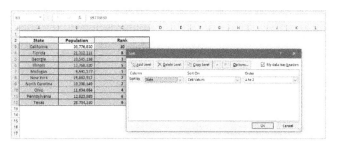

Tip: Since there are three column headers in this example—State, Population, and Rank, you are allowed to sort the data based on these headers.

- Select **Population**, **Cell Values**, and **Smallest to Largest**, under the Column, Sort On, and Order fields, respectively. Then, click **OK**.

- The data will then be arranged according to **Population**, from smallest to largest.

Tip: You may also access the **Sort & Filter** command in the **Editing** group, under the **Home** tab.

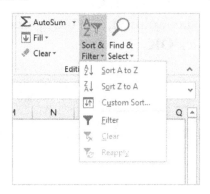

- Click the drop-down arrow below **Sort & Filter** to show options to sort the cells from A to Z, and vice versa, or set a custom sort.

Filtering Data

Searching for a particular data can be difficult, especially in a worksheet with a lot of content. While the **Find** (Ctrl+F) function is always ready to help, it is only useful in locating a single text or a single group of words.

Thus, Excel enables you to filter data. Filtering data narrows down the data in your worksheet, and displays only the information that you need.

Filtering is useful when you have to look for the same data across a comprehensive content.

In the following examples, we will discuss how to apply filter to a given set of data.

Filtering Text Data

To filter data effectively and correctly, your worksheet must first include a header row, which identifies and classifies the content of each column. In this example, we have the following headers: Subject, Score, Grade, and Month.

- Click on one header cell.

SUBJECT	SCORE	GRADE	MONTH
Math	85	Good	January
Science	90	Good	April
English	75	Bad	February
Social Studies	91	Good	June
Physical Education	79	Bad	February
Art & Music	83	Good	January
Math	100	Good	March
English	70	Bad	April
Social Studies	100	Good	February
Physical Education	80	Good	May
Home Economics	85	Good	June
Science	76	Bad	March
Art & Music	70	Bad	January
Social Studies	99	Good	April
Science	93	Good	May

- Click on the **Data** tab, and choose **Filter** in the **Sort & Filter** group.

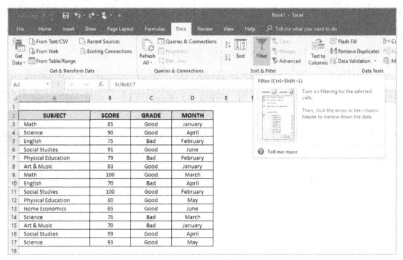

- A drop-down arrow will appear in each column header cell.

- Click the drop-down arrow of the column you want to filter. In this example, we will the filter the **Subject** column. So, click the drop-down arrow in the Subject header cell.

- A filter menu will appear, listing all the data under the Subject column. Here, you can also access the **Sort** command.

• Click the **(Select All)** checkbox to deselect all data. Now, you can choose which data you want to be displayed, by checking the boxes next to the data.

• In this example, we will only select **Math** and **Science** to view more of their content. Thus, click on the checkboxes next to them. Then, click **OK**.

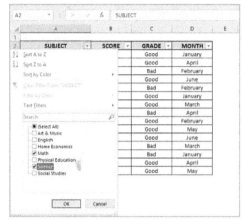

- As a result, only the cells containing Math and Science will be shown, along with other content within the same row(s). Meanwhile, the other subjects and other content within the same row(s) will be temporarily hidden.

- Notice also that the drop-down arrow of the **Subject** cell has included a filter icon, since the data in this column are filtered.

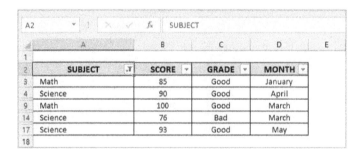

- To view the content of the other subjects, click on the drop-down arrow again, then reselect your preferred data.

Tip: You may also set a **Text Filter**, depending on your preference or requirement. Preset filter conditions include "Does Not Equal…", "Equals…", "Does Not Contain…", "Contains…", "Begins With…", and "Ends With…". Simply supply the necessary information or specific criteria to filter your data accordingly.

Furthermore, in some instances when the generated filter list is quite long, scrolling through it may be a bit difficult. As such, you may want to use the **Search** field to easily find the data that you want to include in the filter.

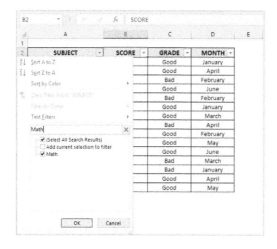

To add another data to the filter, use the **Search** field again to look for it from the list. Click the **Add current selection to filter** box. Then, click **OK**.

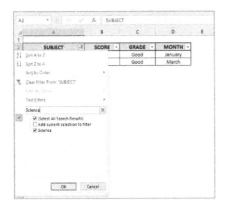 

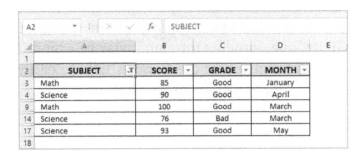

Filtering Numerical Data

In most cases of filtering numerical data, using **Number Filters** is more common, instead of manually selecting or filtering specific values to display.

More often than not, numerical data consist of multiple values. So, when it comes to filtering them, setting a parameter or a condition is more convenient.

Similar to Text Filters, there are also preset Number Filters that can help you easily filter numerical data. These include "Does Not Equal…", "Equals…", "Less Than…", and Greater Than…" to name a few.

In this example, we will apply filter to the **Score** column, to show only the values that are less than 80.

Click the drop-down arrow in the **Score** header cell.

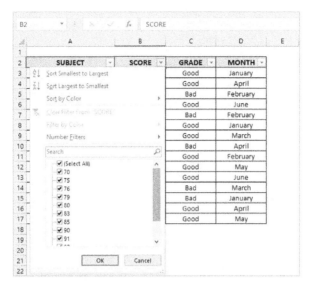

- Hover your mouse pointer over **Number Filters**. Then, click **Less Than**.

- A dialog box will prompt open to ask you to supply the necessary information to complete the number filter condition.

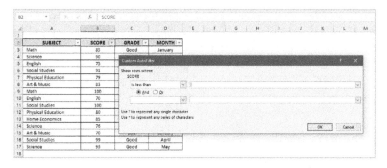

- Enter *80* in the text field provided. Then, click **OK**.

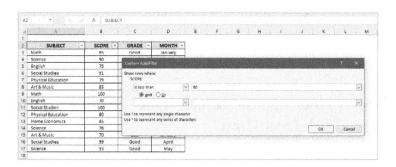

- All cells containing values less than 80 will then be shown, along with other content within the same row(s).

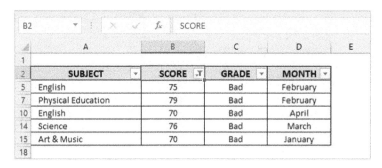

Applying Multiple Filters

Multiple filters may also be applied, especially when you want to narrow down your filtered data even further.

In this example, we will filter the same data, to show only the **Good** grades in the month of **February**.

- Click the drop-down arrow in the **Grade** header cell.

- Click the **Bad** checkbox to deselect it. Then, click **OK**.

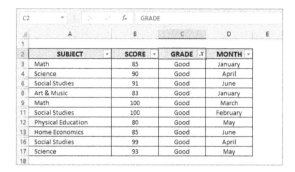

- Now that only the **Good** grades are shown, click the drop-down arrow in the **Month** header cell.

- Click the **(Select All)** checkbox to deselect all data. Select **February**. Then, click **OK**.

- Only the **Good** grade in the month of **February** will then be shown. Notice that the drop-down icons in both header cells have also automatically included filter icons, since we have filtered the data under these columns.

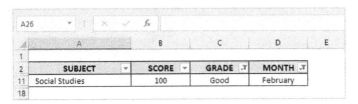

Clearing Filters

You may also clear the filters if you wish to display the data back to its original form.

To clear the filter from a single column:

- Click on the header cell of the column you want to clear the filter from. In this example, we will clear the filter from the **Grade** column. So, click on its header.

- Click the filter drop-down arrow icon to show more options.

- Then, click **Clear Filter From "GRADE"**.

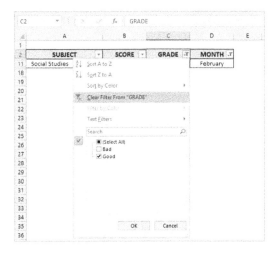

- After which, the **Grade** column will then be cleared of any filter.

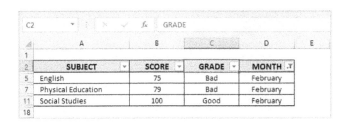

To clear all the filters from a range of data:
- Under the **Data** tab, click the **Clear** command in the **Sort & Filter** group.

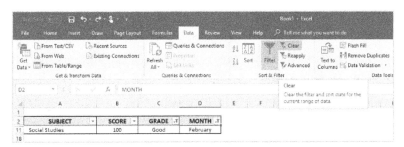

- The data range will then be cleared of any filters.

D2		▼	:	✕	✓	*fx*	MONTH		
	A			B		C		D	E
1									
2	**SUBJECT** ▼			**SCORE** ▼		**GRADE** ▼		**MONTH** ▼	
3	Math			85		Good		January	
4	Science			90		Good		April	
5	English			75		Bad		February	
6	Social Studies			91		Good		June	
7	Physical Education			79		Bad		February	
8	Art & Music			83		Good		January	
9	Math			100		Good		March	
10	English			70		Bad		April	
11	Social Studies			100		Good		February	
12	Physical Education			80		Good		May	
13	Home Economics			85		Good		June	
14	Science			76		Bad		March	
15	Art & Music			70		Bad		January	
16	Social Studies			99		Good		April	
17	Science			93		Good		May	
18									

Tip: The **Filter** command may also be accessed in the **Editing** group, under the **Home** tab.

Grouping Data

Scrolling through a lot of content in a worksheet is certainly difficult, confusing, and tedious. Aside from sorting and filtering data to help you easily reorganize and instantly find the content you need, grouping data is another helpful feature that Excel offers, in order to make your worksheet activities more convenient and more tolerable, for that matter.

Through grouping data, you can show or hide specific sections of your workbook, making it easier to read and less overwhelming. Header cells are also required in grouping data, similar to sorting and filtering them.

For example, in the given data, you only want to view the population from **2014 to 2017**. With this, you may choose to group the columns containing data for **2010 to 2013**, and temporarily hide them, to reduce the data displayed in the worksheet.

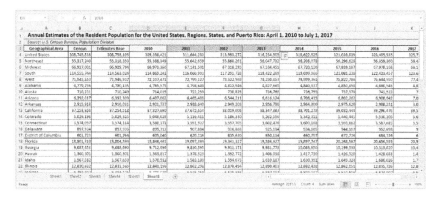

To group rows or columns:

- Select the header cells of the columns you want to group. In this example, select cell range D3:G3 to group columns D to G.

- Under the **Data** tab, click the **Group** command in the **Outline** group.

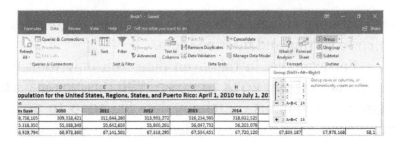

- A dialog box will appear to let you choose what to group— either **Rows** or **Columns**. Choose **Columns**. Then, click **OK**.

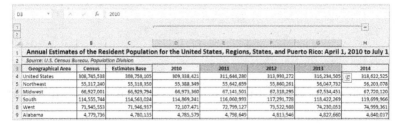

A grouped data is indicated by an outline. Click the minus (-) sign to collapse or hide the group. Subsequently, the minus sign will turn into a plus (+) sign. Click the plus sign to expand or show the group again.

- Click the minus (-) sign to hide the group (columns D to G).

	A	B	C	D	E	F	G	H
1	Annual Estimates of the Resident Population for the United States, Regions, States, and Puerto Rico: April 1, 2010 to July 1							
2	Source: U.S. Census Bureau, Population Division							
3	Geographical Area	Census	Estimates Base	2010	2011	2012	2013	2014
4	United States	308,745,538	308,758,105	309,338,421	311,644,280	313,993,272	316,234,505	318,622,525
5	Northeast	55,317,240	55,318,350	55,388,349	55,642,659	55,860,261	56,047,732	56,203,078
6	Midwest	66,927,001	66,929,794	66,973,360	67,141,501	67,318,295	67,534,451	67,720,120
7	South	114,555,744	114,563,024	114,869,241	116,060,993	117,291,728	118,422,269	119,699,966
8	West	71,945,553	71,946,937	72,107,471	72,799,127	73,522,988	74,230,053	74,999,361
9	Alabama	4,779,736	4,780,135	4,785,579	4,798,649	4,813,946	4,827,660	4,840,037

- Now, you can view the population from **2014 to 2017** with ease.

	A	B	C	H	I	J	K	L
1	Annual Estimates of the Resident Population for the United States, Regions, States, and Puerto Rico: April							
2	Source: U.S. Census Bureau, Population Division							
3	Geographical Area	Census	Estimates Base	2014	2015	2016	2017	
4	United States	308,745,538	308,758,105	318,622,525	321,039,839	323,405,935	325,719,178	
5	Northeast	55,317,240	55,318,350	56,203,078	56,296,628	56,359,360	56,470,581	
6	Midwest	66,927,001	66,929,794	67,720,120	67,839,187	67,978,168	68,179,351	
7	South	114,555,744	114,563,024	119,699,966	121,081,238	122,423,457	123,658,624	
8	West	71,945,553	71,946,937	74,999,361	75,822,786	76,644,950	77,410,622	
9	Alabama	4,779,736	4,780,135	4,840,037	4,850,858	4,860,545	4,874,747	

To ungroup rows or columns:

- Select the header cells of the columns you want to ungroup. Using the same example, select cell range D3:G3 to ungroup columns D to G.
- Under the **Data** tab, click the **Ungroup** command in the **Outline** group.

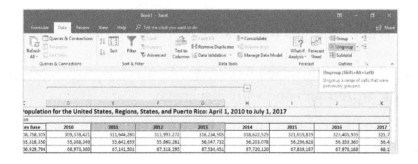

- A dialog box will appear to let you choose what to ungroup—either **Rows** or **Columns**. Choose **Columns**. Then, click **OK**.

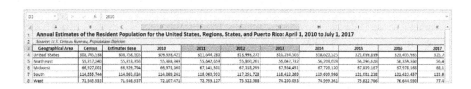

	D	E	F	G	H
›ulation for the United States, Regions, States, and Puerto Rico: April 1, 2010 to Jul					
Base	2010	2011	2012	2013	2014
758,105	309,338,421	311,6		316,234,505	318,622
318,350	55,388,349	55,6		56,047,732	56,203
329,794	66,973,360	67,1		67,534,451	67,720
563,024	114,869,241	116,0		118,422,269	119,699
346,937	72,107,471	72,7		74,230,053	74,999
780,135	4,785,579	4,7		4,827,660	4,840
710,249	714,015	7		736,760	736
392,309	6,407,002	6,465,488	6,544,211	6,616,124	6,706
916,031	2,921,737	2,938,640	2,949,208	2,956,780	2,964

- The data will be displayed back to its original form, without the online.

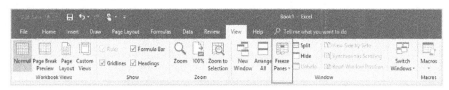

Freezing Panes

While grouping data allows you to show or hide specific sections of your workbook, freezing panes makes it possible to scroll through the entire workbook by keeping relevant sections "frozen" or constantly displayed.

The first column and the top row are usually frozen in a worksheet, as these typically contain constant data—such as headings and main labels—across the entire data range or worksheet.

The **Freeze Panes** command may be accessed in the **Window** group, under the **View** tab.

To freeze the first column of a sheet:

- Click the drop-down arrow of the **Freeze Panes** command.

- Choose **Freeze First Column**.

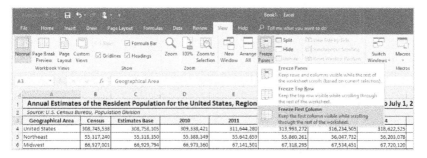

- The first column in the sheet will then be "frozen," and will be constantly visible despite scrolling across the worksheet.

- In this example, even if we have scrolled further through column K, the first column of the sheet still remains visible.

To freeze the top row of a sheet:

- Click the drop-down arrow of the **Freeze Panes** command.

- Choose **Freeze Top Row**.

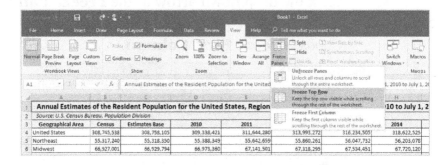

- The top row in the sheet will then be "frozen," and will be constantly visible despite scrolling through the worksheet.
- In this example, even if we have scrolled further down to row 60, the top row of the sheet still remains visible.

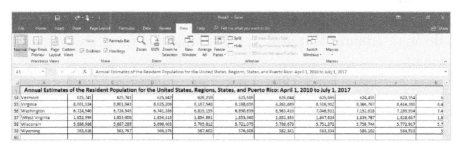

Aside from the top row and the first column of the sheet, it is also possible to select specific rows and columns to be kept visible when scrolling through the entire sheet.

For instance, in the given data, you want to constantly display the column that contains the **Geographical Area** (column A), as well as the row that contains the given **Years** (row 3).

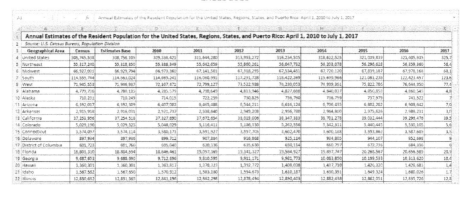

To freeze specific row(s) and column(s) of a sheet:

- Click on the cell located to the right of the column and below the row that you want to freeze. In this example, click on cell B4, because it is the cell to the right of column A, and below row 3.

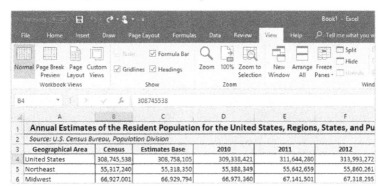

- Click the drop-down arrow of the **Freeze Panes** command.
- Choose **Freeze Panes**.

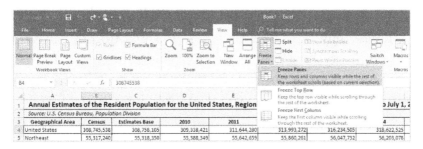

- Notice that column A and row 3 are still both visible, despite scrolling across to column K and down to row 59.

46	Oregon	3,893,920	3,919,664	3,960,673	4,016,537	4,085,989	4,142,776

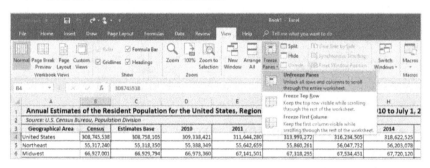

Table showing:

Annual Estimates, States, and Puerto Rico: April 1, 2010 to July 1, 2017
Source: U.S. Census Bu

Geographical Area	2012	2013	2014	2015	2016	2017
Oregon	3,893,920	3,919,664	3,960,673	4,016,537	4,085,989	4,142,776
Pennsylvania	12,768,034	12,778,450	12,790,341	12,791,124	12,787,085	12,805,537
Rhode Island	1,052,761	1,052,784	1,054,782	1,055,916	1,057,566	1,059,639
South Carolina	4,719,009	4,765,862	4,824,758	4,892,423	4,959,822	5,024,369
South Dakota	832,576	842,513	849,455	854,036	861,542	869,666
Tennessee	6,450,632	6,490,795	6,540,007	6,590,726	6,649,404	6,715,984
Texas	26,078,327	26,479,279	26,954,436	27,454,880	27,904,862	28,304,596
Utah	2,854,222	2,899,961	2,938,671	2,984,917	3,044,321	3,101,833
Vermont	625,606	626,044	625,665	624,455	623,354	623,657
Virginia	8,188,656	8,261,689	8,316,902	8,366,767	8,414,380	8,470,020
Washington	6,890,899	6,963,410	7,046,931	7,152,818	7,280,934	7,405,743
West Virginia	1,855,360	1,852,333	1,847,624	1,839,767	1,828,637	1,815,857
Wisconsin	5,721,075	5,736,673	5,751,272	5,759,744	5,772,917	5,795,483
Wyoming	576,608	582,341	583,334	586,102	584,910	579,315

To unfreeze panes:

- Click the drop-down arrow of the **Freeze Panes** command.
- Choose **Unfreeze Panes**.

Formatting Data as a Table

There may be instances when you just do not have the time to manually format your content—add fill colors and cell borders, for example. Fortunately, Excel offers a feature that can automatically transform your data into a table.

Just like regular formatting, formatting data into a table can enhance the look, feel, and quality of your workbook in an instant. In addition, large amounts of data look more organized and more pleasing to the eyes, when presented in a table format.

The **Format as Table** command may be accessed in the **Home** tab. Here, you will discover Excel's various preset table styles and templates that can help you format your data into a table easily and with style.

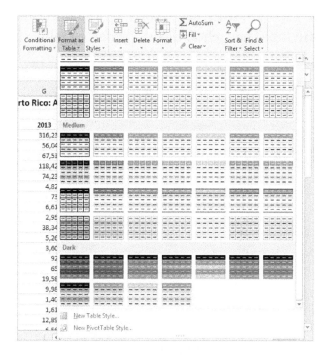

For instance, you want to format the given data into a table:

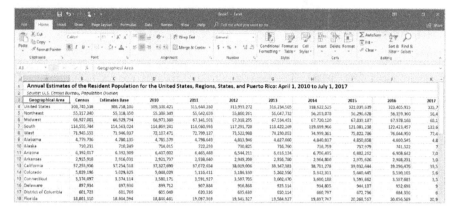

To do so:

- Click the **Format as Table** command, under the **Home** tab. Then, choose your preferred table style.

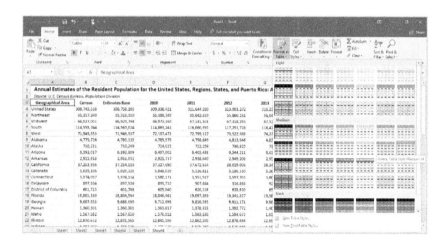

- A dialog box will prompt open to ask you to locate the data for your table.

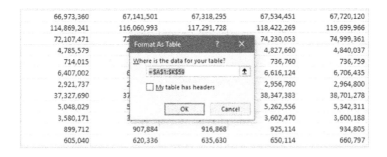

66,973,360	67,141,501	67,318,295	67,534,451	67,720,120
114,869,241	116,060,993	117,291,728	118,422,269	119,699,966
72,107,471	72		74,230,053	74,999,361
4,785,579			4,827,606	4,840,037
714,015			736,760	736,759
6,407,002	6		6,616,124	6,706,435
2,921,737	2		2,956,780	2,964,800
37,327,690	37		38,347,383	38,701,278
5,048,029	5		5,262,556	5,342,311
3,580,171	3		3,602,470	3,600,188
899,712	907,884	916,868	925,114	934,805
605,040	620,336	635,630	650,114	660,797

- Select the cells or cell range that you want to format as a table. In this example, we have selected cell range A3:K60.

- Click the **My table has headers** checkbox, to include headers in your table. Then, click **OK**.

- The cell range you selected will then be instantly formatted into a table.

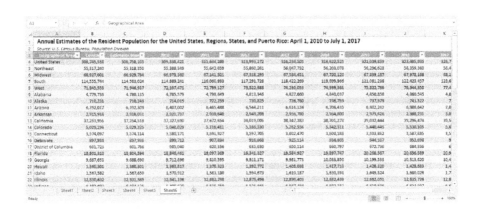

Tip: For your convenience, tables also automatically include filters by default. As such, you can start filtering your data using the drop-down arrows in the header cells, if necessary.

Alternatively, you may also click the **Table** command, under the **Insert** tab, to format data into a table.

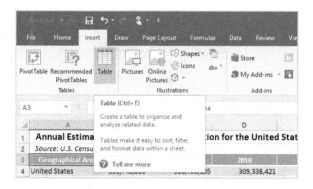

A similar dialog box will appear to ask you to locate the data for your table as well.

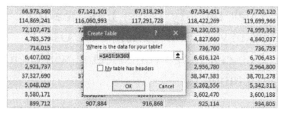

To remove a table:

• Click on any cell within the table to display the **Design** tab under **Table Tools** option.

• Click **Convert to Range**. By doing so, the table will be converted back into a normal range of cells.

• Click **Convert to Range**. By doing so, the table will be converted back into a normal range of cells.

- However, the cells will still retain their data and formatting.

- Select the cells and simply click the **Clear Formats** command, under the **Home** tab, should you want to transform the cells back to their default formatting.

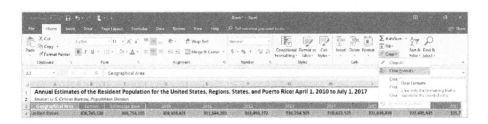

Chapter 6:

Charts

In the previous chapter, you have learned to format data into tables. While tables make your data look more organized, using them in a presentation may come off as dull and boring. Hence, there may be times when you may need to convert your data into charts.

Charts are graphic representations of data that help you interpret data easily and effectively. Through charts, it is easier to compare and analyze data. In addition, charts also enable you to visualize certain trends, that are impossible to see merely through tables.

It is important to first know the different types of charts, understand when to use them, and identify to which types of data are these charts applicable.

Using charts that best represent your data not only adds dynamics to your presentation, but also helps you and your audience to understand your data better.

Chart Types

Excel's charts selection may be accessed in the **Charts** group, under the **Insert** tab.

There are seven major chart options that you can explore in an Excel worksheet:

1. **Column Chart** – uses columns or vertical bars to represent data. Column charts are best used to illustrate data

changes over a period of time, and to visually compare values across different categories.

2. **Line Chart** – uses lines and to establish movements or trends among data. Values are represented by points, connected by lines, to easily determine whether values are increasing or decreasing over a span of time.

3. **Pie Chart** – used to show proportions of a whole. Pie charts represent each value through slices of pie, making it easier to identify which values account for the greatest or least share in a given category.

4. **Hierarchy Chart** – used to present a hierarchical view of a group of data, and to compare proportions within that hierarchy.

5. **Statistic Chart** – used to summarize and visualize key statistical characteristics of data, such as frequency, range, distribution, mean, and median.

6. **Scatter Chart** – compares at least two sets of values and shows the relationship between them. Similar to line charts, scatter charts may also be used to show data trends.

7. **Stock Chart** – combination of a line chart and a bar chart. Stock charts are commonly used to represent a range of price movement over a given period of time.

8. **Combo Chart** – combines two different chart types into a single chart. Combo charts typically consist of a line graph and a column chart.

Converting Data into Chart

• Select the cells or cell range containing the data that you want to be represented through a chart.

• In this example, we have selected cell range A2:C12.

A2	▼	× ✓ fx	State		

	A	B	C	D	E
1					
2	**State**	**Population**	**Rank**		
3	California	39,776,830	10		
4	Florida	21,312,211	8		
5	Georgia	10,545,138	3		
6	Illinois	12,768,320	5		
7	Michigan	9,991,177	1		
8	New York	19,862,512	7		
9	North Carolina	10,390,149	2		
10	Ohio	11,694,664	4		
11	Pennsylvania	12,823,989	6		
12	Texas	28,704,330	9		
13					

- Under the **Insert** tab, select your preferred chart type. For this example, we will use the **Column Chart**.

Tip: To guide you in choosing the chart type for your data, you may also hover your mouse pointer over each chart type to show a preview of your data represented through that particular chart type.

You may also click on **Recommended Charts** to view chart execution samples suggested by Excel based on your data.

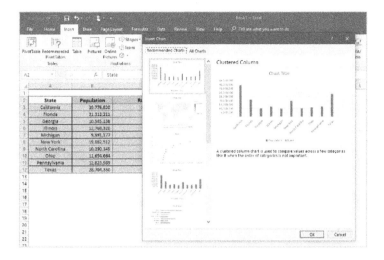

- The selected chart will then be inserted into the worksheet.

Upon inserting a chart into a worksheet, you may still want to modify a bit how it presents your data. Excel allows you to add and modify various chart elements, such as chart title, lines, legends, data labels, and data table, to name a few.

To add a chart element:

- Click the chart to display the **Design** tab under the **Chart Tools** option.

- Click the drop-down arrow under the **Add Chart Element** command. Then, choose your desired element.

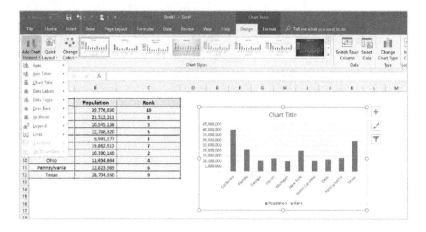

If you do not want to add chart elements manually and individually, you may also choose a preset layout under the **Quick Layout** command.

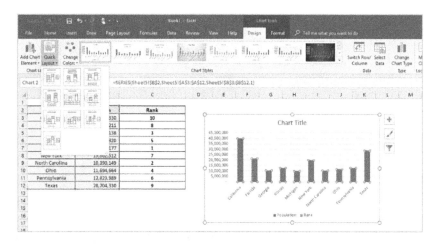

To edit a chart element:

- For instance, to edit the chart title, simple double-click the placeholder, and start typing once the cursor appears.

- Upon double-clicking any chart element, an additional Format pane will appear on the right side of the window to assist you further in formatting chart elements.

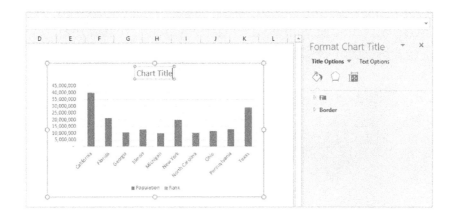

Excel also offers various chart styles that are useful in modifying and beautifying your chart in an instant.

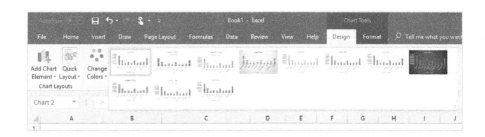

Conditional Formatting

Another helpful Excel feature is the Conditional Formatting. This is used to automatically apply specific formatting—such as fill colors, icons, and data bars—to cells based on certain conditional rules or parameters.

Just like charts, conditional formatting makes it easier to visualize data, and establish trends among data. The conditional formatting command may be accessed in the **Home** tab.

In the given set of data, we will set conditional rules according to the **Scores**, and apply conditional formatting to the values based on the following premises: values lower than

527

80 will have a fill color of red; values between 80 and 90 will have a fill color of yellow; and lastly, values greater than 90 will have a fill color of green.

	SUBJECT	SCORE	GRADE	MONTH
3	Art & Music	83	Good	January
4	Art & Music	70	Bad	January
5	English	70	Bad	April
6	English	75	Bad	February
7	Home Economics	85	Good	June
8	Math	85	Good	January
9	Math	100	Good	March
10	Physical Education	79	Bad	February
11	Physical Education	80	Good	May
12	Science	90	Good	April
13	Science	76	Bad	March
14	Science	93	Good	May
15	Social Studies	99	Good	April
16	Social Studies	100	Good	February
17	Social Studies	91	Good	June

To create a conditional rule:

• Select the cells or cell range where the formatting is to be applied. As an example, we have selected cell range B3:B17.

• Click on the drop-down arrow of the **Conditional Formatting** command, under the **Home** tab.

• Click **New Rule**.

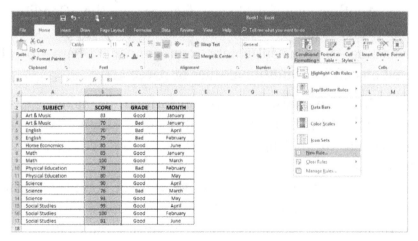

- A dialog box will prompt open for you to set your Rule Type.

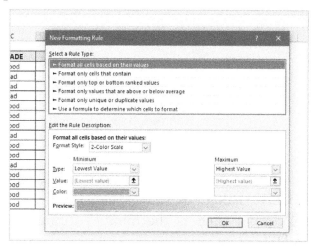

- From the list of Rule Types, select **Format only cells that contain**, since we want to format the cells based on the premises previously mentioned.

- As such, edit the rule description based on the given premises. Select and key in the appropriate options and values in the given fields to set your rules accordingly.
- The first rule is: values lower than 80 will have a fill color of red.

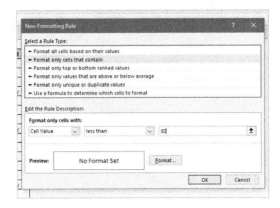

• After filling in the necessary fields, click **Format**. A **Format Cells** dialog box will appear. Here, you can set the specific cell format such as the number formats, font styles, borders, and fill colors.

• Click on the **Fill** tab and choose **Red** as the fill color. Then, click **OK**.

• Click **OK** again on the New Formatting Rule dialog box.

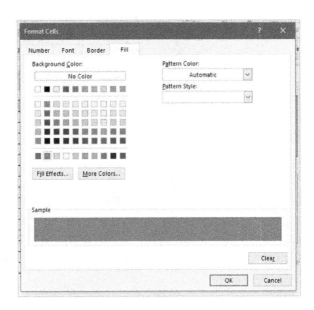

- Now, all cells that contain values lower than 80 have a red fill color.

SUBJECT	SCORE	GRADE	MONTH
Art & Music	83	Good	January
Art & Music	70	Bad	January
English	70	Bad	April
English	75	Bad	February
Home Economics	85	Good	June
Math	85	Good	January
Math	100	Good	March
Physical Education	79	Bad	February
Physical Education	80	Good	May
Science	90	Good	April
Science	76	Bad	March
Science	93	Good	May
Social Studies	99	Good	April
Social Studies	100	Good	February
Social Studies	91	Good	June

- To add another rule, click the drop-down arrow of **Conditional Formatting** again. Then, choose **New Rule**.
- Once again, edit the rule description based on the given premises. Select and key in the appropriate options and values in the given fields to set your rules accordingly.
- Repeat the same process for the remaining 2 rules or premises.
- At the end, your worksheet should look something like this:

SUBJECT	SCORE	GRADE	MONTH
Art & Music	83	Good	January
Art & Music	70	Bad	January
English	70	Bad	April
English	75	Bad	February
Home Economics	85	Good	June
Math	85	Good	January
Math	100	Good	March
Physical Education	79	Bad	February
Physical Education	80	Good	May
Science	90	Good	April
Science	76	Bad	March
Science	93	Good	May
Social Studies	99	Good	April
Social Studies	100	Good	February
Social Studies	91	Good	June

To review and edit conditional rules:

- Select the cells with conditional formatting.
- Click the drop-down arrow of **Conditional Formatting** again. Then, choose **Manage Rules**.

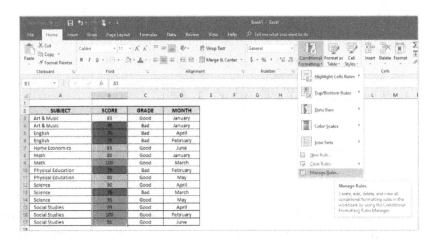

- A dialog box will prompt open to let you view all the formatting rules in the current cell selection, current worksheet, and even in other worksheets within the workbook.

- Here, you can also edit and delete existing rules, or add a new rule.

- Remember to click **OK** upon applying necessary modifications.

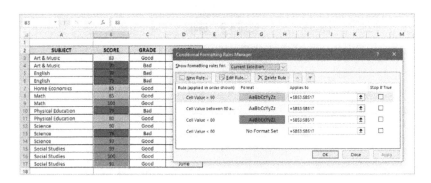

__Conclusion:__

Just like Microsoft Word and Microsoft Powerpoint, knowing how to use Microsoft Excel is such a powerful skill, that can be used not only in school, but most especially at work.

Excel may be a complicated program, but it is among the mostly used programs because of its extensive features and functions.

As taught in the previous lessons, Excel is particularly helpful in storing, organizing, and analyzing data and information. Excel is commonly and widely used to input data that will be later on used for reports, data analysis, and presentations. While it is true that you can also somehow store and organize data in Word or in Powerpoint, the main advantage of Excel lies in its ability to analyze data and perform arithmetic operations, which you certainly cannot do in other MS Office applications.

However, it may also be wrong to entirely conclude that Excel is the best program, since each application is unique in its own way, and has its own specialization—Word is best used for word processing and document creations, Powerpoint is best used for creating slide presentations, and Excel is best used for data storage, organization, and analysis.

As such, to thrive in the corporate world, or as early as in school, a mixture of knowledge and skills of these 3 applications combined is truly essential. As a piece of advice, take the time and the grab every opportunity to learn and know more about these applications. Because, you just might not know, when will these knowledge and skills be put to the test. It is best to be ready by then.

In conclusion, the lessons discussed in this e-book are just the basic and commonly used features and functions of

Excel 2016. There are still a lot of features to discover, and functions to unlock. But do not worry, no one gets to learn all the aspects of Excel overnight. Similar to any other aspect in life, Excel is a continuous learning process. You get to discover more of it, along the process, and as you go on about your daily activities.

Hopefully, you can start applying what you have learned from here, in your daily Excel activities. Likewise, feel free to do more research and read more about Excel. Continue exploring other functions that can help you even further in storing, organizing, and analyzing your data.

After all, you are a step closer to fully excelling with Microsoft Excel.

P.S. As a bonus, we have also included a list of the frequently used Excel keyboard shortcuts that every beginner must know!

35 *Commonly Used Excel Shortcuts:*

No.	Keyboard Shortcut Keys	Function
1	Ctrl + O	Open workbook
2	Ctrl + W	Close workbook
3	Ctrl + S	Save workbook
4	Ctrl + C	Copy
5	Ctrl + V	Paste
6	Ctrl + X	Cut
7	Ctrl + Z	Undo
8	Ctrl + Y	Redo or Repeat
9	Delete	Remove cell content
10	Ctrl + B	Bold
11	Ctrl + I	Italic
12	Ctrl + U	Underline
13	Alt + H, A, then C	Center align cell content
14	Alt + H, B	Add borders
15	Alt + H	Go to **Home** tab
16	Alt + N	Go to **Insert** tab
17	Alt + P	Go to **Page Layout** tab
18	Alt +M	Go to **Formulas** tab
19	Alt + D	Go to **Data** tab
20	Alt + R	Go to **Review** tab
21	Alt +W	Go to **View** tab
22	Ctrl + 9	Hide selected row(s)
23	Ctrl + 0	Hide selected column(s)
24	Alt + F	Open the **File** page
25	Ctrl + A	Select the entire worksheet
26	Ctrl + Shift + U	Expand or collapse formula bar
27	Shift + F3	Insert a function
28	F1	Display Excel Help task pane
29	Ctrl + F1	Display or hide ribbon
30	Alt + Shift + F1	Insert new worksheet
31	Alt + F4	Close Excel
32	Ctrl + F	Find
33	Ctrl + N	Create a new workbook
34	Ctrl + P	Print
35	Shift + Tab	Move to the previous cell

Did you enjoy this book?

I want to thank you for purchasing and reading this book. I really hope you got a lot out of it.

Can I ask a quick favor, though?

If you enjoyed this book, I would really appreciate it if you could leave me a positive review on Amazon.

I love getting feedback from my customers. Reviews on Amazon really do make a difference. I read all my reviews and would really appreciate your thoughts.

Thanks so much.

Timothy C. Needham